EDUCATION FOR URBAN ADMINISTRATION

Monograph 16 in a series sponsored by
The American Academy of Political and Social Science

Co-sponsors for this volume:
The Fels Institute Graduate Associates
The International City Management Association
The National Academy of Public Administration

Editor: Frederic N. Cleaveland
Assistant Editor: Thomas J. Davy

PHILADELPHIA
June 1973

International Standard Book Number (ISBN) 0-87761-164-5

Issued by The American Academy of Political and Social Science at Prince and Lemon Sts., Lancaster, Pennsylvania.

Editorial and Business Offices, 3937 Chestnut Street, Philadelphia, Pennsylvania 19104.

EDUCATION FOR URBAN ADMINISTRATION

This monograph is the seventeenth in a series published by The American Academy of Political and Social Science. Monographs previously issued in this series are:

Monograph 1: October 1962 — THE LIMITS OF BEHAVIORALISM IN POLITICAL SCIENCE

Monograph 2: June 1963 — MATHEMATICS AND THE SOCIAL SCIENCES: THE UTILITY AND INUTILITY OF MATHEMATICS IN THE STUDY OF ECONOMICS, POLITICAL SCIENCE, AND SOCIOLOGY

Monograph 3: August 1963 — ACHIEVING EXCELLENCE IN PUBLIC SERVICE

Monograph 4: April 1964 — LEISURE IN AMERICA: BLESSING OR CURE?

Monograph 5: February 1965 — FUNCTIONALISM IN THE SOCIAL SCIENCES: THE STRENGTH AND LIMITS OF FUNCTIONALISM IN ANTHROPOLOGY, ECONOMICS, POLITICAL SCIENCE, AND SOCIOLOGY

Monograph 6: December 1966 — A DESIGN FOR POLITICAL SCIENCE: SCOPE, OBJECTIVES, AND METHODS

Monograph 7: May 1967 — GOVERNING URBAN SOCIETY: NEW SCIENTIFIC APPROACHES

Monograph 8: October 1968 — THEORY AND PRACTICE OF PUBLIC ADMINISTRATION: SCOPE, OBJECTIVES, AND METHODS

Monograph 9: April 1969 — A DESIGN FOR SOCIOLOGY: SCOPE, OBJECTIVES, AND METHODS

Monograph 10: October 1970 — A DESIGN FOR INTERNATIONAL RELATIONS RESEARCH: SCOPE, THEORY, METHODS, AND RELEVANCE

Monograph 11: December 1970 — HARMONIZING TECHNOLOGICAL DEVELOPMENTS AND SOCIAL POLICY IN AMERICA

Monograph 12: October 1971 — INTERNATIONAL STUDIES: PRESENT STATUS AND FUTURE PROSPECTS

Monograph 13: March 1972 — INSTRUCTION IN DIPLOMACY: THE LIBERAL ARTS APPROACH

Monograph 14: October 1972 — INTEGRATION OF THE SOCIAL SCIENCES THROUGH POLICY ANALYSIS

Monograph 15: February 1973 — PUBLIC SERVICE PROFESSIONAL ASSOCIATIONS AND THE PUBLIC INTEREST

CONTENTS

INTRODUCTION

FOREWORD

In 1957, Thomas J. Davy, Lloyd M. Short, and Stephen B. Sweeney worked diligently together to bring into being a unique volume on Education for Administrative Careers in Government Service. In the preparation of that volume the ideas of practicing public managers were exposed to the penetrating insights of educators, and in turn, practitioners brought the bracing chill of reality to bear upon the propositions advanced by the teacher-scholars. Thirteen years later a group of alumni of Fels Institute of Local and State Government who had gathered at the 1970 Conference of the International City Management Association (ICMA) in San Diego talked about significant changes they had witnessed in the graduate program of their alma mater. They talked about what would be the most important contribution they could make to strengthen the quality of their profession of urban administration. Consensus developed quickly around the idea of seeking to improve professional education for urban administrative careers.

Although the topic was certainly important in 1957, it seemed of even greater urgency in 1970. The special issue of *Public Administration Review* on the "American City Manager," * the ICMA Board's statement emphasizing the innovations needed to strengthen professional education, the efforts underway to pool resources for the creation of a national training center for state and local officials, the extensive investigation of education for the public service by the National Academy of Public Administration (NAPA)—all these reflected the growing concern for developing a more effective educational experience leading to careers in urban government. In addition to these developments, the severe disparity in state and federal funds available to support professional education for urban administration compared to the substantial state and federal investment in education for medicine, business, and other professions set the background for ex-

* *Public Administration Review*, vol. 31, no. 1 (January-February, 1971).

amining the topic closely akin to that of thirteen years earlier—
education for urban administration. And these factors combined
to make the exploration urgent.

A task force of Fels Institute graduates was appointed by the
1970 president of the alumni, Dr. Thomas J. Davy, associate dean
of the University of Pittsburgh's Graduate School of Public and
International Affairs. Graham W. Watt, president of ICMA and
deputy mayor of Washington, D.C., served as chairman and the
membership included John K. Parker and Robert R. Cantine of
the Washington, D.C. administrative staff; Walter E. Scheiber,
executive director of the Metropolitan Washington Council of
Governments; William E. Besuden and Frederick E. Fisher of the
ICMA staff; Elizabeth S. Micheals, assistant secretary of the
Samuel S. Fels Fund; and alumni president-elect Robert B.
Weiss, city manager of Manchester, Connecticut. The Task
Force worked under the general leadership and guidance of Dr.
Stephen B. Sweeney, director emeritus of the Fels Institute of
Local and State Government, and emeritus professor of govern-
mental administration, University of Pennsylvania.

This group met frequently and developed plans for examining
in depth the education of urban administrators. The need for
outside support for this effort was apparent from the outset. The
executive director of the Fels Fund enthusiastically gave administrative support.

The American Academy of Political and Social Science
(AAPSS) agreed to include the project in its generously supported
symposium-monograph program and designated two of its Board
members, Dr. Elmer B. Staats, Comptroller General of the United
States, and Dr. Stephen B. Sweeney, first vice-president of the
Academy, to represent the Academy on the Task Force. Dr.
Staats was elected co-chairman of the committee. AAPSS made
its first pre-symposium grant ($5,000) for the development of a
solid base of information on urban administrators, particularly
their educational needs. ICMA and the National Academy of
Public Administration agreed to be co-sponsors and supporters of
the program—each by lending staff support (William Besuden
and Frederick Fisher of ICMA and Dr. Frederic N. Cleaveland,
provost of Duke University and head of NAPA's Ford Founda-
tion-supported study of public administration education).

From the work of the Task Force emerged the concept of a comprehensive survey-workshop-symposium-publications program. The short-term objective of the project was to develop an authoritative volume on education for urban administration. The continuing and long-term objective was, and is, to stimulate and influence the educational resources of this country to strengthen and improve education for urban administration.

The strategy of survey-workshop-symposium was developed to pursue the short-range objective. The organizing principle of this strategy was to begin the inquiry with the practicing urban administrators, broadly defined. The surveys and workshops* were designed to provide that solid base by drawing from selected practitioners their views on the changes to be expected in the roles of those responsible for solving urban problems and to elicit views on appropriate professional education for these roles. These assessments of roles and their educational requirements were then to be presented to public administration educators. Through the exchange of ideas between practitioner and teacher-scholar in the symposium format, the framework of a pedagogical and institutional approach to education for urban administration would be formulated.

The Symposium was designed to follow the standards in regard to pattern, membership, and procedure established for earlier monographs of the American Academy of Political and Social Science. Thus, writers of basic papers were selected in large measure for their distinguished scholarship. Commentators—two or three for each paper—were invited to prepare brief written critiques. They were drawn from among administrators, educators, and practitioners who have had broad experience and practical knowledge about the area of the paper in question.

Well in advance of the meeting, a copy of most papers was sent to each of the persons involved in the Symposium. This allowed an emphasis on challenge and response and a critical consideration of new ideas presented in the papers and the critiques. Chairmanships of the symposium sessions were shared by Dr. Elmer B. Staats; Dr. John W. Ryan, president of Indiana Uni-

* See the essay by Robert R. Cantine, "How Practicing Urban Administrators View Themselves: An Analysis of the Workshop Deliberations," pp. 1–16 of this volume.

versity and of the American Society for Public Administration;
and Dr. George A. Graham, executive director of NAPA. The
entire proceedings were tape recorded. In addition three re-
porters made notes of the discussion at each session—Hugh H.
Annett, Elizabeth S. Micheals, and Charles Warren. Charles
Warren also prepared abstracts for all basic papers and commentaries. Frederic Cleaveland drew extensively from these notes
in preparing the summary statements at the end of each major
paper and the written critique associated with it. He also relied
heavily upon quotation excerpts prepared from the tapes by
Elizabeth Micheals.

The many who have been associated with this effort share the
hope that this resulting product may gain wide attention from
those who are concerned, as we are, with strengthening the capacity of urban governments to cope with the problems and the
opportunities of our times.

FREDERIC N. CLEAVELAND
THOMAS J. DAVY
STEPHEN B. SWEENEY

How Practicing Urban Administrators View Themselves: An Analysis of the Workshop Deliberations

By ROBERT R. CANTINE

ABSTRACT: While finding some validity in the statement that "management is management is management," the majority of these seventy practitioners-administrators felt that differences in substantive knowledge and skill requirements, outlook, processes, and context were sufficient between urban administrators and business administrators as well as among careers within urban administration, that a fully common educational program would be inappropriate. To the extent that management situations and techniques had general applicability, then common educational experiences would be desirable.

In today's complex and fast-changing world, one of the urban administrator's principal challenges is making the most effective use of his time. He must devote time and talent to building and maintaining a very sensitive information system about the world around him; set his own objectives, and work at achieving consensus among his superiors, subordinates, and citizenry on community objectives; be a salesman for values and actions he believes would be in the public interest; arbitrate conflicts; protect the financial authority of his agency; and "work" the governmental system to get the job done. Demands on his time and talent in the future will involve exercising a greater degree of political sensitivity, developing extended modifications and commitment among members of his organization, and achieving the basic stability essential to successful introduction of change.

Robert R. Cantine, Ph.D., is senior management analyst and chief, management improvement group in the Executive Office of Planning and

Management of the District of Columbia Government. He has served for three years as assistant to the county executive of Prince William County, Virginia. He was also research associate with the systems division of the Government Studies Center, Fels Institute of Local and State Government, where he engaged in the design and application of advanced management techniques, systems science, and computer technology to the requirements of local and state government. He received his Master in Governmental Administration degree in 1963 and his Ph.D. from the University of Pennsylvania in 1970. He has co-authored several studies concerned with the planning of government services. Dr. Cantine serves as a member of the national coordinating board of the Public Technology, Inc./National Aeronautics and Space Administration project on the transfer of technology to cities.

THESE workshop deliberations on the urban administrator and his "real" world can serve appropriately as the introduction to this Symposium. The ideas and themes running through these deliberations furnish the context towards which the symposium papers are directed and around which the symposium discussions held in Philadelphia May 31–June 2 were organized. As noted earlier, the objective of this comprehensive undertaking is to strengthen and improve professional education for urban administration by encouraging open, frank, and critical assessment of this varied career field of urban administration and university approaches to professional education for careers in the field. By bringing together practicing urban administrators and experienced educators for informed and thoughtful interchange the intent has been to enrich the perspectives of all directly involved and, through this volume, to make available generally the essence of that provocative dialogue.

In June and August, 1971 over seventy urban administrators of broad experience participated in workshops designed to elicit, and expose for discussion among colleagues, their views on who the urban administrator is, what kinds of activities demand most of his time and talent, the objectives of graduate professional education for urban administrators, and what knowledge and skills they require to perform effectively. The seventy practitioners had gone through rather extensive preparation for these workshops: each had completed a long questionnaire reflecting the questions described above, and had prepared a written statement of his own views on the emerging roles of urban administrators.

The analysis which follows is focused on the exchange of ideas among these practitioners at the workshops.[1]

Who Is the Urban Administrator?

A very broad definition of the term "urban administrator" had been employed in selecting practitioners to participate in the survey-workshop-symposium series. In the workshops practitioners were asked to examine this expansive notion of the urban administrator. Can urban administrators be considered a relatively homogeneous group for which a common educational program could be developed? Is it true, as some would say, that "management is management is management—whether public, semi-public, or private"? If not, what differences are important to recognize?

These practitioners found no easy answer to such questions. Two views were expressed regarding the similarity between public and private administrators. On the one hand, some contended that differences exist in objectives and "rules of the game" between public and business administrators, differences which influence considerably the knowledge and skill requirements, not to mention the variations in outlook and value commitments. These differences, they assert, work against the assumption that a common educational program can serve satisfactorily for a career in either sector. The remarks of a senior professional association official and those of a Model Cities executive illustrate this position:

I resist the notion that managerial competences are transferable; there is a big difference between the profit incentive and civic effort. They represent two basically different objectives . . . We as [urban public] administrators must have a good feel for social problems; we should be well versed in sociology and basic urban problems. We need that kind of exposure, where a private business executive may not need it that much.

In a 1971 study of private managers who went public, their biggest problem was what to do when someone says, "You can't do that, it's

1. Unfortunately, because of space limitations on the monograph series, a selected sample of the excellent papers by urban administrators could not be published herein. However, it is hoped that such a sample may be published elsewhere in public administration literature.

not politically feasible." They (private managers) tend to say "what do you mean—it's right, we've got the money, and we must do it." The public sector is different. You may waste half a million (by private standards) but you have to take the people's attitudes and feelings into account.

Other practitioners argued not only against a distinction in managerial skills, but also countered that to a certain extent, both public and private sector administrators are held accountable to the same objective standards, especially in terms of efficiency. This feeling was best illustrated by the following comments:

I find a lot of the same management techniques in training sessions of private business and our own profession. Theirs are of interest to me and vice versa. Management principles don't deal with profit, they deal with how to use your people.

There is a basic change in the concept the average constituent has towards the public agency—he considers it as a public business and expects the public business to be run as efficiently.

Despite these differences in viewpoint, there seemed to be agreement that certain analytical skills and "people-oriented" management skills would be of considerable importance to both types of managers. But beyond the similarities in knowledge and skill required to be an administrator in business or public service, differences exist in attitudes, objectives, value commitments, clients, sensitive relationships, and processes which clearly distinguish business and public administration. A common educational program would be beneficial to neither.

Discussion of the important differences among jobs within urban administration led to similar conclusions. Few of the practitioners would agree that a director of public health and a city manager should be products of the same curriculum. At the same time several practitioners recalled their experience in small municipalities where they had performed the functions of public works director, zoning administrator, recreation director, and so on. Some participants saw very practical differences in the amount of face-to-face contact with citizens experienced by the city manager in contrast to a regional federal official, or someone serving as a staff person in support of others. These differences in roles reflect important differences in knowledge and skill requirements. Hence to acknowledge such differences is to question the desirability of a common educational program for all types of positions which comprise the broad category of urban administrator. While practitioners agreed that the jobs of different types of urban administrators share many aspects in common, nevertheless they tended to reject the idea of a common educational program for all kinds of urban administrators. The following statements illustrate these views:

—At the local level there is a striking difference in the amount of face-to-face contact an urban administrator has with his public. It is not necessarily there at the state level, and seldom there at the federal level.

—There are different perspectives even in the public sector—a city versus a council of governments.

—The question is not whether to train someone to be a HUD administrator or a city manager; it's whether education is directed towards a policy analysis role or what we call "man-the-front-lines" role.

—The skill or technique of urban administration is transferable, whereas the substance (health, police, public works, and so on) is not.

In summary, these discussions among practitioners reflected a reluctance to support the notion that urban administrators are a homogeneous group who can be served by a common educational program. The workshop participants recognized that a spectrum of differences probably exists, differentiating between the positions of types of urban administrators. The educational background suitable for certain classes of positions might be common, for example, a senior official of an urban research organization, a city manager, and a senior official in a professional association. In addition, for all management positions—as opposed to strictly staff positions—a core curriculum focused on the development of management knowledge and skills would be clearly appropriate. There are, however, real differences in the substantive knowledge and skill required to perform effectively as a director of public works, a fire chief, a planning director, a school superintendent, or a city manager. These differences in requirements should be reflected in the options available through the educational program beyond the common knowledge and skills that every urban administrator ought to acquire.

CURRENT DEMANDS UPON THE TIME AND TALENT OF URBAN ADMINISTRATORS

What is the urban administrator doing? What occupies most of his time and intellectual talent? How does he allocate his energy now? Will it be the same in the future? How is this behavior influenced by his expectations of what the job ought to be? By his environment? The dialogue among the seventy practitioners on these questions provides a fascinating glimpse into the varied and complex world of the urban administrator.

Information gathering and sensing problems or opportunities

Although not an entirely new or unknown activity, information gathering won high recognition from these practitioners as a primary demand on both their time and talent. This finding should be an important reminder to those planning educational programs. From the urban administrator's point of view this task of gathering intelligence about the environment in which he is working is basic to his performance, not to mention his survival. It is not the kind of information gathering carried out by sitting behind the desk and reading a book or two, or by studying the United States Census. It is the kind of information, often in the form of cues, which comes from being as close as possible to the center of communication flows between people whose actions can have an important impact on his work performance. As one practitioner noted, "The manager needs a sensory system on the dynamics of a situation and where his city government fits in." It requires that the urban administrator work actively to establish and keep open his contacts within the community and with those in other governmental and private institutions. A very brief excerpt in the dialogue between a city manager, a senior executive in one of the nation's largest port authorities, and the senior official of a regional planning agency provides the best illustration of the meaning and significance of this activity:

1st Participant: From my standpoint much of what takes my time is keeping up with what's going on outside.

Moderator: What do you mean by "keeping up"?

1st Participant: Being able to know what is going on so you can cope with it. The external side of the administrator's life is getting so complex that external events occur at considerable cost to the urban administrator's time just in keeping abreast of where he is.

2nd Participant: To keep up with what is going on becomes increasingly important because in most cities what is taking place in other levels of government and in nearby governments is important to you.   Formerly this was not so much the case because what happened in the federal government years ago and in state government was not quite so important to you as an isolated urban administrator.   Now you have to know a lot about federal aid programs, state aid programs, the politics and the policies and things that are going on in other areas around you, to say nothing of the developments within your own municipality.   There are a number of events that take place within your municipality and I don't think you can do very much unless you have a good knowledge of all these programs.   You have to have a background on which to build and insight into what these external and internal bits of information mean.   I see that very much in the work that I do in the COG (Council of Governments).   Here you have three levels of government that are very important and you have a tremendous number of things you have to know about each in order to read meaning into events.

Perhaps as significant as the notion of information gathering, is the practitioners' recognition of the continuing effort urban administrators make to utilize that information to cope with their environment.   As J. Sterling Livingston reminds us, "Success in real life depends on how well a person is able to find and exploit the opportunities available to him, and, at the same time, discover and deal with potential serious problems before they become critical."[2]   To the urban administrator this information gathering activity is his "wellspring" for finding the right things to do at the right time.   In many instances the information is fragmentary,

2. *Harvard Business Review* (January–February, 1971).

disguised, isolated, or indirect. It may come only in the form of an event occurring. In any case it is the administrator's skill at "reading meaning into events (information)" that permits him to identify and define problems and exploit opportunities.

Planning and setting objectives

Information gathering and the ability to use information in support of opportunities at hand presumes the existence of objectives about the future. Otherwise, there would be no basis on which an urban administrator could distinguish between useful and useless information.

Setting objectives and then considering alternative means to reach them is planning. To the seventy urban administrators planning represents an activity they struggle with continuously, but have perhaps less success with than other aspects of their jobs. The task of setting goals or objectives is a particularly difficult element of planning.

The act of setting a course for the future can occur at various levels in the organization, from an individual employee to the most comprehensive organization unit. It can be a conscious and structured activity or informal and instinctive. It can have a long- or short-time horizon. As might be expected, the more formal and systematic the effort of goal-setting becomes, the more difficult and time-consuming it seems to be. One administrator pointed out that "the greater part of weekly staff meetings for nine weeks, as well as an all-day meeting with twenty-two of his key staff, were devoted to the question of goals, not five years out but for the next year." The results appeared to be less than complete success considering the considerable time and talent invested.

The matter of "technique" is of course also involved. Different approaches reflect in part different styles of management. Some practitioners argued that goal-setting is easy: the urban administrator sets the goals and then either (a) he expects them to be accepted because of his position as organizational leader, or (b) he proceeds to persuade and gain the commitment of his subordinates and superiors to his goals. Other practitioners, typified by the earlier example, pursued the more complex but more participative "bottom-up" approach to goal-setting.

No matter how complex the urban administrator finds the task of setting goals and achieving commitment to them within his organization, he faces an even more complex task in working with the community. As one practitioner noted "Model Cities legislation asked that cities state in their Model Cities Plan what their strategies were for allocating resources and attacking city problems; cities had a terrible time complying with that [requirement]." In fact, several practitioners resisted the notion of trying to set community goals around specific values; instead they felt the administrator should try to achieve agreement on specific actions and in this way minimize the polarization of the community over values.

Several practitioners focused on the urban administrator himself. Most saw him developing his own personal set of goals— for himself and the organization he serves. Whether he reveals these goals through the sum of his actions over time or lays them all out at one time for examination, through some formal pronouncement, is a matter of individual style and the situation.

Is all this necessary? Is it a vital part of an urban administrator's performance? The answer seemed to be yes. Despite the time and effort involved, it is a necessary part of effective management. As one practitioner summed it up, "I don't know any other way, particularly where the range of activity is so vast and the number of people so great, that you can actually do the job without management by objectives and management by exception—and goal-setting is a prerequisite to this type of management."

Initiator of change

—The responsibility of a city manager is to persuade the community to move in a certain direction.

—The urban administrator today has a more active role to play in identifying programs needed by the community but not espoused by an articulate pressure group.

—I think the urban administrator has to be a sensor of the need for change. My life is devoted to being an architect of change. You try to change the governmental structure to meet the needs of the city.

These statements of three local government practitioners articulate the view of many urban administrators that their role is one of creating change, or at least adapting the organization to its changing environment.

Although the tendency is to associate such statements with the advocacy of certain social values and policies, the connection is not a necessary one. Indeed, the urban administrators seemed often to approach this issue in a pragmatic fashion, feeling that it was their role to initiate some change, perhaps one time slowing down the rate of change, and on another occasion taking action on a particular social need, depending on the community situation.

Orchestrating the governmental machinery

If the expressions of these practitioners generally reflect the situation in city hall and county courthouse, then the traditional neutrality associated with the British civil service certainly does not hold true for American local government. Indeed, the urban administrator is oftentimes caught in the middle between his subordinates and superiors on a variety of matters. The comments of a Council of Governments executive and city manager of a medium size city illustrate the pressure for an orchestrating role:

—Working with top and middle staff people and dealing with the elected bodies who are our superiors requires a balance of informal relationships and strategies.

—There is a gap between the idealism of my staff and the political realities, represented by my Board. The urban administrator must be a buffer between the staff and the policy setters; a translator, a smoother.

—I see several tasks which require a great deal of time—developing a team relation between the city manager and his assistants and integrating, that is, dovetailing demands and aspirations of his departments with those of the council and those of the public.

Clearly, the "city hall crowd" includes more than passive employees waiting to execute policy originated and decided by others. Indeed, judging from these practitioners, urban administrators continuously feel the pressure to support and be an advocate for the ideas of subordinates who, after all, may be only following the admonition of their bosses to show leadership and be articulate advocates.

As many urban administrators and politicians have found out, making the system work is much more difficult when city employees are disgruntled, feel ignored, have low morale, and are generally dissatisfied with the attention their ideas have received from the administrator or his superior. Several urban administrators at the workshops felt that this role as "buffer" or "orchestrator" is a significant and time-consuming task.

Salesman and consensus builder

General objectives can be set and new policies proposed, but the most universal and time-consuming role of the urban administrator remains the task of building consensus. Here it is that the administrator must invoke his skill in persuading others to accept a proposed action, or his ability to find an acceptable substitute agreeable to all parties. Perhaps among all his tasks, this is the responsibility for which his education and training have least equipped him. As one practitioner saw the situation, at some point in his career, "every student who becomes a city manager ought to sell shoes, automobiles, or something, whether or not for a living, in order to train in the technique of salesmanship. The two roles of salesman and arbitrator run throughout the function of the manager." Most other participants agreed with at least the last sentence of this assessment.

Arbitrator and manager of conflict

Perhaps a corollary of building consensus is the skill of conflict management. The administrator not only has to arbitrate conflict situations but oftentimes must also advise and educate parties to a conflict. One administrator most ably described the nature and intensity of this role in the following way:

We are always mediating strongly conflicting viewpoints on a particular item and I think that what we typically do is pull the threads off conflicting viewpoints and come up with what is practical, what is possible, what is achievable. There is always conflict within our organization. We are in the middle trying to come out with some kind of a feasible thing out of which there will come a meeting of the minds. And it is certainly true with the community groups vis-a-vis each other.

In a backhanded sort of way, this continuous engagement in the settling of conflicts is part and parcel of bringing about conditions which permit agreement to be achieved on other, perhaps more important, community issues. It involves skills which, again, few urban administrators have acquired through their formal education. By and large he has had to "pick himself up by his bootstraps," learning what he can by trial and error and picking up for his own use techniques he has observed being successfully employed by others. Tense confrontations are likely to remain a part of the urban scene for the indefinite future, and the urban administrator will be unable to avoid attempting to arbitrate or manage these conflict situations. As several practitioners pointed out, the urban administrator himself may at times be the creator of tension in the process of working to bring about change, or at least may use tension as an opportunity to move towards change.

Budget and financial management

—I would say that the greatest amount of time and talent is taken up with financial responsibilities. I think it is so because finance, perhaps even more than personnel, is involved in almost any type of activity. I don't mean just getting money but planing for it, using it, and controlling it.

—Younger men coming out of the university today don't have a good foundation in the theory and practice of public finance. Educators should be advised that regardless of problems facing the city administrator in the future, they must understand public finance.

—A constant is the budget problem—allocation of resources. It is a dependable task that won't change in the future.

—The most important task is being able to prepare a sound budget.

Responsibilities for budgetary and financial management continue to loom as time- and talent-demanding activities for the urban administrator. Many of the issues the urban administrator faces, both large and small, are "hassled out" through the budget process. This process provides the forum for a variety of analytical efforts aimed at determining the cost effectiveness of public services. In addition, the management complexity of budgeting and public finance has increased with greater dependence upon federal grants. Who knows how revenue sharing may escalate the importance of effective financial management in city halls.

Last, but probably foremost in importance, he has the heavy responsibility to protect the financial integrity of his community and its government. This requires a basic understanding of urban economics and public finance—as well as a keen insight into the taxpayers' willingness to forego further personal consumption for the benefits of increased public spending.

Getting the job done

—Just sheer active, organizational, driving management.

—The bulk of my time, perhaps fifty percent, is spent with department heads discussing and evaluating programs and policies.

—My time is divided into two parts: (1) keeping things rolling, carrying on what has gone before and improving on it, and (2) desperately struggling to carve out time to think creatively and move ahead.

—Managers tend to delegate anything and everything they can. They end up with a repository of things they haven't figured out how to delegate and these are the things they spend their time on.

—Three activities take most of my time: (1) "working" the government system which is becoming increasingly complex, and helping citizens to do the same. . . .

When all is said and done, all other activities add up to nothing unless time and talent are devoted to execution, to making sure things happen, or as one administrator put it, "to 'working' the system." This involves the traditional management activities of dividing work into tasks and assigning them, seeing that related tasks are coordinated, monitoring performance, and recruiting manpower. Equally important in these times of complexity, the task of getting the "job done" involves facilitating, expediting, and otherwise overcoming the encumbrances of traditional bureaucracy. Perhaps the present-day trend towards co-managers in many medium to large size cities is in reality simply a way to give more attention to "working the system." This is one area of activity where a strong and continuing pay-off can reasonably be expected from a professional urban administrator.

WHAT'S IN THE FUTURE?

In some ways these practicing urban administrators seemed more certain and articulate about the demands of their job in the future than about their current activities. Perhaps it is a natural tendency to be less aware of those things one does instinctively than of the activities into which one has waded knee-deep and about which he is keenly sensitive concerning what may lie ahead under full immersion. The words of the practitioners themselves offer a good glimpse of what may be demanding much of their time and talent in the future:

—The urban administrator must maintain a stable base—a minimum level of organizational and community activity and service to hold the community together—giving the manager the opportunity to devote time and attention to responding to top priority problems of the future.

—The future will place a high priority on organizational maintenance—finding and holding people long enough to get the job done.

—We will be devoting more of our time to developing (educating, training) our people, those who work for us.

—Another aspect of this development will involve people in the community—keeping our eyes open for talent in the community.

—We are seeing more of the trend toward democratic styles of leadership in our organizations. The administrator of tomorrow has to be skillful in developing his people and including them in the decision-making process—it will be a group decision.

—He will have to pay more attention to the needs and sensitivities of elected officials. Now he doesn't understand their goals and pressures.

—Urban managers make decisions and know where they are going but they are extremely isolated from politics in many cities.

Citizens can't get into the system any more—there are no channels into the manager where they [citizens] can negate the influence and effect of elected officials. If we are to continue, the manager must become an astute politician. If citizens can't get to him, he must find a way to feel their wants.

These three themes of creating a stable situation from which to initiate and implement change, organizational maintenance, and developing political sensitivities seem to reflect important "lessons" of the 1960s and early 1970s. First, too much instability can make the management of change practically impossible. Second, to win from employees the personal commitments and positive attitudes essential to improved organizational performance will require something beyond the recognized formal authority of the urban administrator. Last, but not least, for the improved functioning of urban government there must be strong political leadership and strong administrative leadership. They are indispensably related, whether in the hands of one individual or two.

CONCLUSION

If these insights point in a single direction, it is that the urban administrator is a person of action. He is instinctively analyzing, developing strategy, searching for and seizing upon opportunities, and working the system to insure successful execution. A great part of this behavior is "real time" responding to situations, wants, and information as they emerge with little time for relaxed contemplation. Indeed, as many of the practitioners pointed out, one of the more critical problems for the urban administrator is effective use of his time. He can easily let it be consumed by the normal flow of demands made upon him. But if he chooses to take control of his time, the trade-offs in terms of how to invest energy and talent are complex, and a poor choice can have severe consequences.

These insights into the real world of urban administrators represent a challenge to the higher education community and to the individual educator. This picture of the urban administrator at work is not exhaustive. In fact, the image is imprecise in many ways, and it is certainly in flux reflecting the countless variations which can and do occur from situation to situation and with the passage of time. The evidence may be sufficient, nevertheless, for the educator to begin reassessing the thrust of his curriculum and the effectiveness of his instructional techniques in equipping the potential urban administrator for this demanding career.

PARTICIPANTS IN THE FIRST WORKSHOP ON *"Educating Urban Administrators"* HELD AT THE CONFERENCE CENTER, COLUMBIA, MARYLAND, JUNE 1971

ALLOWAY, JAMES, President, New Jersey Civil Service Commission, Trenton

BAILEY, JOHN, Director, Transportation Center, Northwestern University

BESUDEN, WILLIAM, Assistant Director, International City Management Association, Washington, D.C.

BODINE, CORNELIUS, Business Administrator, Newark, New Jersey

BOUCHARD, GERALD, City Manager, Port Huron, Michigan

CANTINE, ROBERT, Senior Analyst, Office of Budget and Executive Management, Government of the District of Columbia

CLEAVELAND, FREDERIC, Provost-elect, Duke University

DAVY, THOMAS, Associate Dean, Graduate School of Public and International Affairs, University of Pittsburgh

FINLEY, ROBERT, Township Manager, Mt. Lebanon Township, Pittsburgh, Pennsylvania

FISHBACH, JOHN, Assistant Director, Professional Development Center, International City Management Association, Washington, D.C.

GASKILL, WILLIAM, Director of Public Utilities, Cleveland, Ohio

HAWKINS, ROBERT, Director for Technical Assistance and Evaluation, Department of Metropolitan Development, Indianapolis, Indiana

KORN, PETER, City Manager, Long Beach, New York

KUNDE, JAMES, City Manager, Dayton, Ohio

McDONELL, ROBERT, Secretary to Board, Montgomery County, Maryland

MATZER, JOHN, City Manager, Skokie, Illinois

MAWBY, NORMAN, Township Manager, Tredyffrin Township, Pennsylvania

MURRAY, SYLVESTER, City Manager, Inkster, Michigan

PARKER, JOHN, Assistant Director for Organization and Management Planning, Government of the District of Columbia

PAULUS, JOHN, Village Manager, Ridgewood, New Jersey

PETTY, DAN, Director of Planning Coordination, Office of Governor of Texas, Austin

PIERCE, CHARLES, Executive Secretary, Mayor's Urban Affairs Council, East Orange, New Jersey

SCHEIBER, WALTER, Executive Director, Metropolitan Washington Council of Governments, Washington, D.C.

SULLIVAN, RICHARD, Director of Public Affairs, Port of New York Authority, New York City

SWEENEY, STEPHEN, Director Emeritus, Fels Institute of Local and State Government and Professor of Governmental Administration, University of Pennsylvania

TERRY, RODERIC, Director, Bureau of Local Government Services, Pennsylvania Department of Community Affairs, Harrisburg

VAN DEUSEN, ROBERT, Village Manager, Glenview, Illinois

WASHNIS, GEORGE, Director of Municipal Studies, Center for Governmental Studies, Washington, D.C.

WATT, GRAHAM, Deputy Mayor and Municipal Manager, Government of the District of Columbia

WEISS, ROBERT, City Manager, Manchester, Connecticut

WHITTLE, RANDOLPH, Assistant Director for Administration, Baltimore (Maryland) Regional Planning Council

PARTICIPANTS IN THE SECOND WORKSHOP ON *"Educating Urban Administrators"* HELD AT THE LYNDON BAINES JOHNSON SCHOOL OF PUBLIC AFFAIRS, UNIVERSITY OF TEXAS, AUSTIN, TEXAS, AUGUST 1971

ASHWORTH, KENNETH, Vice Chancellor for Academic Affairs, University of Texas System, Austin

AYRES, DOUGLAS, City Manager, Inglewood, California

BESUDEN, WILLIAM, Assistant Director, International City Management Association, Washington, D.C.

BROWN, RICHARD, Executive Director, Texas Municipal League, Austin

BURGGRAAFF, WAYNE, City Manager, Richfield, Minnesota

CLEAVELAND, FREDERIC, Provost, Professor of Political Science, Duke University; Director of Education Programs, National Academy of Public Administration, Washington, D.C.

CLARK, ALEXANDER, Associate Dean, Lyndon Baines Johnson School of Public Affairs, University of Texas, Austin

CROW, CHARLES, Executive Director, Coastal Bend Regional Planning Commission, Corpus Christi, Texas

DAVY, THOMAS, Associate Dean, Graduate School of Public and International Affairs, University of Pittsburgh

DOWNS, THOMAS, Administrative Assistant to the City Manager, Little Rock, Arkansas

FERGUSON, FRED, Police Chief, Covina, California

FISHBACH, JOHN, Assistant Director, Professional Development Center, International City Management Association, Washington, D.C.

FISHER, FREDERICK, Director of Professional Development, International City Management Association, Washington, D.C.

Fox, GERALD, City Manager, Wichita Falls, Texas

GILSTRAP, JACK, General Manager, Southern California Rapid Transit District, City of Los Angeles

GRONOUSKI, JOHN, Dean, Lyndon Baines Johnson School of Public Affairs, University of Texas, Austin

HALL, JOHN, Director of Division of Civic Affairs, Texas Christian University, Fort Worth

HARRELL, LLOYD, Assistant City Manager, Stillwater, Oklahoma

HARRISON, RANDY, Assistant to the Director, League of California Cities, Los Angeles

HONTS, ROBERT, President, Christian, Miller & Honts, Austin

KANE, WALTER, City Administrator, Lakewood, Colorado

KELLY, DONALD, Executive Director, Southeast Texas Regional Planning Commission, Beaumont, Texas

KING, NORMAN, Deputy Manager, Claremont, California

KIPP, ROBERT, Director of City Development, Kansas City, Missouri

KITCH, MARK, Model Cities Project, Rock Island, Illinois

LANEY, JOHN, City Manager, Miamisburg, Ohio

LANHAM, FRITZ, Executive Director, Texas Department of Community Affairs, Austin

LEINGER, DAVID, Administrative Assistant to the City Manager, Dallas, Texas

MARKS, LEONARD, Deputy Fire Chief, San Jose, California

McMAHAN, HOWARD, Regional Director, United States Department of Health, Education & Welfare, Dallas, Texas

MICHEALS, ELIZABETH, Fels Fund, Philadelphia

MIKULECKY, THOMAS, Southern Methodist University, Dallas, Texas

MILLER, GIFFORD, City Manager, Orange, California

MULROONEY, KEITH, City Manager, Claremont, California

NESVIG, GORDON, Director of Personnel, City of Los Angeles

OLIVER, JAMES, Assistant for Program Development, Office of Governor of Texas, Austin

PARKER, JOHN, Office of Budget and Executive Management, Government of the District of Columbia

PETTY, DAN, Director of Planning Coordination, Office of Governor of Texas, Austin

PITSTICK, WILLIAM, Executive Director, North Central Texas Council of Governments, Arlington, Texas

RAY, JAMES, Assistant Director, Institute of Urban Studies, University of Texas at Arlington, Texas

REDFORD, EMMETT, Professor of Government, University of Texas, Austin

RUTLEDGE, PHILIP, Director, Department of Human Resources, Government of the District of Columbia

SCHRAEDER, GEORGE, Assistant City Manager, Dallas, Texas

Smiley, Frank, City Manager, Iowa City, Iowa

Sollenberger, David, City Manager, Watsonville, California

Stiff, John, City Manager, Amarillo, Texas

Sweeney, Stephen, Director Emeritus of the Fels Institute of Local and State Government and Professor of Governmental Administration, University of Pennsylvania

Thelen, Al, City Manager, Leavenworth, Kansas

Thomas, Nicholas, Director of Research, Bureau of Government Research, Lyndon Baines Johnson School of Public Affairs, University of Texas, Austin

Watt, Graham, Deputy Mayor and Municipal Manager, Government of the District of Columbia

White, Leslie, Assistant City Manager, Fullerton, California

Some Changing Patterns of American Urbanism

By Martin Meyerson

ABSTRACT: During the past fifteen years, the nation's attitude toward urban problems has shifted because of two major trends. First, there is a changing pattern of population and its location which raise serious questions. Eighty percent of the growth was in metropolitan areas, and more than eighty percent of such growth was outside the central cities. Blacks are approaching a majority in central cities and are resisting their potential loss of influence from a metropolitan government approach. The total population is also younger with forty-five percent under twenty-five. Second, the fiscal dilemma of local government has increased. Costs are escalating rapidly while services are usually deteriorating. Local governments are caught in political and economic patterns which prevent them from increasing productivity and curbing labor costs, on the one hand, and expanding their sources of income, on the other. Without alterations in policies, our society will continue to develop a pattern of urbanization it neither desires nor controls. Widespread citizen participation has compounded the problem, essentially because so much of it has been based on negativism. We require a new optimism, and a new kind of urban leadership that is innovative and willing to experiment. The challenge is for all levels of government to work with private groups, with universities, and other institutions, not only to understand what is happening, but more important, to achieve the potentialities which continue to exist in urban America and which not many years ago seemed on the verge of being realized. For urban leaders and administrators this is no time to lose faith.

Martin Meyerson is president of the University of Pennsylvania and professor of public policy analysis and urban studies. He started his academic

career at the University of Chicago and was Williams Professor of city plan-
ning and urban research at Harvard University and the first director of the
M.I.T.-Harvard Joint Center for Urban Studies. A former dean of the Col-
lege of Environmental Design and then acting chancellor of the University
of California at Berkeley, he was president of the State University of New
York at Buffalo.

Educated at Columbia and Harvard Universities, he holds honorary de-
grees from various institutions and is an honorary professor of the National
University of Asuncion, Paraguay. A specialist in urban problems, he has
been an advisor to the White House, to public and private agencies, the
United Nations and foreign countries. He is chairman of The Assembly on
University Goals and Governance, sponsored by the American Academy of
Arts and Sciences of which he is a Fellow. His books and other writings are
on urban affairs and higher education.

THOSE of us who have been concerned with urban problems
for a substantial length of time cannot help but have a sense
of deja vu in current deliberations within our field. Fifteen years
ago I coedited an issue on urbanism of the *Annals* of this Academy.
At that time I raised various questions, a few of which now seem
dated to me, but some of which I believe as germane today as in
1957. If I had to single out what I consider the most significant
change in the past years, it would be in the attitude toward such
questions rather than the questions themselves. Despite the fact
that there is more serious urban study at more universities, that
professionals have increased severalfold, that data-collecting
methods have enormously improved, that more governmental programs have been started, that we have elevated public and political recognition of urban affairs into a Presidential cabinet post
and department, many doubt that much has been accomplished.

Certain continuities of concern are indicated by some of the
questions I raised fifteen years ago: If population increases, will
the standard of living be raised or lowered? Even more than
fifteen years ago the American population and its standard of
living were overwhelmingly urban. There are now dire predictions—the Club of Rome report prepared by a group from the
Massachusetts Institute of Technology is one of a series of examples—that we will have to return to a nineteenth century standard of living if we do not control population or use of resources
or both. Meanwhile, defying the projections of the demographers,
the actual fertility rate for 1972 appears to be at or below the re-

placement level. Will the acculturation of blacks to middle-class norms be as rapid as their migration to metropolitan centers? The high rate of white exodus from the cities may have made the acculturation of the black less likely. Also the recent movement among blacks is toward definition of black culture rather than absorption. The high and growing rates of violence in the central cities indicate a situation that is troubling to middle-class persons, black as well as white, and often terrifying for blacks who are the most likely victims; it is certainly stimulating the migration of middle-income groups from central cities. At the same time, traditional middle-class values of work, family cohesion, deferral of gratifications seem to be dimming.

Will citizens persist in their present reluctance to allocate personal income to local taxes for public services? The answer to this question is still yes. The voters apparently prefer private solutions to recreation, transportation, and other services. Citizens have become increasingly stubborn about voting monies for many public improvements; the numerous defeats of school bond issues are prominent examples.

If consumer income does increase, how much of it will be allocated to the special goods and services characteristic of downtown centers and to transportation to these centers? The trend toward suburbanization of retail consumer-oriented trade and professional services is continuing. The cosmopolitan centers no longer have the same magnetic attraction they once did; the special mercantile and service assets they offered are now often found in suburban areas which are also more accessible to an increasing clientele.

These are a few questions I chose to emphasize fifteen years ago. The publication of significant portions of the 1970 census, along with other recent statistical material, offers fresh evidence on which to evaluate the implications of these and other earlier questions as well as of new ones. In this essay I shall focus on two sets of characteristics in the changing pattern of American urbanism: the population alteration and the fiscal one.

POPULATION AND LOCATION CHANGES

How many people there are, their characteristics and where they settle determine the services sought from local government.

If there are no great surprises from the recently released 1970 census data—for many of the trends had been previously observed—there are sobering realities.

For example, there are approximately 209 million people in the nation—there were 203 million in 1970—or about double the number fifty years ago. Although the past decade had the lowest rate of growth in the century with the exception of the 1930s, it had the largest absolute gain —about 24 million—with the exception of the 1950s—28 million. Thus even with a relatively modest population growth rate, the housing, utilities, schooling, roads, jobs, medical care equivalent to that in more than seventy-five Charleston metropolitan areas had to be provided in a decade.

More that 80 percent of the population growth took place in metropolitan areas, intensifying the urban character of the nation. In 1970 about 58 percent of the population lived, not surprisingly, on 1 percent of the land; population density in urbanized areas was more than sixty times greater than that of the nation as a whole. Also, by 1970 a majority of the population lived within fifty miles either of the sea coasts or the Great Lakes, reinforcing the concept of large megalopolitan belts on the periphery of the nation.

Growth within metropolitan areas was almost entirely suburban: more than 80 percent of the metropolitan increase was outside central cities. Although the rate of growth for suburban areas has been greater than that of central cities since 1920, the suburban population surpassed that of central cities for the first time in this decade. The implications of this suburban growth are enormous. Consider, for example, revenue rebates to municipalities by state and federal governments: if health or education or recreation programs were to be financed on a per capita basis, the seventy-six million generally more affluent suburbanites would receive larger total amounts than the sixty-four million poorer, less skilled center city residents. Indeed, some of those who hailed the Serrano *vs* Priest California Supreme Court decision (1971) as a great victory for urban school children, now have qualms. Suburban-urban equalization of school expenditures might easily result in decreases of expenditures for central cities, for example, in favor of the areas of rural poor and the smaller blighted communities. Now, worried about equity without fairness, the slogan of reform has become equity with fairness—compensatory education.

Population increases have been most marked in metropolitan areas of one to two million persons. In the last decade, the growth rate of metropolitan areas of one to two million people was double that of larger metropolitan areas and more than one and a half times that of smaller metropolitan areas. This selective settlement may give us clues to the balance sought by people between the benefits of multiple choices in the largest metropolises and the diseconomies and dissatisfactions of very large scale. Large numbers seem to be selecting variety but of a middle rather than a gargantuan order. Associated with this choice is the growth of the newer metropolises of the developing south and southwest compared with that of the older metropolitan areas of the eastern seaboard, for example, Boston, New York, Philadelphia, and Baltimore. The population increase in these four areas was modest: between 6 and 14 percent. Dallas, Houston, and Atlanta, in contrast, showed a growth in population on the order of 40 percent.

There have also been significant shifts in the differences between black and white populations. The white population in central cities declined 1 percent in the nation as a whole. However, this figure masks important variations among metropolitan areas. In the twelve largest metropolitan areas white population in the central cities decreased by more than 13 percent over the last decade. Some of this population loss was due to low natural increase but the vast majority was due to outmigration. Washington, D.C. led the nation with a white net outmigration over the decade of 40 percent of the total white population. Meanwhile the number of whites in suburban areas increased by 24 percent.

The black population has continued its path to urbanization. In fact the moderate growth of central cities was due almost entirely to black population increases. Between 1900 and 1940, black urban population trebled, from 1.3 million to 4.4 million; thirty years later it had trebled again, to 13.1 million. Now almost 60 percent of the nation's blacks live in the central cities of metropolitan areas, constituting 21 percent of their total population. Blacks are a majority in some cities: Atlanta, Gary,

Newark, and Washington. In others—Baltimore, Birmingham, Charleston, Detroit, New Orleans, Richmond, Savannah, St. Louis, and Wilmington—blacks comprise more than 40 percent of the population. Statistically, few blacks live in the suburbs even though their numbers increased substantially—by one million—and at about the same rate as whites during the 1960s. But blacks still account as they did in 1960 for only about 5 percent of the total, but 16 percent in the suburbs of the metropolitan areas with 500,000 or more people.

New service as well as manufacturing jobs are located in the suburbs. Attracted to the suburbs by the presence of land for expansion and its lower cost, a growing population, and fewer problems as viewed by the managers, increasing numbers of firms are moving to the suburbs. In the manufacturing sector the growth rate of employment in central cities in the 1957–1967 decade was 6.8 percent; in the suburbs it was 32 percent. Employment in retail trade grew at a rate of 7.7 percent in central cities but 60.6 percent in the suburbs. For all service activities, the employment growth rate was 25.3 percent in the central cities and 75.3 percent in the suburbs.

During the decade of the sixties in the country's fifteen largest metropolitan areas, the total number of jobs in the suburbs increased 44 percent. But jobs in their central cities decreased by 7 percent, so that by 1970 the fifteen central cities had barely one-half the total number of jobs for their metropolitan areas instead of the two-thirds total of a decade earlier. And only one-quarter of the workers living in the corresponding suburbs commuted to the central cities to work. Reverse commutation—from city to suburb—rose from 4 percent in 1960 to 7 percent in 1970. The remainder held jobs in the outlying areas where they lived.

In 1971, for the first time in the nation's history median family income was above $10,000. Overall, there were important income gains for all groups over the last quarter century—for blacks as well as whites. The income of non-white families has grown faster than that of white families, rising from one-half that of white income in 1947 to two-thirds of it in 1970. Yet income distribution remains relatively constant. Between 1947 and 1972, the poorest fifth of American families received about 5 percent of the total family income and the richest fifth received about 42 percent. In constant dollars the gap widened between these two groups from less than $11,000 to more than $19,000.

The lowest income quintile is very heavily concentrated in center cities. The Census Employment Survey shows that the 1970 unemployment rate in central city survey areas was 9.6 percent. The notion of subemployment, including, for example, those who work part-time but wish full-time work, assumes that this figure is far too low.

If families generally have been getting more prosperous, they are also younger. In 1970 the population of the United States was 1-1/2 years younger than in 1960, the median age decreasing from 29.5 to 28.1. This decrease occurred despite the downward trend in fertility rates over the past decade which has reduced the population under age ten from 22 percent to 18 percent of the total population. There have been sufficiently large gains in the ten- to nineteen-year-old age cohort to lower the median age.

Almost half the nation is under twenty-five years of age, 45 percent. The number of fifteen- to twenty-four-year-olds increased nearly 50 percent during the past decade. Since most crimes are committed by people in that age bracket, much of the increase in crime could be ascribed to that demographic change alone. There will soon be more twenty-two-year-olds than persons in any other single-year age group. They will among other things be candidates for marriage and household formation. The number of women in the work force has increased from 13 million or 26 percent in 1940 to 30.8 million or 40 percent in 1970.

Family size has decreased somewhat during the past decade. Affluence has permitted and current life styles have encouraged more young and old to maintain their own dwellings. The number of such households increased by a startling 50 percent; now every sixth household is composed of only one person. Communal living arrangements, despite the Sunday supplements, have been unnoticeable statistically, but women's liberation, involuntary or voluntary, has not: the number of families headed by an unmarried—including widowed or divorced—woman increased by one-third during the decade. Now more than 10 percent of all families are headed by women; for blacks, the rate is about double. For low-income families, the percentages are very high. Of total white families at the poverty level, a third are headed by women;

for black families three-fifths are headed by women. Women still outnumber men as they have since 1950: the figure has increased since then from 100 women for every ninety-nine men to 100 women for every ninety-five men in 1970.

Not only has the number of households increased dramatically, but the location of new accommodations for singles or small families or households is shifting. In the last years more apartment units have been built in the suburbs than in central cities and the number of such living arrangements about doubled in the suburbs in the decade. There is now one suburban apartment for every two in the city. But the newer units are for the more affluent singles and couples; the youngest, the poorest, and the oldest are still in the central city multiple units.

Although population changes have never had an equal impact upon all localities, the changes of the past decade have reinforced certain differences. The suburbs of the metropolitan communities have the largest concentrations of white, middle-aged, prosperous residents and are offering room for the younger, white skilled, blue-collar workers and their families. Although the suburbs have expansion problems requiring new community facilities and services, and increasingly have growing rates of crime, they do not have the accumulated deterioration and obsolescence of the center cities, nor large numbers of poor people.

Metropolitan government or even cooperation between suburbs and cities has been discussed throughout the twentieth century, but has rarely moved close to reality. Lyle Fitch points out in the *Public Administration Review* for September-October 1970 that in the few cases of recent county-city consolidation, there was little municipal government of consequence outside the central cities. Moreover, recent county-city consolidations have been precipitated by different factors. In the Jacksonville-Duval County consolidation, the precipitant was the exposure of corruption in the municipal government; in Indianapolis-Marion County, it was the desire of the Republican organization to maintain political control; in the proposed Atlanta-Fulton County consolidation, not yet consummated, a strong factor is white fear that the blacks will take over political control of Atlanta.

One current impetus to various forms of metropolitan government is the wish of some affluent whites to protect their city investments and perpetuate their political control. On the other hand, central city residents, traditionally assumed to be eager for metropolitan government, may no longer be so interested, particularly if the growing number of center city blacks continue to flex their political muscle. Blacks may feel that central cities will benefit to no greater degree from metropolitan government than from separate political status, and that they, at least, where numerically strong, could claim a larger share of the jobs and other benefits of local government than would be possible otherwise.

Albert Shanker, the New York City teachers union leader, asserts that schools under neighborhood control are no better than before; they have merely been opened to the spoils system. Blacks, even if they agree with the assessment of school quality, may feel, however, that they have achieved a substantial gain if the school jobs are going to them instead of to the whites. Similarly, they may feel that even if cities function no more efficiently, it will still be a positive gain for blacks to hold substantial numbers of political, administrative, and service jobs.

Fiscal Dilemma

Urban experts from the time of the turn of the century have seen the city as short of funds. But the gap between revenue and desired level of expenditures was a measure of the rising expectations toward municipal services and facilities: halt of blight and deterioration, improved mass transportation, construction of community colleges, new civic centers, summer use of the schools —there were always new or improved programs for which funding was sought. In the past decade, however, costs have been escalating especially rapidly while services at best are stable and, more usually, are deteriorating.

Inflation is certainly responsible for much of the increase in costs. Yet state and local government costs increased more than twice as much as those in the private sector, 54 percent compared to 23 percent, and governmental pay increases have averaged 7 percent per year, equal only to the construction industry in the private sector. Now for many categories of work, municipal employees are higher paid than those in comparable positions in private industry or the federal government and have greater benefits—retirement, vacations, and the like. The number of municipal employees has also increased over the decade—up 33 percent. At present one of every eight employed civilians works for state or local government. If federal employment is added in, more than one of every six employed persons works for government.

Of course, able people will not be attracted to public employment without satisfactory wage and salary scales, so the rise in payroll is worrisome more in relation to productivity than in relation to previous wage bills. The lack of effective cost control in municipal service activities and of improvement of productivity—failings shared by most service activities—will not be corrected just by giving greater financial aid through revenue sharing or by having state or federal governments assume a greater proportion of welfare and education expenses.

On the one hand, local governments are caught in political and economic patterns which have no structural means to increase productivity or curb great increases in labor costs. On the other, these governments are blocked from expanding their sources of income to pay for inflation which is not of their devising and for services and facilities that citizens seem to want but not enough to pay for.

Local governments traditionally have relied on the property tax; they have added sales taxes, fees for services, and in some cases payroll and similar taxes. However, local governments are competitive with each other and cannot raise taxes to the point where residents or firms will vote with their feet, or more accurately their motor cars, moving to another less expensive locality. As sales and income taxes have been added, the percent take of the state and local tax dollar from the property tax has declined: from about 73 percent sixty years ago (1913) to about 38 percent (estimated) in 1971. In absolute terms, the dollar return from the real property tax has been enormous: $40 billion nationally, double that of a decade ago, and rising by almost 10 percent per year. The incidence is about 60 percent on residences and 40 percent on businesses, but assessments vary enormously within and among communities. The property tax has long been regarded as regressive, as inequitably applied, as detrimental to reinvestment, since it is levied against improvements rather than just land. Lately it has been assaulted as well in the courts and it is possible that property tax assessment and collection will become someday a state rather than a local function.

While the property tax has declined proportionately, the fastest growing sources of funds for state and local governments have been the income tax and federal grants in aid. In 1959, state and local income taxes produced less than 5 percent of revenue, and by 1969, 8.5 percent (9.5 estimated for 1970); federal grants in aid were 14.8 percent in 1959 and 17.1 percent in 1969 (18.6 estimated in 1970). State and local governments understandably are demanding more federal funds. The recently inaugurated federal revenue sharing program is one response. At present the federal tax take is 24 percent of the national income (approximately $189 billion in 1970) and the state and local take is 11 percent of national income (approximately $89 billion in 1970). Total taxes have thus risen from 20 percent of the national income in 1940 to 35 percent three decades later.

Over the past years state and local governments have been shifting expenditures for various functions, most notably and steadily in education, which has risen from 31.5 percent in 1950 to 36.1 percent in 1960, to 40.2 percent in 1968. The long-term trend in state and local public welfare expenditures, interestingly, has been relatively steady, and even decreased from 12.9 percent in 1950 to 8.5 percent in 1960, remaining within the 8 to 9 percent range until 1968 when costs began to mount rapidly. In that year it went to 9.6 percent. Since that time welfare expenditures have climbed greatly. Beginning in the mid-1950s, the federal government has paid for the largest share of welfare expenditures. Health and hospitals as a local expenditure remained fairly constant over the eighteen-year period, 1950–68, being 7.7 percent in 1950 and 7.5 percent in 1968. Expenditures for roads and highways decreased from 16.7 percent in 1950 to 14 percent in 1968 and protection and sanitation decreased from 9.2 percent to 7.7 percent over the same years.

The proportionate shifts are significant in terms of priorities and responsiveness to changes in the social and economic and political environment of government. But it is the absolute sum of money expended that most affects the taxpaying citizen: even where expenditures declined proportionately, as they did for highways, outlays were higher. For example, expenditures for highways by state and local governments rose 60 percent in the ten year span from 1959 and 1969, reaching a total of $15.4 billion. The increase in welfare, education, and health expenditures are staggering.

Thus, the fiscal dilemma. State and local governments have strained their tax-generating sources and the look to the federal government is one of desperation. But the pot of gold once anticipated at the end of the Vietnam War may be an illusion: federal officials and others are cautioning that there will be no great funds to be diverted to community and social purposes, and indeed Brookings Institution has prepared a study indicating that public programs are over committed for the period ahead and that taxes must rise just to support what is already under way. The fiscal prospects for urban areas appear bleak.

Raising questions and analyzing data are necessary; however, such procedures, no matter how helpful, are not sufficient to solve problems. Instead of the development of agreement among interest groups on objectives that could be shared, recent years have seen the establishment of vocal splinter groups, each strong enough to veto another group's suggested urban programs, but none persuasive enough to propose programs on which a community could unite. We have had years of negativism and obstruction.

I do not suggest that we should prefer a silent citizenry nor that we should aim only to please the middle of the social-economic spectrum, nor that the old ways were better. Too many reforms have benefited primarily middle-income groups, the ones that were the most articulate and able to propose programs and policies. Now, interest groups who either did not get their share of the pie or who feel they are the most immediately affected by an urban program or project simply block many of the actions that were once unquestionably approved or enthusiastically hailed as answers.

While solutions may not be readily available, I believe that we require a new optimism, a new kind of urban leadership, not on an all-or-none basis, but on an experimental basis. We need to take chances.

We need the national courage to adopt a handful of urban areas as live model cities where major experiments can be tested.

For example, we ought to experiment drastically with education in order to improve it. The numbers of Americans in school and the levels of education attained are impressive. The median number of school years completed for the population over twenty-five is 12.2. Of all persons twenty-five years or older, 55.3 percent have had four years of high school or more and 12.0 percent have four years of college or more. In the eighteen- to twenty-four-year-old cohort 67.5 percent of all persons have completed four years of high school or one to three years of college. A comparison of these two age cohorts reveals that the country is becoming increasingly more educated in terms of number of school years completed. In central cities, not surprisingly, only 57 percent of persons twenty-five years or older have completed high school compared with 66 percent in the suburbs. Among all those aged twenty and twenty-one the median is 12.8 years, almost a year of college—for blacks, it is 12.4. However, encouraging as they are, these figures do not reveal the quality of education received. There are vast differences between, say, a central city all-black high school and a neighboring suburban, upper-middle class high school. Yet both may be deficient. There may also be better ways to learn than through schools. Such experiments as the combination of work and school should be tested.

We should develop test projects on such problems as security. Stockholm monitors some streets with a system of closed circuit TV. Is it too much of a big brother approach for us to attempt and evaluate such a monitoring for an American city? We have never understood why crime in the streets is such a peculiarly American phenomenon. Nevertheless it is not wrong to deal with symptoms when causes elude us.

We should experiment with having private corporations responsible for various city services to see what kind of savings and efficiencies such changes might produce. It may be that much of the future of urban administration will be or should be in the hands of organizations which are not municpal agencies.

Local government had formerly been in the forefront of administrative innovation. Even capital budgeting was borrowed from local government by private industry. There used to be great high schools in our great cities—schools known for the special achievements of their students, based on special programs.

There was an era not too long ago when great city parks and waterfront developments and city planning projects dotted the American urban landscape. The vigor seems gone. Perhaps the malaise is a general one of our country and our world. The vitality that has been lost could be recaptured if more people felt they could devote all or part of their lives to helping America's communities. The energies and talents of the young in particular could be tapped if they saw hope instead of frustration in working within and with city governments—if they could believe that cities can provide solutions to the nation's problems instead of being the problems and that these solutions hold promise for the future of us all. It is then that they might take advantage of the increasing educational offerings in urban affairs.

The challenge is for all levels of government, and all are concerned with the urban community, to work with private groups, with universities and with other institutions not only to understand what is happening—we are already accomplished at description—but to fulfill the potentialities for an economically, socially, and aesthetically rewarding life which continue to exist and which not many years ago seemed closer to realization. Let us not lose faith in urban America.

Commentary on the Meyerson Paper

BY WILLIAM G. COLMAN

ABSTRACT: While in agreement with all of the propositions in Dr. Meyerson's paper as to their importance and relevance, I would have a somewhat different listing in terms of priorities. The basic theme, however, is one that should give us all concern: the slowness of this country and its institutions in responding to long-standing problems.

Urban problems are apparently low on the priority list of the presidential contenders. Significantly, many urban issues are within the reach only of the political leadership at the national level. Few can be successfully met below the metropolitan level.

My own list of issues and problems are somewhat different. While we all differ in their priority, we are agreed on their need for resolution.

William G. Colman has a graduate degree from the University of Missouri and has had wide experience in public administration. He has served with the Oregon Civil Service Commission, Economic Cooperation Administration, Federal Civil Defense Administration, Office of Defense Mobilization, and the National Science Foundation. On retirement from the Advisory Commission on Intergovernmental Relations, where he was executive director from 1960–70, he has broadened the scope of his activities through consultancies with local, state, and federal commissions. He is an honorary member of the International City Management Association and a member of the National Academy of Public Administration.

I HAVE a few comments here * which are rather disjointed— due in part to the wide spectrum of the title of the paper. I agree with all of the propositions in President Meyerson's paper

* Edited transcript of Mr. Colman's extemporaneous reactions to President Meyerson's paper which he had not received in advance.

as to their importance and relevance. I would have a somewhat different listing in terms of priorities, and I think anyone who tries to come up with a comparison of major urban problems would list the issues somewhat differently.

The basic theme in Dr. Meyerson's paper is one that should give us all concern: the very great slowness of the country and its institutions in responding and coping with these problems that have been around for a generation. This I suppose is a manifestation of what we all recognize as one of the attributes of a democratic society, namely, a slowness of response and of deliberate speed and so forth.

I don't think it is any accident that the problems of the cities is fairly low on the totem pole of the current presidential candidates. Mayor Kevin White made quite a point of this is an interview recently. Why is this? It is because these very pressing problems of the center city affect and concern directly only a minority of the voting population, and the fact of the matter is politically that we cannot muster a majority in this country for the conventional wisdom of urban renewal and the low-cost housing programs that has prevailed over the last ten or fifteen years regarding the so-called urban problem—pour more money into urban renewal, revitalize the city, and so on. This does not command a majority today.

My major difference with the scale of things presented in Dr. Meyerson's paper is that these are all relevant urban issues, but a number of them are beyond the reach and scope of the urban administrator and urban political leadership. A lot of these issues are within the reach only of political leadership at the national and state levels and of business leadership at the metropolitan level, representing entire metropolitan trading communities.

In my own list of things in the first category, that is, the challenges to national and state political leadership, I would comprise some that Dr. Meyerson has treated and some that he has not.

I think at the top of the list I would put the increasing squeeze on the public sector in terms of gross national product. Our statisticians still can say that we are fourth or fifth from the top of industrialized countries in what we set aside for the public sector, but what they do not point out is that most of the other industrialized countries alluded to are just two or three percentage points above us now and all in the upper thirties. We are thirty-third, thirty-fourth, or thirty-fifth, depending on how you want to divide the numbers, and we can no longer say that the public sector is starved in this country relative to the private sector. This being the case, one of the major problems confronting the national leadership is reordering priorities and asking ourselves can we any longer afford to put $6–7 billion a year into American agriculture, for example. That is more than the total appropriation of the Department of Housing and Urban Development. Can we any longer afford to spend as much on highways and on various business subsidy programs as we did? And, of course, the whole question of national defense comes in there too.

A second major question confronting national leadership is how to better involve, how to effect a better marriage between public officialdom and private business in coping with public problems. The Committee for Economic Development and others have made stabs at this, and some examples exist of successful local urban coalitions: but these are the exception rather than the rule. We have not yet forged a good public-private partnership in this country in regard to confrontation of major urban problems.

Next I would question the conventional wisdom of orienting our programs to places rather than people. We talk about saving cities, family farms, small towns, and so on. At least in terms of research I think that we need to look at some alternatives. And I would throw out as just one example a study of planned partial or large-scale depopulation and disinvestment in inner cities. Getting the people to where the jobs are and getting the people in the central city into suburban jobs and going with the economic tide rather than fighting it, is what I'm saying. We have been fighting the economic tide for some years without very much success. What are some of the pros and cons? Very little research has been done on that. The disinvestment through such a program would be in the scores of billions obviously but our investment, futile so far in central city revitalization, is also measured in scores of billions.

Another major issue of vital concern in urban areas is income maintenance and effecting some kind of a marriage between workfare and welfare. A great majority of the American people still believe in the work ethic, and we have to work out some compromise between viewpoints epitomizing Russell Long on the one hand and welfare rights organizations and the National Urban Coalition on the other. There must be better methods found for income maintenance but we must also have better methods of assuring an opportunity for work.

Dr. Meyerson has covered very well the whole question of national and state growth policies and this is high on my priority list. I am still talking about the issues confronting national and state political leadership.

Also I would put in here, last but by no means least, equality of educational opportunity and the revolution, fiscal and political, that is going on right now with regard to the financing of education.

In another framework I would put some major issues confronting urban administrators particularly. I think pretty close to the top of the list I would put the whole question of service equity among neighborhoods and doing something about the scandalous discrimination that exists in the delivery of municipal services. I put right along with this the structuring of neighborhood government, as a means of giving an articulate and direct voice to the disadvantaged. Dr. Meyerson has alluded to the shocking decline in municipal employee productivity and very high on my list of issues confronting urban administrators is the development of a higher standard of fiscal integrity and political guts for the municipal bargaining table. We surely don't have that at the present time. We have unfunded pension rights running to frightening levels and if mayors and managers don't shape up on this bargaining matter fairly soon, state legislatures are going to have to shape them up. It has already occurred in New York, and it is liable to occur in a lot of other places unless there is some new approach worked out.

Another big challenge for urban administrators is integrating education with other municipal functions. It has existed for a long time in a watertight compartment politically and physically and this of course is highly unrealistic. What goes on in the city schools is one of the key determiners of the urban future; the urban administrator needs to try to get on top of that.

Also of a similar nature is the complete overhaul of the administration of justice at the urban level, particularly judicial and correctional aspects which we know are a national scandal.

Well, this list could go on and everyone could cut these priorities in a different way, but it is obvious that we have a long shopping list of issues. Some of them are shopping lists for the Congress, the President of the United States, governors, and legislative leaders. Others are on the agenda for mayors and councilmen and business leaders, and several of them are of special concern to city and urban county administrators.

Commentary on the Meyerson Paper

By Mark E. Keane

ABSTRACT: Dr. Meyerson's paper is informative and provocative, but pervaded with despair for the ability of urban leaders and administrators to deal effectively with our urban problems. It is difficult to fully share this despair. Local government, it is my judgment, has not lost its vitality. One important source of this vitality today remains in the city management profession. Urban administrators are concerned about the need for productivity in municipal services, are willing to consider and encourage reform, and are dealing with problems in an innovative and experimental manner. There may be reason for guarded optimism. Although we are making important attempts to deal with problems at the local level, we need time, we need resources, and we need a great many more and better educated urban administrators.

Mark E. Keane has been executive director of the International City Management Association (ICMA) since July 1967. He was city manager of Shorewood, Wisconsin, Oak Park, Illinois, and Tucson, Arizona and immediately prior to coming to ICMA was deputy assistant secretary, Department of Housing and Urban Development. He has been active in the field of public administration since graduating from Purdue University.

FOR urban leaders and administrators this is no time to lose faith. With this admonition, Dr. Meyerson closes a very informative and provocative paper. Strangely enough, however, this paper does not seem to take its own excellent advice seriously. It appears to have lost faith. It is pervaded with despair for the ability of urban leaders and administrators to deal effectively with our urban problems.

The paper despairs of solutions. It cites a number of critical urban problems but is unable to offer much hope for their solu-

tion. Local government, to whom we may reasonably turn for
help in reaching these solutions, has lost its vitality. The steam
seems gone, Dr. Meyerson reasons. Perhaps the malaise is a general one of our country and our world.

Well, perhaps. The problems are difficult to solve. Local
government certainly cannot solve them alone. And some days
in some urban areas would cause even Pollyanna to frown.

But it is difficult to fully share this despair. Local government, it is my judgment, has not lost its vitality. One important
source of this vitality today remains the city management profession. And there is reason to be guardedly optimistic about the
ability of urban administrators to deal with the problems of
America's cities. Within their own jurisdictions, in their relationships with other units of government, and at the national level,
many professional administrators are coming to grips with urban
problems. Not all administrators are performing so admirably,
of course, but a significant enough core of the profession is dealing
effectively with urban problems to warrant looking at them in
some detail.

LOCAL ACTION

At the local level, urban administrators are increasingly concerned about the need for productivity in municipal services.
When I refer to urban administrators, I choose to focus on the
person in local government, a part of it, working for locally elected
officials. They are willing to consider and encourage further reform in the management structure of local government. They are
dealing with the problems of the environment and human services
in an innovative and experimental manner.

Productivity

Take productivity for an example. Urban administrators
have always been sensitive to the need for productivity in municipal services. And they are also sensitive to the need not to con-
fuse productivity with efficiency. A study being jointly conducted
by the Urban Institute and the International City Management
Association (ICMA) has been exploring the issue of municipal
productivity for some time. One of the by-products of the study
is the realization that a great many cities in the nation are con-

cerned with productivity, how to define it in terms of citizens' basic needs, how to measure it, and how to manage to achieve it. St. Petersburg and Tampa, Florida, for instance, have recently begun to define and operationalize productivity in the human service areas. Many other communities are attempting or contemplating similar experiments. So productivity is a growing concern, and no longer in terms of economic efficiency only but in terms of producing services for citizens.

Reform

Another concern of the profession is to perpetuate the spirit of reform that characterized the early city manager movement. It is examining itself and its relationship with the problems of urban America. And it is asking questions about the proper organization of city government in urban areas and the role of professional administrators in this organization. It is no longer wedded solely to the council-manager plan. It believes that the growth of urbanization since the invention of the plan by Richard Childs in the early twentieth century and the multitude of urban political forms require that each city be considered individually. Where modification of the council-manager plan is appropriate, it should be modified. The important thing is to optimize the influence of the professional urban administrator in each setting. So today the profession not only includes city managers, but chief administrative officers in cities with strong mayors, county executives, and council of governments executive directors. The spirit of reform is very much alive and well in the urban administration profession today, although not marching behind a single banner.

Innovation

City managers, chief administrative officers, and other urban administrators are involved in implementing and promoting innovation and experimentation in dealing with the management of all city services, including environmental control and human development. Scottsdale, Arizona, and Simi Valley, California are among a number of cities which have developed innovative and exciting programs related to the environment. In the human services, many cities have experimented with the treatment of drug abuse and with corrections, employing the newest and most innovative techniques. In the field of law enforcement, it is not necessary to travel to Scandinavia to find local officials willing to develop innovative programs. Oakland, California, and Dade County, Florida are just two localities among dozens operating truly exciting experiments in the criminal justice field. In terms of general management techniques, Dayton, Ohio, and San Jose, California have been the testing grounds of literally dozens of radical and workable innovations in city management.

Intergovernmental Action

But many urban administrators have not limited themselves to their own municipalities. Their relationships with other municipalities and their states have also been productive of important social benefits. Consider the housing integration scheme worked out in the metropolitan Dayton area. Or consider the experiment in interlocal revenue sharing in metropolitan Minneapolis. The concern of the profession with metropolitan councils of governments should not be overlooked. The Councils of Government of Atlanta, Southeastern Michigan, and Washington, D.C. are just a sample which have had professional urban administrators at their helm and among their membership. At the state level, a number of urban administrators have been working hard to develop the kinds of policies needed to manage urban areas.

National Action

At the national level as well, professional urban administrators have worked to develop solutions to urban problems. Through ICMA, they have joined with elected officials at the state, county, and city level to form the Big Six public interest groups, which the last several years have worked in concert toward building an intergovernmental consensus on policies dealing with the nation's problems. Among the products of Big Six cooperation have been two of particular importance. The first is Public Technology, Inc., an ambitious and imaginative attempt to apply technology, some of it directly a result of the space age, to urban problems. The second is the National Training and Development Service for State and Local Government, an organization designed to improve the capacity of state and local officials to deal with the problems of our society, including in large part the urban problems.

In the area of legislation, these national organizations of state and local government have played a major role in bringing general revenue sharing close to enactment by Congress. These new resources would do much to attract better talent to local government.

So, at the national, state, metropolitan, and local levels, urban administrators have been involved in a great deal that is vital, innovative, and successful in dealing with the urban crisis.

EDUCATION AND ADMINISTRATION

At this point, some may have cause to wonder whether the pendulum has swung from the extreme of despair in some parts of Dr. Meyerson's paper, to the extreme of unmitigated optimism in this paper. This was not the intention.

The intention was to suggest that there is reason for guarded optimism. Local government has a significant amount of vitality. The urban management profession stands out as one source of this vitality. Unless this were the case, we could hardly justify our concern about their education.

I have tried to deal with the pendulum at the middle of its arc. In so doing, a number of factors should not be forgotten. Urban management at the local level can deal only with segments of certain problems. Others must be dealt with at the state or national level. Although we are making important attempts to deal with many problems at the local level, we need time, we need resources, and we need a great many more and better educated urban administrators.

Here is where Dr. Meyerson's call for a new optimism and the guarded optimism of our profession both meet the question of educating urban administrators, the major concern of those of us gathered here today. Although our moods are greatly at variance and our perception of reality significantly contrast, I would imagine that Dr. Meyerson and I share many of the same concerns about the needs of educating urban administrators.

The education of the next generation of urban administrators must maintain and give us cause to increase our guarded optimism. The education system must seek to perpetuate and expand the willingness to deal with the urban issues at all levels of government. And it must seek to perpetuate and expand within the profession the spirit of innovation and experimentation in dealing with the country's critical urban problems.

Summary of the Discussion of the Meyerson Paper

By Frederic N. Cleaveland

DISCUSSION of President Meyerson's paper among the symposium participants centered around three different focal points: (1) the "nationalization" of urban problems and urban affairs in the United States over the last several decades, and how this process of nationalization has affected the life of the urban administrator; (2) the current fiscal crisis which the urban sector of American society faces, and its implications for urban administrators; and (3) significant changes occurring in the nature of the job of governing the city, the metropolitan region, and the urban place.

On the first of these themes, conference participants were in solid agreement that the national government is fast becoming the determinative force in American society's efforts to cope with urban problems. For the urban administrator this increasing trend means that he is trying to deal with issues, problems, and difficulties present on the urban scene and directly affecting citizens in his community to whom he is responsible, yet the development of policies and the mobilization of resources to combat these problems are out of his hands. Effective approaches to these problems require regional or national decisions involving state and national actions well beyond the reach of the urban administrator. He desperately needs to become a part of a decision-making network which is national in character involving not only the urban administrator, but county, regional, state, and federal decision structures and officials as well.

Frederic N. Cleaveland is provost and professor of political science of Duke University. He has also served on the faculties of New York University, the University of North Carolina, and the University of California at Berkeley. In addition he has been a senior staff member for governmental studies at Brookings Institution, a member of the advisory committee for government programs in the behavioral sciences of the National Academy of

Looking at the situation from a slightly different perspective, this nationalizing trend suggests that the urban administrator is destined to be—perhaps already is—the line administrator working at the cutting edge of what is rapidly becoming a national field service concerned with urban affairs. In this firing-line position the urban administrator will be caught between the trend towards regional and national approaches to urban problems and the equally strong counter thrust towards a higher degree of differentiation in our society as manifested by increasing pluralism in life styles, and in cultural and social values at the urban, community, and even neighborhood level. As one participant observed: "The whole thrust for citizen participation is in part an insistence on the part of citizen groups in the society who have been inadequately represented to have a say as to how they want to live." Another commented: "He [the urban administrator] is trying to adapt and fit into a culturally differentiated segment a national policy of some kind or other. That puts him in a terrific bind because he has to cope with local needs and aspirations and value systems that differ. For this reason, national programs and national policies will have to leave a high degree of elbow room at local levels if we are going to be able to reconcile these counter trends."

To the symposium participants this complex situation indicated the critical importance of taking a fresh look at governmental structure and the political process in our urban areas, especially at its intergovernmental dimensions involving relationships of neighborhood, city, county, multi-county region, state, and even the federal government. Here the concern was both for structure and for process. One practitioner complained: "The United States is the only Western power that has not changed its basic structure in over 200 years." Another practitioner responded: "More than structural change, the urban administrator has got to look at how we mobilize and bring together in some kind of coalition all the forces at work on the urban scene. Re-

Science, president of the Southern Political Science Association, a member of the National Academy of Public Administration and research director of its education programs, and president of the National Institute of Public Affairs. A graduate of the University of North Carolina, he received his Ph.D. from Princeton University in 1951.

gardless of the structure we are still going to have pressure groups which influence that structure and damage it or make it better depending on how we [urban administrators] relate to these groups . . . I do believe that pulling together the forces in some kind of coalition is a major role of the urban administrator, and how we do that deserves our major attention." One of the educators among the symposium participants put this as a challenge to the educators: "We really have to talk about urban administration in the setting of urban political life. Indeed, in dealing with the education of urban administrators in the years ahead, there is nothing more significant that we can do in educational institutions and on the job than to give them a sense of the political process that is evolving and the future of which we can only dimly perceive."

The second theme emerging from the discussion focused attention on the fiscal crisis facing the public sector, especially the urban public sector, in terms of the allocation of gross national product to improvement of public services. No longer can we say in the United States with any conviction that the public sector is starved to benefit the private sector. As one long experienced practitioner observed: "One of the major problems confronting the national leadership is reordering priorities, asking ourselves whether we can any longer afford to put six to seven billion dollars a year into American agriculture. Can we any longer afford this amount which is more than the total appropriation of the Department of Housing and Urban Development? Can we any longer afford to spend as much on highways and on various business subsidy programs as we have in the past?" But besides the question of reexamining national priorities, it is also important to give much greater attention to questions of efficiency in the delivery of services. We need to evaluate alternative approaches to service delivery and explore how to improve management of delivery systems. As observed by the Comptroller General of the United States as he opened this first session of the Symposium, the central problem facing government in the nineteen seventies is not really money, or even the conflict in ideas; the real problem is the critical business of how to implement public programs effectively. In the area of service delivery and program implementation the urban administrator plays a central role.

On the third theme of significant changes affecting the governance of urban places, the participants talked considerably about citizen involvement, about the importance of minorities, about unionism and employee productivity, and finally, looked at whether consensus exists over what urban governments ought to be doing. Increasing citizen participation impressed symposium members as having both positive and negative aspects. Thus on the one hand a principal result of rising levels of citizen participation in local government affairs has been a significant expansion in the number and vitality of "veto" groups seeking to block public action. On the other hand, it was readily agreed that heightened citizen involvement had also proved a source of healthy initiative in many communities, providing constructive proposals for improvement and change in urban policies and programs. Attention was also given to the increasing part to be played by minority groups, especially blacks, in urban affairs. This was approached from two perspectives. One participant observed eloquently: "Pretty close to the top of the list of major issues confronting urban administrators I would put the whole question of service equity among neighborhoods. Urban administrators have got to do something about the scandalous discrimination existing in the delivery of muncipal services. Closely related is a second issue, the structuring of neighborhood government as a means of giving an articulate and direct voice to the disadvantaged." Another participant emphasized the dynamics of central city politics: "Blacks will put blacks in the jobs [of urban administrators] and the question will be how well they have been educated for them. It is the number one responsibility of universities and existing city managers today to educate, to train, to develop blacks so they can carry the responsibilities of urban administration."

Another new development introducing significant change in the world of the urban administrator is the rise in employee unionism. One experienced practitioner observed that in the field of public education militant unionism among teachers is adding very much to the problem of neighborhood disparity in the quality of education. Strong teacher unions are making it possible in some places for teachers with seniority to bid out of the lower quality schools, thus condemning them to a continuing turnover of inexperienced teachers. Another aspect of public employee relations of concern to the symposium participants was the question of union bargaining negotiations and the issue of employee productivity. All acknowledged the serious decline in levels of productivity among municipal employees and noted that an important issue facing urban administrators in many cities is how to strengthen those bargaining on behalf of the city to insure maintainance of a higher standard of fiscal integrity in the bargaining process.

With these emerging changes altering the job of governing the city, with the continuing shadow of fiscal crisis and inadequate resources hanging over the city, and with the complications of urban affairs becoming increasingly nationalized, the situation of the urban administrator is further undermined by a lack of consensus among either the public or the experts over really what urban governments ought to be doing. It was observed that the municipal reform movement of the early twentieth century had been built around a focus of "how to do it better". There was not much disagreement then about what cities ought to be doing, so that major attention could be given to developing ways to carry out tasks more effectively. In the 1970s we are still concerned over how to do it better, but, in contrast to the earlier period, we are also very much involved in debate over what it is that cities ought to be doing. As long as we as a society lack consensus about the appropriate role and function of urban government, then it is extremely difficult to know how to educate urban administrators. This issue lies at the heart of this Symposium.

Roles of the Urban Administrator in the 1970s and the Knowledges and Skills Required to Perform These Roles

By Graham W. Watt, John K. Parker, and
Robert R. Cantine

Abstract: Through a series of surveys, essays, and
workshop discussions more than 130 urban administrators
made known the new pressures they feel on their jobs and
the public enterprise as a whole. They see the urban administrator sitting in the middle of the proverbial kitchen
with the stove going full blast. The urban administrator is
feeling the heat of the disadvantaged, the disenfranchised,
the disenchanted, the establishment, the average taxpayer,
his superiors, and his own organization.

From among such conflicting interests, he will have to
seek a basis for agreement, or when conscience dictates
stand as an advocate of what he sees as the just way.
While he will necessarily be an active participant in determining how issues will be processed through the public system, he will have to have a keen sensitivity for the consequences of these determinations on the participation of
all segments of the community. This goes as well for determinations of the appropriate dimensions of governmental responsibility and response.

He will identify community needs, actively plead for
various causes, serve his superiors and the community as
high-powered analyst, serve as salesman for his ideas,
serve as strategy developer, and act to protect, or promote
change in community values.

Along with these roles he remains the leader of his
organization, responsible for effective, efficient, and sensitive delivery of service. For most of the decisions in this
policy area, the buck stops here. Although this responsi-

bility is often considered the conventional role of the urban administrator, it is, and will be, full of unconventional challenges.

In all of this, the urban administrator will be enlarging his areas of uncertainty. The areas where events and responses are more or less under his control will be diminishing correspondingly. He will face an open system with changing actors and centers of influence.

From this perspective of their roles, these practitioners sensed an urgent need for knowledges and skills which would let them cope more effectively with growing uncertainty. In particular, they attach increasing importance to knowledge of individual and group behavior, political institutions and processes, causes underlying major urban problems (not merely a description of the problems), values motivating people in our urban population, a thorough understanding of themselves, and a deeper appreciation of social, economic, and political philosophies which have shaped and are shaping our institutions.

To act effectively in his changing world, the urban administrator will require skills which will help him bargain and build consensus, cope with sensitive people relationships, size up his organizational and community situation, perform his analytical tasks in a complex world, assess community needs, and effectively delegate authority to other members of the team. Enhanced skills in these areas will contribute to his ability to cope with the ambiguities and uncertainties of his changing job.

Graham W. Watt is deputy mayor of Washington, D.C. A graduate of Washington College, he earned his M.G.A. degree from the University of Pennsylvania where he held a Graduate Scholarship in the Fels Institute of Local and State Government. He began his career in city administration in Kansas City, Missouri, was city manager of Alton, Illinois; Portland, Maine; and Dayton, Ohio. He received the Management Innovation Award in 1969 from the International City Management Association and was elected president of the Association in 1971. He is a member of the National Academy of Public Administration.

John K. Parker is assistant director, planning and management, in the District of Columbia Government. He formerly served as assistant city manager, Alexandria, Virginia, as director of government management research and faculty member, Fels Institute of Local and State Government, and as a management consultant. He is a graduate of George Washington University and has an M.G.A. degree from the University of Pennsylvania where he held a Graduate Scholarship in the Fels Institute. He has been a guest lecturer at several universities and is author of numerous professional publications.

For biographical statement of Robert R. Cantine see: "How Practicing Urban Administrators View Themselves" in this volume.

WHAT ARE WE EDUCATING FOR?

TWENTY, ten, five, even one year ago this writer would have answered this query with a great deal more confidence than he possesses in the Spring of 1971 as we plunge deeper into what Peter Drucker has aptly termed the Age of Discontinuity. . . . Alas, much of what I learned at the collegiate and graduate levels and during a quarter century of public service (at various levels of municipal government) is as naught when facing the problems and issues of today— to say nothing of the near future.

The foregoing quotation is from one of forty-seven papers written by urban administrators participating in the assessment of changing requirements for graduate education for future urban administrators.

What has happened that would cause a top flight urban administrator to feel this uncertainty? What changes in role have occurred? What new situations is he facing? What knowledges and skills are essential to what his job is becoming? Should more time be spent in enlarging his knowledge of services delivered by government, or in enlarging his knowledge of individual and group behavior? Is his understanding of the political, social, and economic philosophies that have shaped our urban institutions as important as his knowledge of techniques in governmental planning?

Those responsible for the design of educational programs for urban administrators must come to grips foursquare with these questions as they make choices of program content and emphasis. The results of these choices, reflected in curriculums and instructional methods, may have an important effect on the career effectiveness of urban administrators, current and future.

Choices made by the educational planner involve assumptions, explicit or not, concerning the roles of urban administrators, the balance among these roles, the relative importance of various program and managerial aspects of those roles, and the relevance of various knowledges and skills to the effectiveness of the urban administrator's performance.

But the educator planning a program works largely without the information about the urban administrators's real work world that would help him design a better education program. This information gap is being closed somewhat through continuing education activities of professional associations and training institutes, and through a limited exchange of persons between the academic and practitioner environment; yet, as a general rule the educational planner is not well situated to secure original information. And what is available through secondary source materials is in scarce supply of questionable quality, and fragmentary in character, with the possible exception of a few case studies.

One of the early efforts addressing this information need of the educator was published in 1957, entitled *Education for Administrative Careers in Public Service*. In addition, the efforts of the former Council on Graduate Education for Public Administration helped to narrow the information gap. But the years that have passed have been characterized by momentous change. The subject is in urgent need of reassessment, for the sake of the educational planner and thus for the sake of the future generation of those seeking careers in the public service.

This particular effort, with its focus on the urban administrator portion of the public service, is intended to contribute toward such a reassessment. Other endeavors with a similar objective, particularly the National Academy for Public Administration's broad study of the needs for education and training in the public service, extend beyond the urban administrator and his needs. We have thus conducted our efforts in developing information about the urban administrator and his world so as to contribute also to greater knowledge of the changing character and requirements of the public service as a whole.

GAINING THE PRACTITIONER'S VIEWS

During the spring and summer of 1971, a series of surveys and workshops was conducted to gain the practitioner's view of the roles of urban administrators and the knowledges and skill requirements they felt important to their performance.

The American Academy of Political and Social Science provided overall sponsorship of these activities to provide a foundation for a symposium, "Educating Urban Administrators." The International City Management Association, National Academy of Public Administration, and Fels Institute Graduate Associates, out of their concern for improving the professional quality of urban administrators, served as general cosponsors and provided staff support for the project. The Lyndon Baines Johnson School of Public Affairs at the University of Texas and the University of Texas Coordinating Board hosted and funded one of the workshops held in Austin, Texas. The Von KleinSmid Center of Public Affairs, University of Southern California, and the Graduate School of Public Administration, University of Kansas, also joined in supporting the Austin, Texas workshop. The main participants were, of course, the more than 130 practitioners who took significant time from their busy schedules either to fill out lengthy questionnaires, prepare written statements, or attend one of the workshops.

It was recognized from the beginning that coverage would be extended only to a selected group of urban administrators and that this sample, limited as it would be, would form the basis for the assessment. Consequently, the sample included as many different job situations as possible, practitioners of various career spans and patterns, various geographic areas of the country, and differing sizes of organization.

Included in the survey were city and county administrators and their assistants; department heads; planning, finance, and personnel directors; professional leaders of regional councils and other regional organizations; senior members of urban research and service organizations; executive officials of civic and community action agencies; principal staff members of professional associations; and key officials in state and federal programs directed at urban areas.

Participants initially were asked to complete an extensive questionnaire focusing on their participation in various service program and managerial activities, the assumed importance of these activities in the future, and the importance of various knowledges and skills for the effective performance of urban administrators.

A smaller number of participants, approximately fifty, prepared short papers, expressing their own ideas, in their own language, on the roles of urban administrators—now and in the future—and the knowledges and skills they felt were important to those roles.

Finally, two workshop sessions were held to bring approximately seventy-five participants together for a face-to-face, in depth discussion of the topic, "Educating Urban Administrators." These discussions were taped and transcribed.

We think the information is of considerable value to educators. We will use extensively in this paper the questionnaire responses, prepared papers, and workshop discussions to provide the content and tone of what practitioners see the job of urban administrator becoming, how the urban administrator participates in the various aspects of community governance, and what knowledges and skills he sees necessary for effective performance. In doing so we have necessarily provided a framework for this information derived from our own experience as urban administrators.

What Is the Job Becoming?

Yet this very fact—that of coping with accelerating change—is what has made urban administration so challenging, interesting, and dynamic. Truly it is the job where the action is, where there is never a dull moment, and where no two days on the job are ever alike.

This statement is from a paper prepared by the manager of a suburban township. It emphasizes the environment of change within which the urban administrator continuously seeks to find his various roles. These roles are forged from the urban administrator's own expectations concerning his behavior and from the expectations that others have of him.

The context within which these roles can be assessed centers on the critical choices made by the body politic concerning community governance. As we see these choices in broad perspective there are at least three:

1. determining the procedural aspects of how the community should be governed, that is, who does what, when and how;

2. determining the appropriate dimensions of governmental responsibility and response for the safety, health, and welfare of the community;

3. determining how best to manage public resources to get the job done.

The urban administrator continuously searches for his appropriate role in making these determinations, and based upon his findings exercises the future responsibilities which follow. Each of these three critical choice situations bears further exploration. Here are some of the conclusions that emerged from our inquiry.

Determining the procedural aspects of community governance

Of fundamental significance to the urban administrator is the matter of his participation in the task of developing and applying the procedures manual for how the community will be governed. The central problem is one of determining how issues will be processed. Who will participate and when? How will issues be presented? This aspect of community governance involves not only internal rules within his agency or community but also relating each of these to their environment, including other agencies and levels of government.

The urban administrator brings to his task two perspectives, not necessarily separate: (1) his own role in making program and managerial policy as it is affected by the rules; and (2) the public interest as it is similarly affected. To what extent, and in what way, the urban administrator participates, or has an opportunity to affect the process, is determined partly through formal instruments such as the city charter and position controls. However, the English language is often ambiguous. Moreover, there continuously arise situations for which there are no established precedents to govern the urban administrator's behavior. Under these conditions there exists considerable flexibility for the urban administrator's participation.

In their own essays, practitioners described in a variety of ways their changing role in determining procedural aspects of community governance:

1. The urban administrator will increasingly be expected to assist in the process of allocating responsibility to various governmental units—that is, defining what are local, state, and federal affairs.

2. Administrators should push for the inclusion of the disadvantaged and speak for those who do not sit at the decision-making table.

3. The emerging formality of citizen participation is placing new demands on the urban administrator. He is being called upon . . . to decentralize services and increase opportunities for citizen involvement in the decision-making process . . . He must strive to increase the visibility and accessibility of municipal agencies by using such approaches as ombudsmen, community advocates, and neighborhood city halls and service centers. New mechanisms need to be developed for obtaining citizen input before decisions are made and for monitoring feedback regarding ongoing programs.

These three practitioners point to the urban administrator's increasing obligation to be aware of whom the system serves, whose voices are heard in the formation of policy, and where responsibility rests for the resolution of various issues. His actions in the future will call for the application of values that are fundamental to determining how the community will govern itself.

Many of the tough issues reported by practitioners in the survey reveal more pointedly the nature of the urban administrator's participation in determining how issues will be processed. Consider these examples:

1. whether to develop a Citizen's Advisory Committe for preparing a Comprehensive Plan and select its composition;

2. whether to recommend appointment of a Citizen's Advisory Committee for Housing;

3. whether and how to establish a system of ward-based town meetings;

4. whether the city should divest itself of health functions

and organize an area-wide agency for the same service at lower cost;

5. whether to bargain for employees before city council or let employees unionize and bargain with city council directly;

6. how to get the city council to listen to the administrator's advice before taking public positions;

7. whether to continue executive briefing sessions for the council;

8. how to determine the most effective methods to inform the public on city activities and problems;

9. how to communicate with thirty-six community groups;

10. how to deal with private interest groups and individuals who wanted to strengthen the roles of advisory boards;

11. how to keep the council out of purely administrative matters.

This list easily can be expanded to illustrate other aspects of the urban administrator's involvement in determining how the system is to function. What items should be placed on the meeting agenda? When should they appear? Should the departmental budget be submitted to the community?

These specific choice situations go on almost ad infinitum, some more critical than others, some with longer-term effect than others, some initiated by the urban administrator, while others are thrust upon him. But each reflects his participation in determining which issues are processed through the governmental system, how they are to be processed, and who participates at various stages in the process.

In a slow-moving situation these choices may occur less frequently and permit the luxury of intense analysis. In other cases, the urban administrator may be bombarded with several crises simultaneously, severely straining his ability to do more than note the events as they fly by. But by and large, simply by virtue of his position, he is an active participant in this procedural aspect of community governance. In these times of criticism of the system, the task is becoming ever more delicate and sensitive. It goes almost without saying that what happens in this area of policy reflects directly upon the urban administrator's roles in other policy areas.

Determining the dimensions of governmental responsibility and response

In addition to choices about functioning of the system, the body politic makes choices concerning governmental responsibility for community life. Several determinations are encountered. First, in what areas of community life is it desirable for government to assume responsibility? Second, what should be the nature of this responsibility, for example, regulator, operator, enforcer? Third, to what level of service should the government commit itself? Fourth, what is the appropriate response to bring about the desired effect?

These questions call for the application not only of values, but also of analytical ability, legal judgments, political acumen, salesmanship, and a host of other skills and tools that may be essential to the resolution of the issues.

However, in these times of questioning, habit and tradition are challenged for their consequences. Furthermore, there is widespread recognition that the public sector can have a critical impact on the community's standard of living, even in well-to-do communities. In addition, the rapid pace of change in knowledge, values, and technology has contributed to experimentation with new living styles and a feeling that very few things are impossible if commitment and resources are available. In this environment the political system faces a real challenge in responding to questions of responsibility, scope, type, and level of service.

What is the role of the urban administrator? What is expected of him and what does he expect of himself? Excerpts from the short essays written by practitioners help us understand what they see their role becoming:

Thus, the generalist administrator might spend his time . . . faithfully advocating the consumer while drawing elected officials into a common camp with the oppressed and disenchanted; and developing a sense of community whereby neighborhoods not only have clean streets and fire protection but neighborliness, life, jobs, opportunity, hope, and dignity. Not a small order but not unreachable.

Administrators now and in the future must seek to achieve a more equitable way of allocating benefits and resources to groups that have been omitted from participating in our society.

He must acquire political acumen that will cause him not to be labeled as purely a nuts and bolts paper-shuffling, accounting, internal management administrator but rather a politically responsible, effective policy executive who can marshal total community and regional resources to solve community problems and meet community opportunities.

The most significant role of the urban administrator today is his influence on policy formulation. He has the facts about existing conditions. He has the data on the unmet needs and unsolved problems. He has access to the literature and his peers to learn of possible solutions. Hopefully, he has some creativity to develop new solutions.

The urban administrator has to be a developer of new programs. Once he has demonstrated the competence to find new solutions or encourage his subordinates to do so, he must help persuade their acceptance by the legislative body or the public.

Managers should throw themselves into the role of political leader of the community if this is necessary to fill a vacuum that often exists. . . . If this is not done the urban community may not get the leadership it so desperately requires to bring itself back together as a viable entity.

The urban administrator must be a social engineer responsive to the community's social needs as well as its physical needs. He must be able to respond effectively to needs of the disadvantaged who are increasingly becoming a very vocal element within the urban area.

It is my contention that the major role of the urban administrator is to act as a catalyst for the reallocation of resources to people-oriented programs.

Advocacy role: here, the job is to plead the case of the disadvantaged— the poor, the minorities, the young—before his own agency.

The role of administrators as consensus seekers of conflicting interests and the conversion of those interests into policy recommendations and programs is a growing and vital role.

The urban administrator seems to function best as a broker, in the old sense of the word; as one who is paid a fee for acting as an agent in the making of an agreement. The urban administrator never fully understands the process he goes through, or does he need to. The manager, as broker, must know what the demands for change are and what is possible within the system. In most cases the manager serves as the one who searches for the possible. The manager's influence and authority rests on his ability to seek and find the possible. This is what his expertise is built upon.

This image of the manager (as broker) seems to work smoothly as long as there are no absolutes for managers. The manager, however, always seems to have to face the moment when there is no possible way, only the just way. That moment varies with every manager, and so does the response. It can only be said that every manager must leave his (broker's) role when his own conscience dictates. Every manager is a man, and his moral problems are no less complex than those of Hamlet.

One of the most vital roles of the urban administrator is as a planner. This role involves policy formulation and a determination of what is in the public interest in a given situation.

For these practitioners the role of the urban administrator is more and more one of continuous and intensive involvement in all aspects of determining the dimensions of governmental responsibility and response. He becomes both philosopher king and high-powered analyst. He becomes sensor of the human situation, pleader for the cause, and searcher for the possible. He becomes a needs identifier for all segments of the community; special advocate for the disadvantaged; broker of differences, seeking the possible; moral human being who must live with his conscience; developer of solutions to bring about the desired effect; salesman for his ideas; action clock for the community with a sense of timing for action; and protector of, and promoter of, change in community values.

Yet not all urban administrators agree with these role concepts. The disagreements are illustrated in the following terms by two urban administrators, one a city manager and the other a Model Cities Program executive:

With all these new roles added on to the importance of preserving the essential administrative role, the question becomes, can the urban administrator be all things to all people? This is a very real question for which I have no answer than to observe that many urban positions are being created which are essentially man killers. . . . The only area of remedy I can suggest is . . . the role of facilitator of change. I would suggest that with everything else, the urban administrator should not take it upon himself to become a forcer of change. The role of primary policy leadership should be left to others. This permits him to play a more appropriate staff role to the policy changers and does not draw as greatly upon the energy which is required for him to play his other roles.

It is my opinion that the structure of local government will materially change during the 1970s. . . . I foresee an emphasis on placing more responsibility and authority upon the elected offices of mayor and councilmen. . . . Such a change in the environment within which urban administrators operate will result in the administrator acting more as a technician and less as an outward initiator of policy and political spokesman for the city.

For different reasons both statements argue that the urban administrator's role as outward advocate of various social, economic, or political policies will be limited. Both arguments are strong—job survival, and the possible advent of structural change affecting leadership roles. However, the projection of a stronger advocacy role prevailed among the majority of these urban administrators.

Evidences of what these roles mean in operational terms are illustrated by the types of tough issues encountered by urban administrators as reported in their questionnaires, including:

1. seeking to strengthen citizen planning board responsibility even though its members were not supported by the council;

2. providing personnel and equipment to black citizens groups to help them clean the neighborhood;

3. deciding whether to assert the administrator's own recommendations in a highly volatile citizen participation setting;

4. seeking legal action by federal authorities to halt local discriminatory practices;

5. pushing for equalization of refuse collection in all neighborhoods;

6. obtaining consensus on a major new administrative position to deal with youth needs of the community;

7. seeking modification of civil service rules to open jobs to the disadvantaged;

8. recommending against using the city housing agency for suburban, low-income housing;

9. deciding whether to recommend funding new neighborhood grants to build neighborhood action if it meant cutting other services;

10. choosing whether to recommend the enactment of local open housing regulations in light of federal action;

11. facing a split council over the building of public housing;

12. determining how stringently to enforce the new housing code;

13. selling realtors and developers on a public housing program;

14. deciding whether to play the leading role in achieving local consensus on expressway routes;

15. choosing among economy, environment, the travelling public, and the neighborhood in aligning major streets;

16. developing and proposing very strict controls on commercial uses along major arterials;

17. determining whether to assume public operation of a hospital;

18. undertaking conversion of private mental health operations to public funding and control;

19. recommending increases in the welfare department budget that were opposed by a large segment of the community.

A far greater number of tough issues/problems were actually cited by the urban administrators, illustrating the nature and extent to which they have been, and are now, involved in determining the dimensions of governmental responsibility and response. This role is intensive, continuous, and full of hazards. What these practitioners have said to the educational planner about the future is to expect a further extension of their participation in raising and seeking resolution to the people problems of urban areas, with all the consequences this portends for their need to perform as brokers, salesmen, analysts, and so forth.

The urban administrator, like the educational planner, is faced with choices in terms of where he concentrates his energies among various program areas. How he allocates his involvement is partly a reflection of his community's needs, but also is partly a result of his personal choice among competing needs. For those

surveyed, Tables A and B illustrate career-to-date involvement
in various service programs and how the importance of these
services is expected to change in the future.

If an educator had to choose the five service categories for
which greatest substantive knowledge should be imparted through
continuing or pre-entry professional education, responses of this
group of practitioners concerning career-to-date involvement
might turn the educator's attention towards ecology/environment,
public order, land use, transportation, and employment. Least

TABLE A—EXTENT OF CAREER-TO-DATE INVOLVEMENT BY SERVICE CATEGORY (n = 133)

Category	No Answer 1/	Limited	Moderate	Extensive	Weighted Score 2/
Ecology	7	25	51	50	2.20
Public Order	5	32	42	54	2.17
Land Use	10	30	44	48	2.13
Transportation	15	32	42	44	2.10
Employment	15	36	38	44	2.07
Economic Development	15	35	47	36	2.01
Housing	12	38	47	36	1.98
Race Relations	12	50	38	33	1.86
Education	27	48	39	19	1.73
Public Health	15	66	29	23	1.64
Welfare	30	73	16	14	1.43

1/Includes "no involvement" and unusable responses.
2/Weighted score is formed by weighting responses as follows: Limited = 1, Moderate = 2, Extensive = 3, and then dividing the sum of these products by the number of respondents.

attention would be given to welfare, public health, and education.

Such a conclusion, however, would be too simplistic. Broad
differences of involvement exist within several of the categories,
particularly public order, housing, transportation, employment,
economic development, and race relations. In several of these
service categories significant proportions of these practitioners
have experienced limited, moderate, or extensive involvement, reflecting perhaps their unique local situations.

Secondly, if their assessments of the relative future importance of these categories prove correct and bear any relationship

to future involvement, then such service areas as ecology, housing, and race relations will take on increasing importance. These assessments, it should be noted, are highly consistent with the practitioner's role descriptions quoted earlier, in which they stressed their growing responsibilities as advocates and pleaders for the disadvantaged and minority groups, and as active participants in the formulation of policies affecting the human situation in urban areas.

TABLE B—FUTURE IMPORTANCE BY SERVICE CATEGORY

Category	No Opinion	Less Important	No Change	More Important	% More Important
Ecology	12	1	14	106	88%
Housing	21	1	16	95	85
Race Relations	22	3	26	82	74
Public Health	27	4	28	72	68
Employment	20	4	34	75	66
Public Order	14	4	36	79	66
Transportation	20	5	38	70	62
Welfare	44	14	22	53	60
Education	37	3	39	54	56
Land Use	19	2	48	64	56
Economic Dev.	21	5	59	48	43

How best to manage public resources

Whatever decisions are made concerning the procedural aspects of community governance and dimensions of governmental responsibility and response, there remains the conventional task of managing the public enterprise to get the job done. Despite the image of management as the urban administrator's traditional role, there are many cases of promise outstripping performance— of severe breakdowns in effective, efficient, and sensitive delivery of service. For the disadvantaged this failure has often meant further suffering. For the average taxpayer it has often added to frustration and anger, leading to the not-so-pleasant taxpayers' revolt. How do urban administrators view their management role? Consider these excerpts from their own statements;

To me the vital part of the urban administrator is his administrative sense. This intangible commodity is that knowledge and ability needed to get a job done, including the division of work into subordinate tasks, the identification of the sequential logic between tasks, and the ability to assign limited and specialized resources to the accomplishment of the various subtasks in a reasonably efficient manner.

He must be an organizational leader employing concepts of team management and management by objectives. He must seek out and cultivate the talents of his staff and integrate them with a coordinated management team.

The manager provides the leadership for change within the organization. He creates the atmosphere for innovation.

In managing his organization the urban administrator sets goals, shapes strategies for their fulfillment, marshals resources, sets them into motion, monitors progress, and takes corrective action when necessary. . . . He has to be constantly aware of and sensitive to what is going on both inside and outside his organization and what the implications are for the organization.

There are at least two important facets to the role of any urban administrator—(a) conducting the ongoing affairs of the organization for which he is responsible, and (b) reshaping the organization as necessary to better meet the responsibilities set upon it.

The urban administrator is or can be a leader of the administrative organization. He can provide direction, energy, and moral tone for the staff. He can encourage career development through further education, training, and increased responsibility.

The urban administrator must be an evaluator, not only of the new programs he has developed as they move into fruition but also of those which he has inherited. . . . The conclusions [of his evaluation] must be put into effect to modify the activity when it is needed.

While highlighting the general nature of their managerial role, several practitioners viewed the managerial function from a different perspective:

The urban administrator will delegate to functional specialists the management of, and decision-making involving the traditional local departments. In so doing, his role in departmental matters will become more passive except for major items or interdepartmental disputes.

Secondly, the administrator will be further removed from operational line and staff matters which have consumed much of his time and energy and these matters will be increasingly handled by better trained technicians.

Basically, these practitioners see their managerial role becoming one of using the organization creatively, adapting it to new circumstances, and orchestrating the responses of its various components. While not contradictory, the emphasis on delegation of authority does stress a fairly commonly held viewpoint among these practitioners that, for reasons of developing and retaining an effective management team as well as to achieving more effective allocation of his time, the urban administrator will delegate whatever tasks he can. As one practitioner put it:

Managers tend to delegate anything and everything they can. They end up with a repository of things they haven't figured out how to delegate and those are the things they spend their time on.

From the standpoint of fulfilling managerial responsibilities, the most interesting part of this statement is the repository of things they haven't figured out how to delegate. For along with some of the more routine managerial tasks the urban administrator ends up performing, his managerial role has come to involve some very unconventional challenges. The nuts and bolts of management have taken on new dimensions.

The old concept of budgeting as a control mechanism is made secondary to its critical importance in policy formulation. Skyrocketing costs, slow revenue growth, and citizen outrage at growing tax bills have forced the urban administrator to squeeze more performance out of his organization. The old concept of the executive budget, open to citizen scrutiny on sort of a referendum basis, is giving way to the notion of early community input. The remolding of the budget document and process to focus on results and performance has introduced a new complexity into the program planning and budgeting process, requiring new analytical and communication skills.

In the medium- and larger-size cities and counties the pressure continues to mount for neighborhood or area management, requiring development and experimentation with new organizational structures oftentimes involving large overhead costs. If the movement to pattern decentralized management after the Model Cities concept succeeds, many of the old forms of organization and the principles upon which they were based are in for a real wrenching.

The systems approach has also taken its toll on organizational arrangements as the conflict is exposed between old organizational boundaries and the need to coordinate a complex network of resources necessary to accomplish specific results.

For the urban administrator, internal organizational and management problems are also compounded by changing patterns of intergovernmental relations. While there is movement towards decentralization at the local level, at the same time there is pressure for allocation of certain responsibilities on a regional scale, generated in part by urban administrators working at the regional level. Moreover, with the increasing entanglement of local, regional, state, and federal governments, it becomes more essential for the urban administrator to gain knowledge of, and access to, these centers of influence. In addition, the management burdens of high overhead costs, inflexible use of manpower, excessive paper pushing, and intricate grants procedures associated with state and federal assistance programs have further complicated the management task.

At the community level the community organization movement has added to the unconventional challenges facing the urban administrator. In particular, the maze of quasi-public enterprises, such as non-profit housing corporations, have added to the expanding range of management requirements associated with coordination of service delivery.

These unconventional management challenges emphasize perhaps most heavily the task of communication—upwards, downwards, and outwards. The intensity of exchanges, complexity of the information to be exchanged, and the points to which communication is directed have all multiplied. The characteristics of those for whom the message is intended are also varied and must be considered in the communication.

The types of tough issues or problems urban administrators mention in describing their managerial roles reflect some of the conventional and unconventional challenges that make up their real world, including:

1. handling a walk-out by sanitation employees;
2. averting strikes with four employee unions;
3. taking action when council refuses to accept a negotiating agreement with employees;
4. modifying civil service rules to open jobs to disadvantaged;
5. seeking to persuade cities, counties, and other special districts to join a regional sewerage program;
6. recommending only a two percent raise for all city employees;
7. cutting personnel drastically while maintaining essential services;
8. hiring social workers to do police work related to narcotics abuse;
9. determining when to break up an existing organization and remold and restructure activities;
10. directing municipal activities during student demonstrations;
11. coping with complexities introduced by the use of new management approaches such as Program, Planning, Budgeting (PPB), management by objectives, and so on;
12. administering the personnel system equitably in the face of a need to reduce staff;
13. helping to shape up subordinates for job responsibilities; firing incompetents;
14. changing organizational structure to handle urban development problems;
15. achieving an equalization of refuse collection;
16. granting a request from the Human Relations Commissioner for a community relations program over objections of public safety employees;
17. determining the level of police service;
18. developing an adequate executive reporting system for managerial decisions—without entailing extreme overhead costs;

19. determining an appropriate allocation and means of co-ordination of central and departmental planning;

20. achieving increased employee productivity;

TABLE C—EXTENT OF CURRENT PERSONAL INVOLVEMENT BY
MANAGERIAL CATEGORY (n = 133)

Category	No Answer 1/)	Limited	Moderate	Extensive	Weighted Score 2/
Determine budget and other financial strategies	14	12	27	80	2.57
Develop and maintain relationships with governing body or other superiors	16	13	33	71	2.50
Determine organizational structure	24	13	35	61	2.44
Plan and design governmental programs	33	13	42	45	2.32
Determine policy and program priorities	29	21	31	52	2.30
Direct and administer program operations, particularly under emergency conditions or in politically sensitive situations	34	28	32	45	2.29
Determine operating systems and procedures	19	19	45	50	2.27
Administer personnel systems and procedures including recruitment, selection and discipline of key employees	16	24	40	53	2.25
Seek the cooperation of other governmental levels and neighboring jurisdictions whose cooperation is critical to success of a program	13	23	44	53	2.25
Develop and maintain a communication system both for sending directives and for keeping informed about community and organizational development	29	26	44	34	2.08
Negotiate with employee unions and other employee groups	15	53	30	43	2.07
Involve citizens, particularly minorities and disadvantaged persons, effectively in the decision-making process	16	33	52	32	1.99

1/Includes "no involvement" and unusable responses.

2/Weighted score is formed by weighting responses as follows: Limited = 1, Moderate = 2, Extensive = 3, and then dividing the sum of these products by the number of respondents.

21. achieving coordination of housing and human resource programs within the organization and with outside agencies and community organizations.

TABLE D—Future Importance by Managerial Category (n = 133)

Category	No Opinion	Less Important	No Change	More Important	% More Important
Involve citizens, particularly minorities and disadvantaged persons effectively in the decision-making process	22	1	23	87	78
Seek the cooperation of other governmental levels and neighboring jurisdictions whose cooperation is critical to success of a program	14	1	28	90	76
Negotiate with employee unions and other employee groups	25	19	27	62	57
Determine organizational structure	31	2	44	56	55
Determine budget and other financial strategies	16	7	53	57	49
Develop and maintain a communication system both for sending directives and for keeping informed about community and organizational developments	38	1	49	45	47
Direct and administer program operations, particularly under emergency conditions or in politically sensitive situations	36	5	46	46	47
Plan and design governmental programs	41	1	40	41	45
Develop and maintain relationships with governing body or other superiors	24	2	60	47	43
Determine operating systems and procedures	26	14	59	34	32
Administer personnel systems and procedures including recruitment, selection and discipline of key employees	24	8	67	34	31
Determine organizational structure	35	12	58	28	29

Some feeling for how these practitioners extend themselves in various managerial activities, and the importance they see these activities taking on in the future, is shown from their questionnaire responses set forth in Tables C and D.

In terms of current personal involvement, the educator would find that determining the budget and related financial strategies, maintaining effective relations with superiors, and determining appropriate organizational structures stand out as demanding the most extensive involvement of urban administrators.

Responses to the survey also suggest that urban administrators are extensively involved in planning and designing governmental programs, determining policy and program priorities, directing program operations under emergency or politically sensitive situations, determining operating systems and procedures, administering personnel management, and seeking the cooperation of other jurisdictions or levels of government.

Finally, their responses suggest the urban administrator is least personally involved in establishing communication systems for sending or receiving information about his organization or community, and for involving citizens, particularly minority groups, in the decision-making process.

However, the educator would want to look further at the extent of variation in these responses for additional clues to guide his educational planning. If he did, he would find several very different patterns.

On the one hand, there exist cases of near unanimity on the extent of the urban administrator's involvement. This is particularly true with respect to their extensive involvement in determining the budget and related financial strategies. On the other hand, the educational planner would find a second pattern that reflected broad differences in the involvement of urban administrators within a particular managerial activity, for example, involving citizens in the decision-making process. Here there is almost an equal likelihood that an urban administrator will have limited, substantial, or extensive involvement.

Finally, the educator would find at least one case of very sharp differences reflecting a situation in which the urban administrator is either involved extensively or almost not at all in a particular managerial activity, for example, negotiations with labor unions.

When the educator looks at how urban administrators assessed the future importance of these managerial activities, he might draw the following inferences. First, few, if any, categories of managerial activity will be less important to the effective performance of an urban administrator in the immediate future.

Second, urban administrators indicated strongly that intergovernmental relations and citizen involvement will take on increasing importance to the effective performance of urban administrators.

Third, such aspects of managerial responsibility as personnel management, an appropriate organizational structure, and established operating systems and procedures will remain nearly constant in their importance.

Finally, for several managerial activities, including budgeting, program planning, developing and maintaining a communication system, and directing program operations under emergency or politically sensitive situations, there is an absence of agreement about their changing importance in the future.

The Urban Administrator's Need for Knowledge and Skills

Although it is tempting to recommend that a modern urban administrator needs the skill and knowledge of a Renaissance man, the administrator must always be learning. (Excerpted from an urban administrator's comments on graduate programs.)

The educator, in order to market his program or to fit it within a fixed time frame, must make choices among what skills and knowledges he will try to impart. What should the content of his program be? What knowledges and skills are important to the effective performance of urban administrators?

This was no easy question for the practitioners themselves, despite their continuous experience with situations calling for the application of particular knowledges or skills. With their enlarged domain of activities has come a sense of need for new knowledges and skills. Tables E and F, taken from their questionnaire responses, reveal what they sensed as most or least important for the future in terms of knowledge and skills.

TABLE E—IMPORTANCE OF VARIOUS CATEGORIES OF KNOWLEDGE (n = 133)

Category	No Answer 1/	Least Important	Moderately Important	Most Important	Weighted Score 2/
Knowledge of human relations i.e., theories of individual and group behavior relevant to managing organizations	6	9	34	84	2.59
Knowledge of values motivating the behavior of people in urban areas	6	16	44	67	2.40
Knowledge of causes underlying major urban problems	6	9	57	61	2.39
Knowledge of various political institutions and processes	6	19	59	49	2.24
Knowledge of social characteristics, institutions and processes of urban areas	11	18	63	41	2.19
Knowledge of concepts in personnel administration, including labor relations	6	15	84	28	2.10
Knowledge of urban economic development including both public and private sector	7	27	56	41	2.08
Knowledge of the history and aspiration of minority and disadvantaged groups and how these characteristics are reflected in contemporary behavior	7	25	78	23	1.98
Knowledge of organization principles and practices	6	37	59	31	1.95
Knowledge of principles and practices of governmental planning	6	49	60	19	1.78
Knowledge of specific services government provides its citizens: health care, welfare, model cities, etc.	6	62	44	21	1.68
Knowledge of various techniques such as data processing, information systems, etc.	6	65	43	19	1.64
Knowledge of engineering principles	6	110	12	5	1.09

1/Includes "no response" and unusable responses.
2/Weighted score is formed by weighting responses as follows: Limited = 1, Moderate = 2, Extensive = 3, and then dividing the sum of these products by the number of respondents.

In terms of knowledge areas, the practitioners assigned greatest importance to knowledge of human relations, knowledge of values motivating people in our urban population, and knowledge

TABLE F—Importance of Various Categories of Skills (n = 133)

	No Answer 1/	Least Important	Moderately Important	Most Important	Weighted Score 2/
Skill in situation analysis i.e., "sizing-up" the community political milieu, organization, and staff	6	16	39	72	2.57
Skill in bargaining, negotiation & other consensus-seeking techniques	6	13	32	82	2.54
Skill in handling interpersonal relations	7	13	47	66	2.42
Skill in analytical thinking, problem solving and associated techniques of analysis including those employed in program evaluation	6	18	42	67	2.39
Skill in assessing community needs	7	23	49	54	2.25
Skill in the process of delegating authority and responsibility to subordinates	7	20	55	51	2.25
Skill in relating to and understanding minority, disadvantaged, and other culturally distinctive groups	8	23	69	33	2.08
Skill in audience-oriented communication, i.e., speaking effectively	8	31	55	39	2.06
Skill in financial analysis	7	59	49	18	1.67
Skill in organizing and writing policy statements, reports, etc.	7	74	37	15	1.53
Skill in systems design and operations analysis	8	94	25	7	1.32
Skill in job analysis, i.e., assessing the requirements and responsibilities of positions	7	106	14	6	1.21

1/Includes "no response" and unusable responses.
2/Weighted score is formed by weighting responses as follows: Limited = 1, Moderate = 2, Extensive = 3, and then dividing the sum of these products by the number of respondents.

of causes underlying major urban problems. During later workshop sessions and in their essays, knowledge of one's self and knowledge of various social, economic, and political philosophies also stood out prominently. They would have the educator place least importance on knowledge relating to technological innovation, engineering principles, the specific services rendered by government, and the principles of governmental planning.

These emphases are consistent with the urban administrator's role perceptions requiring sensing of the human situation in urban communities, dealing directly with individual people and their values, and achieving improvement in the quality of community life. These responsibilities are not accomplished by the urban administrator in solo—but by working with people—individual citizens, community groups, elected officials, employees in his own organization, and so forth. Success must also be achieved in the context of political institutions and processes—existing or new—set up to handle the processing of community issues and management of the public enterprise. And to deal with the challenges, frustrations, disappointments, and successes of his job, the urban administrator must understand not only others, but himself as well.

Although he may be possessor of considerable knowledge relevant to his roles, achieving their fulfillment demands the acquisition of particular skills which facilitate the application of knowledge to the situations he encounters. Here the urban administrator would have the educator turn most of his attention towards skill in bargaining and related consensus building techniques, skill in handling interpersonal relations, skill in situation analysis, skill in analytical thinking and processes, skill in assessing community needs, and skill in the process of delegating authority.

The practitioner's emphasis again focuses on the challenge of dealing with people and their problems and seeking to achieve agreement from among different points of view. This applies not only to people in the community but also to those in his administrative organization. In the case of the latter, there is a clear implication that if the urban administrator is to devote such a substantial part of his energies to outside roles—developing effective relations with superiors, developing effective community participation, and seeking the cooperation of other jurisdictions and levels of government—the orderly functioning of the public enterprise will require that he be capable of, and skilled in, the process of delegating authority and responsibility. Reflected in his assessment of what skills are least important is his rejection of the role of technical expert and his view of the changing nature of the nuts and bolts of his managerial role.

Summary

Our analysis and review of the practitioner's responses, prepared statements, and workshop discussion have been outlined in the foregoing sections.

It has been clear throughout their responses that these urban administrators feel new pressures on their jobs, and upon the public enterprise as a whole. These new pressures stem partly from society's enlarged expectations concerning the appropriate dimensions of governmental responsibility. The pressures are also partly a product of the complex and quickly changing environment in which public issues get raised, debated, and acted upon.

These practitioners see the urban administrator sitting in the middle of the proverbial kitchen with the stove going full blast. He is feeling the heat of the disadvantaged, the discriminated-against, the disenchanted, the establishment, the average taxpayer, his superiors, and his own organization.

Among the many conflicting interests he will have to find the possible, or when conscience dictates, stand as an advocate of what he sees as the just way. While he will necessarily be an active participant in determining how issues will be processed through the public system, he will have to have a keen sensitivity for the consequences of these determinations on the participation of all segments of the community. His sensitivity must extend equally to determinations of the appropriate dimensions of governmental responsibility and response.

He will identify community needs, plead actively for various causes, serve his superiors and the community as high-powered analyst, serve as salesman for his ideas, serve as strategy developer, and act to protect, or promote change in community values.

Along with these roles he remains the leader of his organization and responsible for effective, efficient, and sensitive delivery of service. For most of the decisions in this policy area, the buck stops here. Although often considered the conventional role of the urban administrator, management is, and will be, full of unconventional challenges.

In all of this, the urban administrator will be enlarging his areas of uncertainty. The areas where events and responses are more or less under his control will be diminishing correspondingly.

He will face an open system with changing actors and centers of influence.

From this perspective of their roles, these practitioners expressed an urgent need for knowledges and skills that will help them cope more effectively with growing uncertainty. In particular, they attach increasing importance to knowledge of individual and group behavior, political institutions and processes, causes underlying major urban problems—not merely a description of the problems—values motivating people in our urban population, a thorough understanding of themselves, and a deeper appreciation of social, economic, and political philosophies which have shaped and are shaping our institutions.

To act effectively in his changing world, the urban administrator will require skills that will help him bargain and build consensus, cope with sensitive people relationships, size up his organizational and community situation, perform his analytical tasks in a complex environment, assess community needs, and effectively delegate authority to other members of the team. Enhanced skills in these areas will contribute to his ability to cope with the ambiguities and uncertainties of his changing job.

STEPS TOWARD IMPROVED EDUCATION FOR URBAN ADMINISTRATORS

For many practitioners it would probably be a real awakening to return to the campus and observe the skills and knowledges being taught to the new generation of urban administrators. Some parts would be hailed as significant advances, other parts would be judged irrelevant.

But if there is to be a reasonable degree of correspondence between the career being prepared for and what is imparted through the formal and continuing education process, then many curriculums and approaches to instruction will have to be revamped. Educators will have to be concerned with the development of the whole individual and the situations he will face, not just with certifying that he or she has made passing grades.

Access to knowledge and skills must not be dependent upon whether a person is pursuing a master's or doctorate, but rather geared to meeting the end product objectives of an educational program which corresponds to the dimensions of the real world toward which the student is oriented. Too often, other criteria prevail in determining program content.

Underlying all of this is the necessity and desirability of increased collaboration between educational planners and the practitioners. This collaboration can take a variety of forms, including consultation between professional associations and educational planners, participation of practitioners in the development and conduct of the educational program, and participation of educational planners in the world of the practitioners.

For the practitioner who sits back and complains about the quality of education for urban administrators, he should be reminded that there is a two-way street to improvement. Only an active partnership between educators and practitioners can enable higher levels of achievement for each and it is incumbent on both groups to take intiative to bring about this partnership.

Commentary on the Watt-Parker-Cantine Paper

By Thomas M. Downs

ABSTRACT: The Watt-Parker-Cantine paper accurately records the self-perceptions of administrators toward their jobs. It does not necessarily describe any part of the reality of urban government today. The manager has created for himself a job that is essentially either a man-killer or a city-killer. Help will come to the urban administrator when he sheds the notion of aloneness, solitude, and sole self-dependence that pervades his job concept and begins to spread the load. The Master of Public Administration certificate will not suffice. The one thing that will severely damage the future prospects of urban administration is the urban administrator's lack of ability or willingness to continually expand the skills and knowledges necessary to solve urban problems.

Thomas M. Downs, assistant city manager of Little Rock, Arkansas, received a master's degree in political science from the University of Missouri and an M.P.A. degree from the University of Kansas. He recently served as chairman of the International City Management Association Task Force on Young Urban Administrators.

WANTED

CITY MANAGER: Large, progressive central city seeking a professional manager. Individual must have skills in bargaining and related consensus building techniques, skills in handling interpersonal relations, in situational analysis, in analytical thinking, in assessing community needs, and in delegating authority. He must have a knowledge of human relations, of the values motivating people in our urban population, of causes underlying major urban problems, of himself and of various social, economic, and political philosophies. He must push for the inclusion of the disadvantaged, speak for those who do not sit at the decision-making table, increase opportunities for citizen involvement, decentralize services, increase the visibility and accessibility of municipal agencies, and assume an advocacy role. He must have legal judgment, political acumen, and sales ability. He must set goals, shape strategies, marshal resources, provide direction, energy, and moral tone for the staff. He must be a policy executive, political leader of the community, a social engineer, a catalyst for the reallocation of resources, consensus seeker, broker, planner, sensor of the human situation, pleader for the cause, searcher for the possible, needs identifier, action clock, and an evaluator. He must be able to use the organization creatively, adapt it to new circumstances, and orchestrate the responses of the organizational components. He must also be able to direct program operations under emergency or politically sensitive situations, to seek the cooperation of other levels of government, and be able to establish complex communication systems. Pay is commensurate with ability.

THIS lengthy job description was not written as a vehicle for humor, but to pull together the various skills, roles, and talents of the urban administrator described in the Watt-Parker-Cantine paper. Each of the above qualities, along with many more, are catalogued as being a part of the fabric of urban administration. The entire Watt-Parker-Cantine paper was an attempt to provide a job description for the position of urban administrator. If the job description spread all over the first page is an adequate recap of that article, then it is obvious that not even Spiro Agnew, with the Holy Grail in his right hand and The Book of the Dead in his left, could adequately fill this position.

REAL PICTURE?

In actuality the urban administrator is sometimes more than the sum of the qualities described in the Watt-Parker-Cantine paper, but he is more often much less. There are many other views of urban administrators in existence that are much less flattering. If you are interested in a description of urban administrators that is reasonably accurate, but not very favorable, read the last half of Thomas Wolfe's book *Radical Chic and Mau-Mauing The Flak Catchers*. The view presented there is from the outside looking in, the view from the other side.

Why then does this paper present such an obviously expansive and all-encompassing view of the urban administrator's job? It is simply because this is how the practitioner sees his job, how he sees his participation in the community, and what knowledges and skills he sees as necessary. What this paper does is accurately record the self-perceptions of administrators. It does not necessarily describe any part of the reality of urban government today. Does this mean the paper is not useful? Far from it. Perhaps the most valuable information about a profession is its self-image. This paper has provided a good look at that self-image and it allows certain observations to be made about that image.

Choke Point

An obvious place to start is with the observation that urban administrators see their role as extremely expansive. The urban administrator sees himself as "the" center of the urban system. He sees himself performing functions that hold together the warp and woof of urban society and in most cases he sees himself doing this singlehandedly. This brings to mind a question first asked by Frank Sherwood and later asked by Keith Mulrooney in the January-February 1971 issue of *Public Administration Review*. That question was, restated somewhat, does the role structure of the city manager often have dysfunctional results for the city he manages? That question has never received an adequate answer, but given the job description urban administrators have worked up for themselves and the expectations of the communities they work for, this would seem to be the case.

It is not the impossibility of the job description that is dysfunctional, it is the fact that urban administrators see themselves inside of that role and try to perform all of those functions. The problem is greatly compounded when they attempt to perform all of these functions alone, or at least with very little help.

The urban administrator himself becomes the choke point in a system when his self-perceptions are as broad as those reflected in the Watt-Parker-Cantine paper. The manager becomes the point where all of the bucks stop, where all decisions must be made, where all communication is routed, where all urban change is implemented, where all solutions are created, where all evaluations are made, and where plans are laid. This self-concept of responsibility soon gets the manager to the point where he does not have time to adequately perform any of his self-assumed tasks. At that point the manager has created for himself a job that is essentially either a man-killer or a city-killer. If the manager attempts to fill all of his self-assumed roles, he begins to work fourteen-hour days, six days a week. He performs in a manner barely adequate to his self-perceptions, but puts such a strain on himself that he soon burns himself out. Perhaps this is one reason so many managers leave the field at such an early age. This is the man-killer side of the problem.

City Killer

If the manager does not have the drive, ability, skill, or knowledge to perform in the man-killing fashion, yet continues to demand that he still be considered the filler of that gigantic self-perceived role, then he is acting in a fashion that is harmful to both his organization and to the urban area he serves. One vivid example stands out in the Watt-Parker-Cantine paper that illustrates how managers become victims of their own rhetoric, when their reach exceeds their grasp. In an almost understated manner, the Watt-Parker-Cantine paper notes that the response to a questionnaire designed to find out how managers actually spend their time suggests the urban administrator is least personally involved in establishing communication systems . . . for sending or receiving information about his organization or community, and . . . for involving citizens (particularly minority groups) in the decision-making process. How managers deal with the role of advocate bears directly on this communication process.

Most managers accept the role of advocate, but few have ever fully examined it. In accepting the function of speaking for those who do not sit at the decision-making table, citizen involvement advocate, sensor of the human situation, and needs identifier, the manager often acts as if he is actually performing these functions. Since it is easy for the urban administrator to convince himself that he is speaking for those not present, he often tends to cloak his actions and programs with an advocate's rhetoric, yet he is seldom able to perform the advocate role with any degree of representativeness. Given the absolute bottom priority managers actually give to creating communication links, it is easy to find the reason for this lack of accurate representation.

The urban administrator who has become a victim of his own rhetoric in this manner becomes a dysfunctional part of the urban system. The urban administrator who feels that he represents those who are not present, but does not expend much energy to find out the actual needs of those individuals, makes actual participation an impossibility. Who will ever listen to the complaints of a minority group if the manager has already spoken for them? This is but one example of how urban administrators get trapped by their own rhetoric and become a part of the city-killer process. Other examples of reach exceeding grasp are plentiful.

Vestige of the Past?

Given the vastness of the problems that faced a manager in the past, given the old traditional corruptness of local government, and given the fact that the manager was often the only mobile, educated professional in city hall, it is easy to see where this role concept came from. Managers were actually the center space, the funnel point, of the entire organization. Today's increasingly complex urban environment and the availability of professional urban assistants has made this role concept obsolete in most cities.

Help

A start on a solution to this problem can be found in the quote by a manager who said, "Managers tend to delegate anything and everything they can. They end up with a repository of things they haven't figured out how to delegate and those are the things they spend their time on." Unfortunately most managers take that "everything they can" in an extremely limited sense. Two quotes in the paper talk of delegating to functional specialists and to better trained technicians. Unfortunately there is nothing in that man-killing job description that can be delegated to a better trained technician. The tasks, roles, and skills described are those of general management. The choke point will not be loosened by hiring more data people, more budget analysts, or more technicians.

Help will come to the urban administrator when he sheds the notion of aloneness, solitude, and sole self-dependence that pervades his job concept. This dependence is highlighted by the earlier mentioned questionnaire that showed managers spending the least amount of their time building communication links.

Urban administrators will begin to find their jobs are less man-killers, less city-killers, when they begin to spread the load. Managers will find they can fill their role expectations, and can perhaps even exceed them, when they function as a group. Managers do not need more technicians, more helpers; they do need more comanagers. Urban administrators have got to eradicate the idea that the top of the pyramid is occupied solely by a godhead. The center of an urban system is peopled increasingly with entire management teams. These teams contain the mix of talent, perspective, temperament, interest, skills, and background which can fill that man-killing job description. As the rate of change increases and cities keep up their out-of-control growth, more and more managers will be forced to seek out and build their own management teams. Many large cities have experimented with this type of management, most notably Dallas, Texas and Kansas City, Missouri. John Taylor in Kansas City has probably done more with the concept of comanagers than anyone in city government today.

QUESTION?

Toward the end of the Watt-Parker-Cantine paper they say practitioners expressed an urgent need for knowledges and skills that will help them cope more effectively with growing uncertainty. This is indicative of the fact that the knowledges and skills needed to be an urban administrator change from day to day, from situation to situation, and from town to town. These urban administrators obviously did not receive the necessary skills and knowledges when they were in school because they are now in urgent need of new skills. In view of their job concept and their inability to deal with this concept in an adequate fashion, managers are in urgent need of help. The situation is all the more serious because that help is available now, but is often unused. Why don't they get this urgently needed help?

EDUCATION

Given the obvious fact that urban administrators cannot be filled up with all of the skills and knowledges needed in one short course, given the gargantuan job description managers have staked out for themselves, and given the obvious need for role perspective, along with the self-professed urgent need for skills and knowledges, it would seem a sure bet that managers are beating a track to every training opportunity available. No such luck.

The International City Management Association has to practically browbeat its members to attend training sessions. Why? It is probably the self-created job concept again. Urban administrators have created such a demanding, all alone, I'm the only one who can run this city, choke point type job that they cannot leave city hall long enough to learn the skills they need for the job. Managers are in a sense caught in a death spiral. They cannot get away from the job long enough to learn the new skills that would allow them to cope with the new urban environment, and they cannot get away because they do not have these new skills and knowledges. Managers continue to try to fill impossible roles by themselves because they know of no other way, and they know of no other way because that attempt robs them of all of their time. If there is any one thing that will severely damage the future prospects of urban administration, it is the urban administrator's lack of ability or willingness to continually expand the skills and knowledges necessary to solve urban problems. The spiral of job too big to take time to learn and job too big because of no learning has got to be broken.

Hopefully this paper has pointed out the fact that the real need for new skills and training does not lie with those who are entering the profession, but with those already in it. The need for education and training is at the urban administrator level and given the rate of change in urban societies, it will probably continue to be.

After seeing how urban administrators have an overly expansive view of their job, after seeing how the rhetoric of this job can become dysfunctional, and seeing that this situation has trapped the urban administrator in a spiral he cannot escape, where does the urban administration educator start? First, urban educators are going to have to try to gently break into this spiral and point out some of the contradictions in it. They are going to have to bring the outside perspective to the manager. All too often urban educators only tend to reinforce the current rhetoric without attempting to make this rhetoric functional. After that, urban educators have a chance to expand the function of the university beyond the traditional concept of filling up captive audiences, certifying these audiences as educated, and leaving them with the impression that they have been, for all time, educated.

Perhaps it is time to realize that traditional university based education for public administration may do many other things, but it does not educate. One shot, fill up programs may cause more harm than good when they leave the individual with the feeling that he has been educated. The traditional method is also a failure in that it interfaces with an urban administrator only once, and then only briefly, during his career.

It may now be time to base graduate level urban public administration education in the city instead of in the university. Because of the need for continuous learning and growth at all levels of urban administration, cities could now afford to hire a full-time Ph.D. public administration type whose only function is the continuing education of the middle and upper management levels of the organization. This person would insure that the skill levels of all urban administrators in the area were kept current. He could also guide the development of newcomers to urban administration by preparing a series of work experiences for them, and supplying the framework to relate those experiences. The concept could be expanded so that a large central city could also provide this type of experience for the staff of surrounding smaller cities.

In this continuing education experience both the urban system and the academic system can be greatly strengthened. This interaction between administrator and educator could benefit the manager in that he could obtain an outside perspective on his job, would have a vehicle with which to articulate and expand upon his self-concepts of his job, and would have a seemingly bottomless reservoir of knowledges and skills from which to draw and learn. The urban educator in turn would find himself participating to a greater extent in urban affairs, would increase his work world contacts, and obtain insights into the needs of urban administrators at any one given time.

In view of the role urban administrators have carved out for themselves, in view of the demands of society on urban administrators, and in view of the blinding rate of change in urban society, it is obvious that a correctly designed, one shot, Master of Public Administration certification is not an answer. A continuous growth and education process is an absolute necessity if urban administrators are going to gain the perspective, skills, and knowledges to perform adequately. Urban administrators and educators can form a valuable partnership for the future—the question really is, can either break out of their traditional molds long enough to form that link?

The answer to this question is extremely important. As Robert Dahl pointed out in *After The Revolution,* some people govern in our society because they are acknowledged as competent. Urban administrators, both individually and as a profession, can easily lose the competence attributed to them. When that competence is lost, because of inadequate job concepts, inadequate skills, or inadequate knowledge, then their chance to professionally administer our urban society is also lost.

Commentary on the Watt-Parker-Cantine Paper

By Henry Reining, Jr.

ABSTRACT: There is little quarrel between this commentator and the authors of the report as far as the substance is concerned. As an educator, one learns a great deal of the practitioners' views from this report. One gains a tremendous appreciation of the public spiritedness of our urban administrators today. The quality of personal leadership is absolutely essential yet difficult to gain through education. The report stresses the quality of synthesis, the ability to make the judgment of a Solomon, and the problem of transmitting this quality through the educational process. The report raises the question of admissions policies in the educator's mind. How do we identify the creative tendencies, the change agent proclivities in prospective students? These views of practitioners demonstrate once more that there is no such dichotomy as politics and administration. Therefore, it would seem that those of us who have been giving our students in the urban administration curriculum lots of politics to chew on have been hitting in the right direction.

Henry Reining, Jr. is dean and professor of public administration, Von KleinSmid Center of International and Public Affairs, University of Southern California. He has also served on the faculties of Princeton University and American University, was assistant director, Port of New York Authority (1945–47) and educational director, National Institute for Public Affairs (1935–45). He served as president of the American Society for Public Administration and is a member of the National Academy of Public Administration.

ONE supposes that since the three authors of the paper are all practitioners and they wrote forty pages on the role of the administrator and the knowledge and skill he thinks he needs and only one and a half pages on his proper education, one as an educator should write forty pages on the administrator's education and a page and a half on his practice. But that righting of the balance would curtail the fun of joining in on the speculation as to what a city manager, a county chief administrative officer, et al. must and should do on the job. It is an open secret that there is not complete agreement among the practitioners, as this report brings out. And there are differences in executive styles among public executives, depending upon the motivation, values, and personality of the executive and what he gets his satisfactions out of, into which this report does not go. Be that as it may, what does one, as an educator—the head of a program which for more than forty years has been purporting to training urban administrators—what does one learn from this report?

One gains a tremendous appreciation of the public spiritedness of our urban administrators of today, at least those several score who responded to the questionnaire and wrote the papers from both of which the authors liberally quote. Obviously, these public executives are highly intelligent, unusually skillful, exceptionally able to express themselves, and impressively dedicated to the public weal; and yet with all that quality one detects self-doubt as to the practitioners' ability to deal with the ever more difficult problems of the future. One respondent used the phrase Renaissance man as required. To the educator this may well be a signal that besides all considerations of skills and knowledge and values, the student-administrator had better be not only of high but of superlative intelligence before he is admitted into the educational program in the first place. The question of admissions policy is therefore very much in order if the educational institution cares to acknowledge its role as gate-keeper and customs-guard at the entrances into the profession of urban administration. Superlative intelligence, rare quality though it be, can be measured.

But what of such quality as personal leadership referred to again and again in the urban administrators' responses—the quality is essential, that is clear, but can it be gained through education? Probably not; enhanced perhaps. Then should its possession not be an admissions requirement? If so, how could it be measured? Peer judgment? Review of past record of leadership of any kind of group? Personal interview? This commentator would wager that there is not an educational program in the country which would attempt such an assessment; is there?

Not just intelligence and leadership is required but that quality which is such a curious blend of the two plus moral integrity, that is, wisdom, the ability to make the judgment of a Solomon. The report says it is also required of the urban administrator of today and will be even more in the future. This quality of synthesis with an answer is referred to variously in the report: analyzing a situation; sizing up a community, an organization, a staff; assessing community needs; evaluating program; formulating policy alternatives; designing systems. How is the educator going to test for that one? Can it be transmitted in the educational process program? Partly, probably yes; but in essence, no. Is there not an inbred quality or set of traits involved which might be searched for in the admissions process? What is it—perspective, judicial demeanor, constructive imagination? Can we identify it in sufficient specificity to make it a parameter—this essence of wisdom?

Finally, as to admissions considerations, at least, there is great emphasis in the report on the rapid rate, indeed the rapidly accelerating rate of change in the job of the urban administrator. Nothing ever remains the same; no things stand still. New mechanisms need to be developed for obtaining citizen inputs, to decentralize services, to improve the delivery of services. It is part of the role of the city and county managers and others such to faithfully advocate the consumer and the disadvantaged, to develop new programs, to be a social engineer, to plan for change. Change, change, change. And yet those of us who have been training city managers for a generation or two remember many of them as conservators in their motivation, devoted to maintaining the status quo rather than pursuing the new and the improved; socially conservative; and politically Republican. What now, educators? How do we identify the creative tendencies, change agent proclivities? Shall we accept only Democrats? It is an admissions problem as well as a curriculum and training objective, is it not?

The rapidly accelerating pace of change needs to be discussed in another context as well, since it cuts throughout the consideration of public affairs education. One is much struck in reading the report, Tables A and B, with the difference that the respondents suggest between today and the future, what the important service fields have been to them to date and the future importance of these same fields. Only the first of the list of five appears in the same ranking, namely, ecology. In ranking as to future importance, the respondents have ecology first again, but housing comes second, race relations third, public health fourth, and employment fifth—in both lists, and public order drops from second in the now list to sixth in the future list.

One is really inclined to quarrel with the 133 respondents in the way in which they listed these service categories. They have education, land use, and economic development as the last three service categories in terms of future importance! And welfare only comes off one position higher. Could it be that most of the respondents were city managers who were not accustomed to dealing with education, because in so many places education is under a separate school district; nor with welfare, because in so many places welfare is handled by the county? This still does not account for land use and economic development being so low, especially since the planning and zoning function is generally to be found in city halls. This is indeed a puzzlement; perhaps our statisticians can help us out when they reassess the composition of the statistical tables.

Tables C and D in the report also bring out the change which the respondents anticipate. The first five elements of personal involvement on the part of the manager are listed in Table C as Determine budget and other financial strategies, Develop and maintain relationships with governing body or other superiors, Determine organizational structure, Plan and design governmental programs, Determine policy and program priorities. Then as to changes anticipated, Table D ranks the following among the first five, and please note that there is only one listing in common; and that falls from first to fifth. The five elements as seen by the 133 respondents in terms of not current but future importance are: (1) Involve citizens, particularly minorities and disadvantaged persons, effectively in the decision-making process; (2) Seek the cooperation of other governmental levels and neighboring jurisdictions whose cooperation is critical to success of a program; (3) Negotiate with employee unions and other employee groups; (4) Determine organizational structure; and finally (5) Determine budget and other financial strategies.

The importance of this changed ranking can hardly be over-stated. The element denominated involvement of citizens goes well beyond the customary definition of government and enters deeply into the realm of governance. It also contains a social justice element in its reference to the minorities and disadvantaged persons. And it belies the old politics-administration dichotomy in using the phrase the decision-making process!

Likewise, the second element, intergovernmental cooperation, gets the manager into decidedly extramural matters.

The collective bargaining element is radical enough; it has been commented on frequently enough and extensively enough in other places than this one so as to merit no further comment here except to indicate the great change which it produces in the supervisory and management situation.

Although the final two tables in the report are not set up on a comparative present time, future time basis, it is extremely interesting to note that the first three categories, Table E, call for knowledge of human behavior, that is, psychology and social psychology; and the fourth calls for knowledge of political insti-tutions, and fifth, of social institutions and characteristics.

The first elements in Table F are equally interesting. They rank in importance of various categories of skills: number one is situational analysis; number two is skill in bargaining and negoti-ation; number three is the handling of interpersonal relations; and number four is that element, wisdom, which was referred to above—it is called in the listing, skill in analytical thinking, prob-lem-solving, and associated techniques!

One is tempted to continue to underscore and emphasize, but this would essentially be repeating the substance of the report. One more comment, once and for all, that there is no such dichot-omy as politics and administration: a great deal is said in the report about the policy role of the administrator. One respondent is quoted even as saying that he thought the city manager ought to step forward as the political leader of his community if no other such leadership showed up! The great majority of the respondents, however, felt that the manager should not go that far; he should content himself with a background, behind-the-scenes role, a policy-formulating rather than a policy-determining role. Therefore, it would seem that those of us who have been giving our students in the urban administration curriculums lots of politics to chew on have been hitting in the right direction.

It will be apparent to the reader if he has gotten this far that there is little quarrel between this commentator and the authors of the report so far as the substance of the report is concerned. One small fight, however. At the very end of the report is the statement that access to knowledge and skill must not be dependent upon whether a person is pursuing a master's or a Ph.D. Maybe so, but given the organization of academic programs, there may be some value, despite what the authors of the report say, in talking about different levels of training and education of urban administrators as related to such customary levels as the master's degree and the doctor's degree. Two years ago a group of city managers came into our School of Public Administration and asked for doctorates for urban administrators. A year or more of discussion followed as to the special instruction which was to attach to this program—the Doctor of Public Administration degree fortunately does not adapt itself to an area of concentration such as local government administration. A program of study was worked out and the first group of fifteen started September 1971. What these men are after is a deeper understanding of human behavior, of politics, sociology, and psychology in the community; a better understanding and a greater skill with analytical techniques and the process of synthesis; and so on. Even though the faculty did not initiate this program—as a matter of fact, had to have some of its doubts dispelled by its management clientele before being persuaded to start it up—there is considerable enthusiasm now behind that doctorate. It will take several years to tell, but it does give the above statement in the report some challenge at least. Such instruction could simply not be imparted at the level of the master's degree.

Commentary on the Watt-Parker-Cantine Paper

By GEORGE J. WASHNIS

ABSTRACT: The Watt-Parker-Cantine paper covers the subject matter clearly and with sufficient thoroughness that anyone reading it should have an appropriate but broad understanding of what urban administration is all about. While the paper provides a complete catalogue of functions and issues, it fails to describe the human conflicts that enter into the urban profession. The urban administrator's role needs to be dramatized, so that the realities of the job will be understood by those students attracted to it. The personal attributes and human skills required of the urban manager cannot be developed in the classroom, thus it will take continual field work and a comprehensive internship to fulfill these objectives.

George J. Washnis is director of municipal studies, Center for Governmental Studies, Washington, D.C. His undergraduate and graduate study was at the University of Pennsylvania where he earned an M.G.A. degree and held a Graduate Scholarship in the Fels Institute of Local and State Government. When he joined the Center, he was chief administrative officer of East St. Louis, Illinois, a post he had held for seven years. The findings of his study of municipal decentralization have been published and he has also conducted a study of the Model Cties Program. He is an active member of the International City Management Association and has served on its Task Force on Management Criteria.

THIS paper covers the subject matter clearly and with sufficient thoroughness that anyone reading the material should have an appropriate but broad understanding of what urban administration is all about. Its principal defect may be that it is largely a shopping list of issues, covering such a broad category of subjects that if one, never having read the report, were asked to define the role of an administrator, he could choose any of several subjects bothering American society and be right on target. Of course, this reflects the nature of the survey questionnaire leading to these conclusions and must be reviewed in that context.

DRAMATIZING THE ROLE

Reader interest and motivation for this subject matter could be considerably increased with the addition of a few pages describing human conflicts, pain, and joy that enter into the urban profession. Regardless of contemporary belief that the administrator's role is one concerned largely with ecology and housing and race relations, it should be stressed that much of the same personal agonies and difficulties which confronted the administrator yesteryear confront him or her today. And to more dramatically demonstrate this role, examples might be used showing how one is pushed to the brink of psychological limitation in such things as disagreements with the mayor, dismissal hearings before the city council, sit-ins, and some others. Only in this manner can a fair assessment of the role be portrayed. The result may be enough to frighten or encourage those with some feelings about entering the profession, and it may attract more appropriate talent, eventually able to withstand the pressures of the job.

ADMINISTRATOR AS ARCHITECT

Today's society is issue-oriented and seeks exciting jobs which deal with these issues. This report appropriately defines many of the issues but does not show clearly enough that the management profession needs to continually reflect current issues and solutions to be able to stay in business. If urban administrators avoid dealing with matters of race, poverty, slums, and citizen participation, some other type of administrator will take over the responsibilities. This could include directors of model cities, community action, human resources, and similar programs. It needs to be more clearly pointed out that the true administrator not only must stay abreast of a changing world but be one of its architects as well.

The administrator is a thinker, planner, and doer. From his broad knowledge and extensive reading, he must judge how this nation should proceed in the future and formulate concepts for new energy resources, new towns, sense of community, national priorities, distribution of wealth, and other issues. He must be ahead so that no matter how the world and its problems look, he is dealing with appropriate and timely issues. If he is not, his city is probably withering away.

Fusing the University and the Real World

All of this is so appropriate to the university mind that there hardly needs to be much of a fusion between student ideals and sound administrative practice. Professors have been slow catching up to the real world and administrators have been too busy with old things. Perhaps the two can now mesh, but the question of how the university keeps abreast of unrecorded experience must be answered.

Proper curriculum development and coverage can only go so far in the education of future administrators. Most importantly, today's training should include extensive field work and internship programs for students, in order to keep abreast of a rapidly changing world and to develop a sense of the working world. As one junior year college student stated after spending a short time on a field assignment with the Conference of Mayors and visitations to some cities, "I have learned more in three months on the job than in three years in college." Time after time similar expressions are heard from students in training. The expression of this one student dramatizes the need for intern programs and how best to add substance to any curriculum.

This paper places human relations and motivation highest on the scale of important knowledge, and sizing-up the community and bargaining and negotiation highest as necessary administrative skills, and rightly so. But these traits will not be developed in the classroom. It will take continual field work and a comprehensive internship to fulfill these objectives. Greater importance could be made of this fact.

Career Strength versus Political Strength

The professional urban administrator is supposed to know more about how to manage his city or county or region successfully because it is his career and because he has received in depth training and experience over a long period of time. On the other hand, mayors and most other local elected officials, with rare exceptions, survive in local government leadership positions for much briefer periods. Recent perspective shows that most mayors in the difficult problem cities remain for one four-year term and depend considerably on career department heads and managers to conduct the business of running the city.

Although the urban administrator's average term is not much longer in any one city than that of most mayors, he carries with him valuable experiences from a much longer urban career; therefore, his chief role is to quickly size up the community, coalesce forces, and get things moving in the direction of creating a viable city. And he must do this without letting political, partisan, or any regressive elements slow the process. In short, the survival of cities and counties depends much on the expertise of professional administrators who are non-partisan political animals and who take the responsibility of subtly leading citizens and politicians on a successfully proven course. No longer can the progressive administrator sit back and wait to be guided by elected officials. He must take the position that he is one of them and has as much right and a duty to do whatever is necessary to improve society. As a citizen advocate, at times he may have to be the balance of power on the side opposite the mayor and city council, which may make his position less tenable but more significant. His ability to select department heads who are less political and more technocratic than himself may determine the stability of his administrative machine. But for himself he must be willing to take whatever challenge is necessary to get the job done.

Conclusion

The paper covers well the disciplines needed to confront pressing current issues of urban government management, perhaps because it is the product of experiences of practitioners. In effect, it says that we live in a rapidly changing environment, and in order to keep current we must continually survey the real world and be unafraid to tackle its most serious problems, recognizing that these problems are not the ones that have traditionally confronted administrators but are the more basic ills of society.

Approaching solutions by cosmetic means becomes frustrating and unrewarding. The urban administrator must immerse himself in top priorities and more permanent solutions. And at the same time, in order to train those who wish to assist or follow him, he must encourage on-the-job training as part of the university's curriculum.

Summary of the Discussion of the
Watt-Parker-Cantine Paper

By Frederic N. Cleaveland

THIS paper is based upon empirical data gathered especially for that purpose, and discussion of the paper, therefore, began with questions about the nature of the sample of respondents and about interpretations of the data presented. Participants in the Symposium tended to agree that the composite image of the roles of urban administrators emerging from the paper probably reflects with reasonable accuracy the perceptions held by younger, more activist urban administrators about the nature of their jobs. Some educator participants questioned the wisdom of defining the job of the urban administrator solely in terms of the generalist administrator. They suggested that the conception should be broad enough to include as urban administrators those who manage functional line agencies such as a public works department, a public school system, or a city department of planning or health. Most of the discussion, however, turned on generalist urban administrators typified by the city manager.

One practitioner expressed concern that the complex roles as defined by the paper were indeed impossible for any one person to perform. "The manager sees himself increasingly as the man who runs it all—the godhead figure in city government. This is dangerous because these managers do not take the time to fulfill all their own self-perceptions. They can't take the time, they don't have it to give. One way for him to get out is to resort to delegation, but he can't fulfill all of the functions by himself. The role he has created is impossible to perform." Another practitioner agreed, observing that the urban administrator's job requires a team approach. The generalist administrator must work closely with the political leadership of the community—the elected officials—and with heads of more specialized agencies like the Model City director and the head of the Community Action program. Thus one significant skill the urban administrator requires is the ability to identify the key people in the community and within the city government with whom he must work to achieve a team effort.

In summary participants accepted the description of the generalist urban administrator emerging from the paper as representing a whole series of roles. No one urban administrator performs all these roles or even very many of them at any one time. City managers vary in style, they vary in the emphasis they give to particular role dimensions. Moreover, situational factors help to determine the emphasis any particular urban administrator brings to his work at any point in time. Again there is wide variation introduced by the unique character of each urban community, its structure of power and influence, the particular problems that require urgent attention, the extent and character of citizen involvement in the community, and many other factors. So the picture emerging from the paper can be considered properly as a composite of the various roles and role dimensions of the urban administrator as identified by a group of some 130 practicing urban administrators responding to a common set of questions, some quite detailed and some very general.

One participant experienced both as educator and practitioner supported the idea of paying attention to what a group of city managers have to say about their roles. In his view managers have a realistic view of their own profession. Indeed a city manager does not really feel he has earned his spurs until he has been fired at least once. This tough-minded approach gives added credibility to what city managers say about themselves. Another experienced practitioner suggested that much could be learned about the views of city managers by studying the transition of the International City Management Association (ICMA) over the past ten to fifteen years. The way ICMA has changed reflects the changing views of city managers about what is important in their jobs and what kinds of help they look to their professional association to provide.

In the course of the discussion two alternative models of the role of the urban administrator were developed, each different from that presented in the paper. The first can be derived from traditional democratic political theory which conceives of people in the community represented in their city government by elected officials. The urban administrator then is the "hired hand," responsible for carrying out the wishes and instructions of the elected officials. The second alternative model comes from the traditions of professional guilds characteristic of modern industrialized urban society. This is the "doctor knows best" model which looks to the norms and values of the profession for prescriptions about what the professional—in this case the urban administrator—is expected to do. Ordinary citizens have no in-put, for they are the "unwashed" and what they think is unimportant. These two alternative models probably shape the perception and thinking of some within American society today. Some elected officials, for example, probably view urban administrators in terms of the model based on democratic theory. No doubt some city managers and some managers of functional departments in city government reflect the "guild" model, viewing themselves as anointed professionals charged with responsibility for performing in accordance with standards set by their profession.

One participant experienced both as academic and as practitioner observed that what was being said about urban administrators in the paper and in the discussion could be said as well about managers generally in the public sector. His comment is further confirmed by the findings of the Delphi study concerning the nature of the public service in the 1980s. The judgments expressed by public administration educators and practitioners in the Delphi exercise indicated that more and more in the future managerial roles in the public service will require highly developed interpersonal skills and skills in bargaining and negotiation. As the Delphi participants look ahead they see an increasingly complex environment for managers in the public service involving such elements as activist citizens groups, aggressive employee unions, and more fluid organizational structures employing project teams demanding more participative management. If these descriptions of managerial roles are indeed applicable generally to public administrators and are not unique to urban administrators, this fact has important implications for curriculum planning and for the kinds of students for which such curriculums should be designed. Indeed, one experienced educator among the symposium participants observed that this discussion of administrative roles and categories of knowledge and skill had as much to contribute to formulation of admission policies in educational institutions as it did to the design of curriculums. "There is a definite limit to what can be accomplished in education. Most of the process of personal formation or development is complete by the time a student gets to us at the master's level. Maybe one way out is to pay more attention to admissions policy. If we are looking for the personal leadership, the personal adroitness and dexterity that this urban administrator's roles call for, and if we acknowledge that we can't hope to achieve this through educational effort, then we have got to insist that the man or woman have traits before acceptance into the educational program."

Participants generally agreed that the kinds of roles set forth as characteristic of the urban administrator would prove increasingly attractive to today's young people concerned to make the political system more responsive. But it was also agreed that if young people act upon the basis of their interest in preparing themselves to fill such roles in urban government and enter one of our educational programs, many are likely to become disillusioned and "turned off" to the point of dropping out. Despite their excitement about the goal, these young people are not prepared for what they find both in the educational process and in their first year or two on the job. Two issues were raised for serious consideration and study by those engaged in educating urban administrators: Do educators recognize the great importance of starting the process of socialization into the profession of urban administration seriously at the initial point of contact with potential students expressing interest in the field? These considerations might suggest building into the educational program an early contact for the students with the real world of the urban administrator through such devices as a field work course in the first term or a pre-entry internship in the summer even before the academic program begins. A second issue for the educator to ponder is what kind of image of the urban administrator and his role is assumed by the academic program? Do faculty members share a common conception? Do their conceptions reflect the realities

of the roles these administrators are performing in the urban
world? Or does the academic program either lack a clear assumption about the nature of the urban administrator's job, or are
these assumptions simply those derived from the more abstract
concepts of social science disciplines? Hopefully, this paper expressing what a group of practicing urban administrators perceive
their roles to be will prove a useful guide to educators in evaluating the underlying assumptions of their programs for educating
urban administrators.

Attracting and Stimulating a New Generation of Urban Administrators

By JAMES M. BANOVETZ

ABSTRACT: While the number of applicants for graduate study in urban programs has increased, numerous clues exist which suggest a scarcity of excellent students as a career option. The challenge of attracting and stimulating a new generation of urban administrators is one which must be met through the availability of funds to make graduate study possible, the provision of internships to win student commitment to urban administration careers, and, most importantly, by the availability of information within the educational process which makes municipal administrative careers a viable and distinct possibility for the student as he makes his vocational selection.

James M. Banovetz is professor and chairman, Department of Political Science, Northern Illinois University. Editor and co-author of Managing the Modern City, *he has served as director of the Center for Governmental Studies at NIU, and as a director of the Graduate Program in Urban Studies and Center for Research in Urban Government at Loyola University, Chicago. For the last three years he has chaired the Urban Studies Fellowship Advisory Board for the Department of Housing and Urban Development. Other key assignments include five years as chairman of Illinois' Community Service and Continuing Education Council and executive committee membership on the Illinois Commission on Urban Area Government. He started his career on the staff of the League of Minnesota Municipalities.*

A T FIRST glance, any effort to assess student interest in careers in urban administration, in this era of the "now" generation with its new, people-oriented morality, seems almost redundant. According to popular commentators and self-proclaimed spokesmen for the generation on the other side of the gap, today's student population has rejected materialism, racism, hypocrisy, and self-concern in favor of honesty, community involvement, and the public good. Among such persons, presumably, the self-evident appeal of careers focused directly on the scene of most contemporary social disorder—the urban scene—should be more than sufficient to produce tidal waves of applications for admission to graduate programs in urban public affairs, including urban administration.

There has, in fact, been a swelling in the ranks of applicants for graduate study in urban programs. Such programs, particularly at the graduate level, have proliferated in higher education, and particularly in the emerging state universities. National fellowship programs, such as the urban studies fellowship program of the Department of Housing and Urban Development and the minority fellowship program in urban affairs sponsored jointly by the Ford Foundation and the National Association of Schools of Public Affairs and Administration, have come forth with dollars to attract students into the field. Traditional academic programs in law, social work, engineering, economics, health, and other fields have developed urban components in response to student demand for relevance in their subject matter content.

Yet, unfortunately, the demand for professionally educated graduates in urban administration has not been satiated. To be sure, the tightening job market has assured, perhaps for the first time, a plentiful supply of applicants for administrative positions in urban governments. Some communities, for instance, already have developed qualms about advertising position vacancies in the job opportunities listings of the national professional associations because they are unable to cope with the number of inquiries they receive. Yet, there remains a problem. It is threefold. First, careers in urban administration must be made sufficiently attractive so that the plentiful supply of applicants will persist even when jobs are no longer scarce in other occupations. Second, the supply of applicants must be kept sufficiently large to insure the availability of persons of high quality and competence for these public service careers, thus keeping the public service from filling up with the dregs unwanted by other kinds of employers. Finally, the problem is one of assuring a flow of job applicants comprised of persons who have been properly equipped with the professional education and skills appropriate to the positions for which they are applying. Job vacancies in urban administration should be filled by persons educationally prepared for them, not by the graduates of teachers' colleges who have been unable to secure classroom positions or by retiring military officers looking for a second career.

There are numerous clues which suggest that a scarcity of excellent students seeking preparation for careers in urban administration continues to exist. The intensified efforts of governments at all three levels to encourage careers in urban-related occupations, including administration, can suggest no other conclusion. That the scarcity persists can be attributed to one or more of several causes, including: the spirit, motivations, and goals of the younger generation might have been misconstrued, and today's young people might not be particularly interested in social service occupations; careers in urban administration might not offer meaningful forms of involvement in the solution of societal ills; existing academic programs in urban administration might be an irrelevant basis for meaningful careers; urban administration, as a viable career route, might not be sufficiently visible to students; or incentives might be lacking which encourage young people to translate their aspirations into careers in urban administration. This paper will argue that a major share of the blame must be attributed to the latter two causes, and that these causes can be remedied. Specifically, it will suggest that urban administration is largely invisible to students as a career option, and that increased opportunities for personal contact with the field and for financial support of graduate study in it can pay handsome dividends in attracting and stimulating a new generation of urban administrators.

THE APPEAL OF CAREERS IN URBAN ADMINISTRATION

The appeal of careers in urban administration is different for today's college-age student. By contrast with a decade ago, more students today are interested in such careers, and for more reasons.

Historically, there have been two basic sources of urban administrators. Urban governments secured the preponderance of their administrative employees from the pool of local manpower looking for home town jobs. Such persons continue to be the principal source of such manpower today, particularly for sub-professional and paraprofessional positions.

Most persons attracted to local government jobs are not look-ing for any particular kind of job, or even necessarily a job in government. Their principal motivation is to find work by which they can support themselves while they pursue their life style in the community in which they have chosen to reside, usually the community in which they grew up. Even when employed in a particular governmental job, such persons rarely identify them-selves as professionals; they are simply home town residents working in the best available job. Traditionally, such persons have had little or no college education, but more recently an in-creasing number of them possess some junior college background.

Persons holding such positions can be reached by educational programs in urban administration, and particularly by short courses aimed at mid-career employees. The success of subpro-fessional and paraprofessional educational programs in the com-munity colleges, such as the growing number of community col-lege programs in law enforcement, indicates: such programs can reach and upgrade the quality of persons holding positions in urban government; such programs can raise the educational pre-requisites for urban government employees at these levels; the existence of such programs can and will attract growing numbers of persons with some higher education to these career oppor-tunities.

The evolution of the good government movement of the early twentieth century, the development of public administration as an academic specialization at the master's degree level, and par-ticularly the emergence of the council-manager plan of local gov-ernment combined to give birth to a second category of persons attracted to careers in urban administration. These are the professionally trained, career-oriented, nationally mobile em-ployees whose primary allegiance is to the profession in which they are engaged and only secondarily to the particular com-munity that happens to employ them at any particular time. This professional species emanated from the ranks of civil en-gineers, the first professional specialization employed by most urban governments, who tended to evolve into the newly created position of city manager. Following this lead other professional positions have also evolved in urban government, including specialized professionals in planning, public health, finance, law, and urban renewal. Meanwhile, the city manager's job has evolved from its civil engineering origins, through a managerial technician phase, to its present specialization in public policy processes, and in the process it has spawned a new profession: specialists in urban program administration. It is to such professionals that society has been more frequently looking for leadership help in resolving the increasingly severe problems of racial injustice, poverty, urban decay, urban dispersion, community development, and environmental deterioration. Consequently, it is the problem of recruiting new and better talent to this profession that must be a matter of primary concern.

To be sure, there has always been a steady flow of graduates professionally educated for urban administration, haphazardly attracted to the occupation by a variety of inducements, including relevant individual experiences, professorial encouragement, attractive job opportunities, or similar inducements of an indeterminate nature.

More recently, with the advent of a stronger social concern among young people, there have been sources of motivation encouraging students to consider careers in urban administration. The first of these is an ideological commitment to reform, to set right the wrongs of contemporary society. Manifested principally among white students with a liberal orientation, this motivation is most frequently associated with a lack of a clear-cut perception of how the student can best express himself, or achieve his goals. A few of the persons so motivated commit themselves to experimental activities, such as communal living; many immerse themselves in activist political causes, such as Students for McCarthy; and a too small percentage ultimately find their way into academic programs designed to prepare them for some form of public service career. Persons with this motivation are much more likely to be attracted to graduate programs in urban studies than to graduate programs in public administration, perceiving the latter to be much too staid and establishment-oriented for their tastes.

Properly motivated and instructed, such persons can make very productive public servants. Undirected or left to their own devices, however, such persons can encounter problems as public servants. Ideologically committed to reform, for instance, they are much more likely to experience dysfunctional frustration at the slow pace at which society typically permits reforms to occur. The ideological commitment, furthermore, can rob them of the air of impartiality and neutrality that is: (1) a frequent requirement of administrative leaders; (2) an absolute requisite for the competent analysis of policy alternatives and the design of strategies to implement desired policies; (3) a necessity to diagnose accurately the causes of problems, the motivations of people, and the effective constraints relevant to any given situation. Unfortunately, too, given the transitory and faddish nature of public concerns, little reliance can be placed upon this sort of motivation as a long-run supplier of applicants for professional careers in urban administration.

A second new source of persons interested in urban administration are minority students who are searching for ways to help impoverished minorities in general, and their own people in particular, to achieve a better life style. Although ideologically committed to this objective, such students rarely have a definitive notion of how they can best fulfill this commitment. In truth, there is no single best way. The welfare of most minority groups in the United States can be fostered by almost any kind of a contribution from their educated members. Accordingly, there is a bewildering array of paths laid out before the competent black, Chicano, or other minority student, all promising to lead the student toward a career which will enable him to make a meaningful contribution to the welfare of his people. Lacking any meaningful yardstick by which such paths can be compared, and typically needing outside financial assistance to underwrite the cost of further study, such students frequently fall back upon a simple and immediate financial criterion in making their selection: which path offers the most promising and remunerative source of support for further study. Careers in urban administration will be successful in attracting such students, for the most part, only to the extent that graduate programs in the field are able to compete with other fields of graduate study in the amount of money they can offer to prospective minority graduate students.

There are, then, only two clearly identifiable motivational patterns which can be exploited to recruit applicants for the field of urban administration. There are those seeking careers in their home town area—these can best be reached by appropriate academic programs offered by colleges and universities in their locale. Thus can be constructed a very strong argument for a much wider dispersion of academic programs in urban administration than presently exists; without such dispersion, a large proportion of the potential student supply for such careers will not be reached. Conversely, the greater the geographic dispersion of colleges and universities offering a concentration of work in urban administration, the greater will be the number of students attracted to the career field.

The second exploitable motivations are those held by the minority students seeking careers which will contribute to the betterment of society's disadvantaged. For these students, financial support for graduate study is frequently the marginally discriminating factor in specific career selection. Thus, fellowships in urban administration for minority students are not only the most effective, but frequently the only way, to attract these students to the career field.

For other students, there is no clear set of motivations which can be exploited. There is little recent evidence of any kind which suggests that particular kinds of students are more likely to be attracted to the field of urban administration.[1] The general literature on vocational choice also offers little insight.[2] But there are, nonetheless, clues which suggest ways in which these other students can be reached and attracted to urban administration. These come from the students themselves.

STUDENT INCLINATIONS

Clues can be gained both from undergraduate students, who have yet to finalize their career choice, and from graduate students

1. Thomas J. Davy, "Education of Urban Administrators: Considerations in Planning and Organizing Graduate Degree Programs," *Public Management,* vol. 54, no. 2 (February, 1972), pp. 5–9, 10. This author's search for studies bearing on this matter produced a similarly fruitless conclusion.

2. Perhaps the best treatment of the subject of vocational choice is Donald G. Zytowski, *Vocational Behavior, Readings in Theory and Research* (Chicago: Holt, Rinehart, and Winston, 1968). Also useful is Robert Calvert, Jr., *Career Patterns of Liberal Arts Graduates* (Cranston, R.I.: The Carroll Press, 1969).

in urban administration, who have just recently made a career commitment to the field. To acquire information about undergraduates, a survey of the occupational inclinations of Northern Illinois University (NIU) undergraduates enrolled in political science courses was undertaken late in 1971. More than half the respondents were juniors; two-thirds were either majors or minors in political science; few, if any, had taken courses taught by the university's senior faculty in public administration.

In the survey, very few students indicated any interest in urban public service careers; most planned to undertake graduate study in some other professional or academic field, principally in law or education. Urban public service careers were more frequently listed as a second or third choice of the respondents, suggesting that recruitment for urban administration programs might depend as much upon how crowded law schools are, or the employment prospects in high school teaching, as on any other factor.

When students who did express an interest in an urban public service career were isolated from their peers, and subjected to further scrutiny, no significant correlations were unearthed regarding their background. Interest in such a career did not appear to be related to age, sex, racial background, socioeconomic background, nature of home community, grade point average, or years of schooling. Furthermore, students interested in an urban public service career are not more motivated than other students by a concern for a career which would have social importance or provide an opportunity to resolve societal and urban problems. In fact, the respondents in general tended to rank such motivations quite low on their personal value scales.

The one distinctive characteristic of the urban administration-oriented student that did emerge from the survey was reliance upon faculty advice in selecting a career. Half of the students interested in an urban administration career reported a principal reliance upon faculty advice in career selection, while only sixteen percent of the remaining students gave such advice a similar ranking. On the other hand, in the NIU experience, senior faculty with interests in urban administration will receive a number of unsolicited inquiries from students in each of the related undergraduate courses they teach, and such inquiries usually result in several applications for admission to graduate study in the field. This suggests that students become interested in urban-oriented careers only when such careers have been suggested to them by faculty members or others whose advice and counsel they trust.

In point of fact, urban administration is not a highly visible career option. There are comparatively few practitioners: students are not apt to have a father or neighbor in this field. Urban administrators receive relatively little publicity in the media, compared, at least, to lawyers, doctors, authors, and similar professions which dominate the news reports, soap operas, and Hollywood productions. Few classes in political science, furthermore, encourage an interest in urban administration by the nature of their subject matter. Public administration itself often is not taught in relation to the federal government, and in any event as the subject becomes more analytical, it ceases to have professionally relevant content or appeal. Local government courses may more often provide the information which would encourage a student to choose a career in urban administration, but the typical political science curriculum contains relatively few such courses. Most college and university faculty, in political science as well as in other disciplines, have had limited, if any, exposure to urban administration and thus do not think of it as a viable career option for students.

The consequence, of course, is that the typical college or university student receives relatively little motivation to choose a career in urban administration. It is also true, as Donald E. Super has pointed out, that the nature of an individual's career pattern is guided significantly by the opportunities to which he is exposed.[3] It would seem to follow, therefore, that the recruitment of more and better persons to careers in urban administration is dependent upon improved systems for making urban administration a recognized, viable career option for undergraduate students. In fact, there is evidence that even small efforts in this direction can have very significant success.

The International City Management Association, for instance, reports that its college visitation program, in which city managers

3. Donald E. Super, "A Theory of Vocational Development," in Zytowski, op. cit., pp. 121–129 at 127–128.

are asked to visit particular college campuses and spend a day talking with undergraduate students, has been overwhelmingly successful. The theory behind the program is quite simple: by spending a day talking with groups of undergraduate students, a city manager not only identifies urban administration as a viable career option, but is also able to answer questions regarding desired academic preparation, career entry problems, and subsequent career development possibilities. At a relatively small Colorado college, for instance, the program has been credited with success in encouraging seven students in the last two years to undertake graduate work, and ultimately careers, in the urban administration.

A recently completed survey of graduate students in urban public administration at Northern Illinois University suggests that two factors were of crucial importance in encouraging students to make urban administration their career choice. The first, and by far the most important, factor was faculty encouragement. Seventy percent of the students now in the program listed such encouragement as a principal reason for their career choice; ninety percent indicated they made this choice either because of faculty encouragement, because of contact with professionals in the field, or because of their contacts with students in graduate public administration programs. In other words, personal contact with someone in the career field, or with someone who knew and spoke encouragingly about the career field, appears to be virtually a prerequisite for the selection of urban administration as a career choice.

The second factor of major importance in the attraction of persons to careers in urban administration is the availability of financial aids to defray the cost of professional studies. In the NIU survey, sixty percent of the students in the urban administration program indicated that the school's internship program, which provides work-study opportunities with support stipends during the students' period of graduate study, was an important factor in their selection of urban administration as a field of graduate study. In some cases, the internship played a key role in encouraging students to choose that particular vocational specialization; in other cases, it made possible the implementation of a predetermined choice of municipal administration as a vocational field. The financial aspects of the internship played a particularly crucial role in the vocational selection of the NIU program's minority students. Without this inducement, none of the NIU students would be studying either at that institution or in the field of urban administration. This is not because money is unusually important to minority students, nor because money blinds such students to other considerations, but simply because student support money is the decisive factor in choosing between several attractive career options, each of which offers the desired opportunity for social contribution.

Since NIU has not achieved national reputation among students as a place to study in the field of urban administration, furthermore, the internship played the determinate role in attracting students to the university from schools outside the immediate midwestern geographic environment of the institution.[4]

The internship also has a second, equally important effect. For the vast majority who serve in an urban administration internship, it is the adhesive which binds the student to the urban career pattern. Over ninety-five percent of the graduate students placed on internships at Northern Illinois University, for example, have found that the internship either strengthens their resolve to go into municipal administration, or has built such resolve where none previously existed. In a small minority of cases, the internship clearly demonstrated that urban administration is not the preferred career line of the student, thereby permitting him to alter his career path before he has made commitments not easily reversed.

The success of the internship format would seem to be indicated by the growing support for this device which has developed during the last ten years. Internships have existed nearly as long as professional training for municipal administration, but typically as adjuncts to graduate programs in public administration. More recently, governmental agencies and professional associations, recognizing the recruitment value of these experiences, have begun to promote internship opportunities on their own. Thus the International City Management Association, for example, has

4. All of the conclusions described above from the survey of current NIU graduate students would undoubtedly be similar for earlier students in that program.

been promoting and helping to finance summer internships; the Department of Housing and Urban Development is using internships, financed through special project 701 funds, to attract more minority students into urban development careers; an increasing number of state departments of local government affairs are encouraging, and in some cases even helping to finance, internship programs in local government agencies; and a rapidly increasing number of urban administrators are making internship positions an institutionalized component of their staff organization.

Properly used, the internship may also be able to fill another critical need: it can serve as the source of badly needed money to help students finance their graduate, professional studies in urban administration. Part-time internships in local government agencies can be substituted for graduate assistantships and blended with full-time academic work both to support the student during his studies and provide him with a work-study learning experience.[5] Such an arrangement, particularly available to graduate programs in or near metropolitan areas, can prove beneficial to the cooperating governments as well: the local agency can secure part-time, professionally-developing staff assistance at a monthly cost well below the market rate. A growing number of city managers in the Chicago metropolitan area are also using the part-time, work-study internship as a device for the screening and recruitment of future, full-time administrative assistants.

Three factors, then, seem to be of prime importance in directing students of all racial and national backgrounds toward urban administration careers. The first is personal contact, preferably with undergraduate faculty members who are familiar with the opportunities and possibilities of careers in urban administration.

5. This has been the basis upon which the graduate program in urban administration has been built at Northern Illinois University. Located in close proximity to the Chicago and Rockford metropolitan areas, the university has developed working realtionships with local government agencies in those areas under which the local agencies employ full-time students as part-time (twenty hours per week) interns for nine to fifteen month periods. The students receive stipends of approximately $280 per month from the local government agency and a waiver of tuition and out of state fees by the university. This arrangement, almost singly, has been responsible for the program's development at NIU.

The second is money—money to make attractive and possible the study necessary to enter urban administration as an educated professional. The third, and most dynamic, is personal experience—the internship. Taken together, the three factors constitute a powerful motivational force. The task of attracting more and better students to urban administration is, essentially, one of optimizing the impact of these factors, individually and in unison.

These factors cannot be optimized, however, under present conditions. Recruitment for careers in urban administration must face a grim truism: today, as in earlier years, college students are almost universally unaware both of the existence of the career opportunities in urban administration and of the service opportunities such careers afford. Students do not contemplate careers for themselves in fields with which they are unfamiliar and particularly in fields of whose existence they are unaware. Unfortunately, urban administration is not a visible career option to the general public, and is no more visible to the typical undergraduate. As a result, the typical student does not even consider a career in this field; this is true both for students imbued with the new concern for service to society as well as for students with more traditional aspirations.

Graduate support stipends and internship opportunities, by themselves, will not correct this situation, they will not stimulate the desired increments in the number and quality of applicants for urban administration careers. Someone must first present such an option to the students. Unfortunately, most career counselors and faculty members, even faculty members in political science, know virtually nothing about urban administration as a career field. The challenge, then, is to stimulate student interest in a profession about which very little information is typically known or available.

A Program of Action

A response to this challenge might appear to be complicated, as indeed it would be if the customary campus information-dissemination devices had already been properly and customarily exploited. Fortunately—or unfortunately—they have not yet been mobilized to the cause; hence an exhaustion of available remedies would appear to be indicated. Career counselors, undergraduate advisors, teachers, and placement officers must be made more aware of the opportunities—job-wise and service-wise—which exist in the field. Courses must be introduced into undergraduate curriculums which would lead to an interest in the field. Opportunities for personal involvement at city hall and the county courthouse must be expanded for undergraduates. Professionals already in urban administration must continue to assume an expanding responsibility for making their occupation more visible.

Stated in yet another way, urban administration must be more readily used as a response to the commonly heard student question, What can I do with a degree in political science—or economics, or sociology, or geography, or other field—besides teach? With the answer, furthermore, there must be concrete information about such a profession: the modes of entry, the opportunities available, the challenges, the career development possibilities, and the personal satisfactions.

Related to this is the need for more systematized paths for career entry. Presently there is no easy way of directing students into the urban government job market. In the larger urban centers, at least, it should be possible to develop a single, centralized local government recruitment office to facilitate career entry and mobility. Such an office could contain registers of job opportunities in local government agencies throughout that area, and perhaps in other urban areas as well, along with registers of individuals interested in pursuing any of the variety of professional opportunities available in local government. The centers might provide standardized applicant testing and screening services, advertise the availability of careers in local government, and offer individualized career counseling services to persons at career-entry and mid-career levels.

Most importantly, however, is the need to enrich the contribution made by faculty members to the recruitment process. This has two dimensions. First, more information about careers in urban administration must be made available to faculty members in general, and particularly in the social sciences. Special attention in this respect should be paid to the faculty members teaching at liberal arts colleges and other institutions where graduate and professional training in public affairs and urban administration is not available and who, hence, are less likely to have contact with the field during the normal course of their work. Second, faculty already associated with urban administration programs must seek exposure to a wider range of students, particularly students at the undergraduate level.

Finally, more students would be attracted to careers in urban government if undergraduate course offerings in the urban field, and particularly in urban government, were significantly expanded. Such offerings usually are often a most effective recruitment device. They provide the student with an intensified introduction to the dynamics of urban governance, the problems to which such governments address themselves, and the possibilities for individual participation in efforts to resolve those problems. They project urban governments and their problems into the consciousness of students, and pose potential new career paths for them. Yet, even in this day of national concern with urban problems, there remains a distinct shortage of urban-related courses in the typical social science curriculum, and a complete absence of them in many liberal arts college curriculums.[6]

The challenge, in other words, is an informational challenge: appropriate, career-oriented information about municipal administration must be available and transmitted to students. This can best be done by proper exploitation of the time-honored mechanisms for communication with students—through the classroom, counselor's office, and, most particularly, through faculty influence and faculty-student contacts.

CONCLUSION

The question for the future is not really whether or not an adequate number of students can be attracted to careers in municipal administration. The tightening job market will assure a plentiful supply of job applicants. The problem of the past,

6. James M. Banovetz and David R. Beam, eds., *Higher Education and Urban Service* (DeKalb, Ill.: Northern Illinois University Center for Governmental Studies, 1970), esp. chap. 4, pp. 15–24.

the problem of securing enough warm bodies to fill administrative positions, now seems to have been resolved. The problem of the future is one of equipping the warm bodies with the requisite professional skills to perform their functions, and meet challenges of urban administration, in a professional, confident manner. That, in turn, is a challenge which must be met by professional schools in urban administration, and by the urban administration profession. It is a challenge which must be met through the availability of funds to make graduate study possible, the provision of internships to win student commitment to urban administration careers, and, most importantly, by the availability of information within the educational process which makes municipal administrative careers a viable and distinct possibility for the student as he makes his vocational selection.

Commentary on the Banovetz Paper

By H. George Frederickson

ABSTRACT: It appears that James Banovetz and I are in more than a little disagreement. Most major schools of public affairs are highly visible on their campuses and have no trouble attracting students in quantity and quality. As more public or urban administration schools evolve and develop their own faculties and degree programs, and begin to do effective placement, I am confident that good students will be both attracted and stimulated. In fact, the major programs in urban administration do get excellent students, and many of them. I also very much doubt if fellowships are a fundamental determinant of either the quantity or quality of urban administration students. The keys to attracting the next generation of urban administrators are separate schools and degree programs, strong bridges to the schools for urban public service occupations, and more effective relationships with governments and a pedagogical and paradigmatic reassessment. If the programs are good, I am certain that first quality students will be in ample supply, will pass successfully through the programs, and will provide greatly improved leadership for the urban public service.

H. George Frederickson is chairman of the graduate program and professor of public affairs at the School of Public and Environmental Affairs, Indiana University. He is the editor of a recent special issue of the Public Administration Review *on "Administration and Politics in Urban Neighborhoods." He also edited the recent book* Politics, Public Administration and Neighborhood Control. *He is co-author with Linda S. O'Leary of the book* Power, Opinion and Policy: A Study of Syracuse, New York. *A member of the National Council of the American Society for Public Administration, he was program chairman for the 1972 conference.*

THE task at hand is to spend my allotted 2,500 words responding to Professor James Banovetz's essay "Attracting and Stimulating a New Generation of Urban Administrators." Ordinarily such a task would not be difficult but in this case it is, because it appears that Jim Banovetz and I are in more than a little disagreement. Because of this limitation in words, I am unable to defend in detail the reasons for my differences with the Banovetz essay; consequently, my commentary might be interpreted as flip or cavalier. So, it is at the risk of appearing both disagreeable, and cavalier, that I spend my remaining 2,400 words.

Banovetz contends that urban administration jobs are not made sufficiently attractive to students; there are too few persons of high quality and competence in the urban public service; and urban administration incumbents and applicants need to be properly equipped with the professional education and skills appropriate to the position for which they are applying. He further suggests that there is a scarcity of excellent students seeking preparation for careers in urban administration and this is probably because such career routes are not made sufficiently visible and there are too few incentives, such as internships and scholarships, to lure first quality people to the field. He is especially concerned that the ideologically committed young might not be properly motivated and instructed to become good urban administrators, because they might experience frustration and may not develop an air of impartiality and neutrality that is: (1) frequently required of administrative leaders; (2) demanded for the competent analysis of policy alternatives and the design of strategies to implement desired policies; (3) necessary to diagnose accurately the causes of problems, the motivations of people, and the effective constraints relevant to any given situation. To get better students into educational programs designed to prepare them for urban administration there must, in Banovetz's view, be an increase in scholarship and fellowship money, wider use of internships, and the development of greater personal contact between students and undergraduate faculty who can better describe opportunities in urban administration. And there should be much wider dissemination of information on urban career possibilities, because what we have here is primarily an informational challenge.

While never defining or describing what he regards as urban administration, Banovetz uses the city manager as the arch typical urban administrator, leaving the impression that his conception of urban administration is focused on city managers, chief administrative officers, those heading auxiliary operations such as budgeting and personnel, and possibly department heads. With such a narrow conception of urban administration it is no wonder that he does not find these activities visible, because they are not. When compared with the urban public service professions—education administration, law enforcement administration, social services administration, health and hospital administration, and so forth—his urban administration does lack visibility. In fact, urban public occupations are highly visible but they are just not related, in the mind of the student, to general city management or public administration.

Students, in my view, see real careers when they can associate them with actual schools and programs. Schools of business, education, law, public health, social services, and the like, all prepare prospective administrators and in ways that students can see and understand. And these schools educate many more people for urban administration than are educated in urban studies or public administration programs. With the exception of the fewer than a dozen major schools of public or urban administration most larger university campuses give a Master of Public Administration (M.P.A.) degree or its equivalent as a vest pocket operation out of a political science department or a business school. The faculty of these degree programs are minuscule, and most courses are taken cafeteria style in the traditional social science disciplines and applied to the degree. Such programs are hardly calculated to attract students either in great quantity or quality. Most students can spot bogus degree programs and jerry-built institutes and avoid them in favor of real schools that prepare for real occupation, unless, of course, they are really dedicated to some particular occupation such as city management. The major schools of public affairs with which I am familiar are highly visible on their campuses and have no trouble attracting students in quantity and quality. As more public or urban administration schools evolve from political science departments (in much the same way that schools of business administration disengaged from economics), develop their own faculties and degree programs, and begin to do effective placement, I am confident that good students will be both attracted and stimulated.

Now, to the question of the quality of students preparing for urban administration—compared to schools of education, social work, business and the like, we really have very little to offer a perceptive student, either in visibility or in substance, with the important exception of a few major schools of public affairs. And, in fact, the major programs in urban administration do get excellent students, and many of them. I am continually impressed by the education, sophistication, energy, dedication, and ideological commitment of contemporary students of urban administration. I worry much less about the quality of our students than I worry about the low quality of educational preparation we provide. Given the quality of most university programs for educating urban administrators, we are probably getting much better students than we deserve.

Professor Banovetz contends that fellowships, internships, and information dissemination are the keys to attracting and stimulating a new generation of urban administrators. Fellowships are a very great help in aiding those who are disposed to study urban administration, particularly if they are poor. But I very much doubt if fellowships are a fundamental determinant of either the quantity or quality of urban administration students. The student search for fellowship support customarily follows his occupational decision. Once the student chooses law, or business administration, or social work, he may select between schools on the basis of fellowship availability; but few students, I believe, choose their life occupations on the basis of fellowship availability. Consider, for example, the fact that law schools are experiencing an unprecedented overload in applications; and they traditionally offer very few fellowships. Still, fellowships are important to the development of urban administration education and should be expanded. Similarly, internships have had a positive effect on the development of urban administration education programs and should be expanded. And information on urban administration occupations and educational programs that prepare students for such occupations should be widely distributed. But information will not make quality schools out of marginal programs.

In fact, one of the basic problems in urban administration education are those programs that are more information than they are substance. There is a kind of credibility gap in the presentation of urban management programs causing one of my students to hypothesize an inverse relationship between the quality of a degree program and the flashiness, claims, and length of faculty described in its brochures. Surely there is a place for small urban administration programs in universities, but such programs should exercise the greatest of prudence in presenting themselves to the potential student.

In Banovetz's essay he expresses some skepticism as to the capacity of ideological young reformers to be effective in the urban public service. After almost six years of working at the Maxwell School with some highly ideological young M.P.A. students, and an occasional radical, and probably the largest group of black graduate students of urban administration in the country, my views are almost the reverse of Banovetz. The strong ideological commitment of the young and their determination to make the public service more humanistic and equitable, and more productive is one of the few really exciting characteristics of a field that is too often dull. The spirit and élan of these young administrators must be somewhat like that of urban administrators in the early days of public administration, although rather more humanistic. Very senior public administrators were reformers in their day but their spirit and vision was lost in the 1940s or 1950s. Certainly the young reformers are frustrated, but what administrator does not get frustrated, given the complexity of contemporary organizational life. From all I am able to determine when I see or hear about students who have finished M.P.A.'s in the last five years, they are doing very well in the urban public service, and especially the reformers. The young reformers who select themselves out to go into urban administration programs are, it seems to me, among the most responsible and constructive forces in the country; and I am convinced that they will improve the administration of urban government significantly.

If, as I contend, fellowships, internships, and personal contacts are not the keys to attracting and stimulating a new generation of urban administrators, what are those keys. There are four. First, we must create many more independent schools and programs in public and urban affairs at both the graduate and undergraduate level. The vital point here is separate status as schools with separate faculties and degrees. Surely these schools should relate effectively to the traditional social science disciplines but they should not be dominated by them. Medicine broke away from the biological sciences but still retains strong bridges to those sciences. Business broke away from the social sciences but still retains links especially to economics, sociology, and psychology. And public and urban administration must break away.

Second, schools of public and urban administration must relate in consistent and systematic ways to those other professional schools that educate the bulk of urban administrators. When there is a strong public management presence in schools of social work, schools of engineering, schools of education, and schools of law because they are firmly bridged to a separate and strong school of public or urban affairs, we can have a real impact on the conduct of government administration. When the school administrator or the social services administrator, because of his training, thinks of himself as an urban public manager first and an educator or social worker second, we have done our job. As more universities recognize and adopt this model, not without strong resistance particularly from political science departments and schools of business, the urban public management profession will grow.

Third, schools of public and urban affairs must be much more effective in relating to local government agencies and officials. Our student placement efforts are weak compared to other professions. Our internship programs are often not well managed, and our continuing education programs need work. If all three of these were substantially improved, both local and state governments would become accustomed to working closely with schools of urban and public administration, and both the schools and the governments would profit from it.

Fourth, the quality of the next generation of urban administrators will depend, in part, on what they are taught. I am much less sanguine than Jim Banovetz on this matter. He encourages properly motivated and instructed administrators, and an air of impartiality and neutrality and at several other points in his essay seems to indicate that those of us who design urban administration curriculums and teach urban administration courses know what we are doing.   In fact, we do not have an agreed upon paradigm and we hardly have a paradigmatic dialogue. There is a common core of knowledge in urban affairs—politics, economics, demographics, and the like—and we can instruct as to how urban systems work.   But that is not the same thing as urban administration, and we are not in agreement as to how urban systems should work.   More serious, we do not have much in the way of shared and tested theories, models, or paradigms for effective urban administration.   Is change agentry the center of contemporary urban administrative theory, or is it impartial and neutral policy analysis?   In sum, we need deep and continuing assessments of questions of pedagogy, theory, and curriculum in urban administration.

The keys to attracting the next generation of urban administrators are separate schools and degree programs, strong bridges to the schools for urban public service occupations, more effective relationships with governments, and a pedagogical and paradigmatic reassessment.   The uniqueness of each university will cause it to respond to this model in different ways, but the most successful schools of urban administration over the next decade will, I believe, be some variation of this model.   And, if the programs are good, I am certain that first quality students will be in ample supply, will pass successfully through the programs, and will provide greatly improved leadership for the urban public service.

Commentary on the Banovetz Paper

By Philip J. Rutledge

ABSTRACT: Dr. Banovetz has identified some major areas of concern, such as the shortage of professionally trained administrators, the increase in numbers of applicants for graduate study mainly due to financial stimulus as opposed to commitment, and the invisibility of public administration as a profession. Current fellowship and internship programs are techniques toward which we should direct considerable attention as a useful mechanism for solving the problems of attracting and stimulating new urban administrators. There are two other major considerations to explore because of their cause-and-effect relationship to the problem of retaining new administrators in the system. They are the quality of bureaucracy into which we are trying to attract this new breed of administrators, and the question of whether public administration is indeed the arena in which the new breed can contribute best to social change. Present administrators should be aware that the degree of involvement they demonstrate is a factor in increasing the visibility of the profession. The very fact that they are visible and dealing with the complex problems of today in an innovative manner will attract larger numbers of the new generation. The greatest challenge to us all—public administrator, poor, middle class, and affluent—is change, and our adaptiveness to that change. And that would be our greatest asset in attracting and stimulating a new generation of urban administrators.

Philip J. Rutledge is presently deputy administrator, Social and Rehabilitation Service, Department of Health, Education and Welfare. A graduate of Roosevelt University, he has an M.A. in Public Health from the University of Michigan. He has served on numerous commissions and task forces dealing with higher education and urban problems, and prior to his present position was director, District of Columbia Department of Human Resources.

ATTRACTING and stimulating a new generation—a new breed, if you will—of public administrators are challenging tasks that should be at the forefront of the problems causing concern to our profession. Dr. Banovetz has identified several major areas of concern, such as the shortage of professionally trained administrators, the increase in the number of applicants for graduate study drawn mainly by generous stipends, not commitment, and the invisibility of public administration as a profession.

We should direct considerable attention to current fellowship and internship programs as useful mechanisms for solving the problems of attracting and stimulating new urban administrators. Dr. Banovetz names some of the fellowships currently offered and suggests that their dollar value is attracting more applicants into the field. At present-day costs of education, the availability of economic assistance is a major concern of students in all fields. Yet the provision of economic assistance is not the only attractiveness of fellowships. A close examination of one fellowship program now operating can best demonstrate the effectiveness of such programs as instruments of change.

The National Urban Fellows Program, sponsored by the National League of Cities-United States Conference of Mayors and supported by grants from the Ford Foundation, has affiliated itself with Yale University and Occidental College to provide a combination of academic training and practical experience. The program has averaged thirty-one interns each year since it began in 1969, selected from applications submitted from practically every state in the Union and every minority group. The number of applications has increased each year since 1969, indicating that interest in the field of public adminstration has increased or that the high visibility of the interns is attracting more and more potential urban administrators.

Perhaps as much emphasis should be placed on attracting the older student as on attracting the student who enters graduate school immediately on completion of undergraduate work. For the National Urban Fellows, the age limit is from twenty-four to thirty-nine and the median age has been thirty-four. Students this old bring to the program maturity, sophistication, and expertise, particularly because one of the requirements is that a candidate have two years or more administrative experience. Fellows receive academic training through the university affiliation, practical experience in a supervised internship working with a public administrator, and exposure to other administrators, selected for ability and experience, through seminars.

Dr. Banovetz emphasizes two types of students attracted by fellowships and no doubt they exist: the liberal white student in urban studies programs, and the minority group students ideologically committed to bringing about some changes to their people but attracted to those fields providing the most economic assistance. However, the requirements of a program like the National Urban Fellows often eliminate the less serious student. The initial effort necessary for each applicant for the fellowship has a twofold effect: candidates who are not serious are discouraged immediately, and the keen competition for the slots easily rivals the competition for entry into law and medical schools, thereby stimulating interest in careers in urban administration.

The fellowship program concept can solve many of the problems of attracting and stimulating the new urban administrators, if actual programs are as well structured as the National Urban Fellows Program. Of course, fellowship programs are not the answer to all the problems. Career counselors, undergraduate advisers, college instructors, and placement officers must be made more aware of career opportunities in the field. Courses more applicable to graduate work should be introduced into the undergraduate curriculum, and greater exposure to practicing administrators could be afforded even in secondary school.

As in any other profession, practicing professional public administrators are going to have to assume greater responsibility for increasing the visibility of urban administrators. They should advise schools of urban administration of the educational needs of students and work for a better, more pertinent curriculum. Last, but far from least, is the need for them to dispel the popular belief that most public service jobs are obtained by political patronage. Few if any students would be willing to expend time and money preparing for a career that may not be open to them when they have fulfilled the requirements.

A mechanism for attracting young people into the field of urban administration exists in the fellowship program idea. If the idea is used to the best advantage by making full use of the university affiliation as well as by providing good internship programs, students completing the work in urban administration will be a credit to the profession.

There are two other major considerations to explore because of their cause-and-effect relationship to the problem of retaining new administrators in the system: the quality of bureaucracy into which we are trying to attract this new breed of administrators, and the question of whether public administration is indeed the field in which the new breed can contribute best to social change.

Public administrators should be applying the ideals and principles of this society to make them work to ameliorate the problems born of a changing era. Instead, we are witnessing a period of situation management in which our tools, techniques, and resources have no substantial impact on our problems, but merely forestall greater catastrophe. No amount of professional training can alleviate the frustrations experienced by a conscientious administrator who has observed all the rules of classical administrative principles, only to find that his agency has solved no problems, that he has no measurable results to point to, and that the conditions his agency has sought to end have actually gotten worse.

The ideal recruit to the new generation of public administrators should be a young person so fired with enthusiasm that he is seeking greatness in himself and in his profession. But perhaps Clifton Daniel, associate editor of the *New York Times*, is right, He was quoted recently in the *San Francisco Chronicle* as saying:

We don't require great men at the moment. We require good men, men who'll do their jobs well, get on with business and not go around creating crises and antagonizing people. Great times turn up great leaders and we're just not at a "great and challenging" period of history right now. And that may not be such a bad thing.

The lives of public administrators will become increasingly nerve-racking and unsatisfying if we do not as a nation find practical solutions for today's urgent social problems. Our recent solutions to problems in social welfare, health, manpower, and juvenile delinquency, to cite a few, have been out-and-out failures. Some say they were designed and administered to fail because of the divine preordination conceptual framework of those in decision-making positions.

Representatives of the groups to be served are seldom part of the final decision-making process regarding the crucial issues on program and policy formulation. Given the structure of our society, the problem of citizen participation is not likely to be solved soon. But we can tackle immediately the operations end of program implementation by the wholesale drafting of new ethnic groups into public administration where the rubber hits the road.

This new breed must include significant numbers of talented people from among the nation's ghetto-dwellers, black and white, Spanish-speaking newcomers, American Indians, Mexican-Americans, members of other oppressed minorities, and women. The new systems should be designed so that members of minority groups are a very inextricable part of them. With these kinds of changes in our systems design, we could provide the incentive that will make public administration attractive to them.

Redesigned systems call for redesigned education for the new generation, the re-education of some present administrators, and additional training for lower line employees. The new education must provide opportunity for self-expression and creativity and instill in the student flexibility; it must provide opportunity to acquire the skill necessary to function adequately. Administrators must feel confident in decision-making. When they do, their work will become a product of self-expression, culminating in creativity rather than in the dull, routine, task-oriented drudgery that can accompany the most prestigious position.

Present administrators need not be considered passé in this changed system. If they demonstrate the ability to change with the system, their years of experience could be invaluable when put to use in a new system, for we are dealing with continuing growth and awareness. We must build the model for the new administrator from many elements of the old.

Education (on-the-job training) for lower line employees should be completely revamped. College credit could be granted on the basis of training and experience. Building a cadre of new administrators from within the agency should be inherent in any new system.

Redesigning education at several levels, then, would be one of the functions of the new system. The design would not fit people to the system; rather, the system would work for the people—and bright, talented people would be attracted to it. Such people would actively seek positions when they could be sure they would not be lost in an overwhelming and impersonal bureaucracy.

Another function of the changed system would be to increase the visibility of administrators. In the new complex system, administrators would work more closely with small community-based delivery systems and neighborhood subunits of government that have been delegated some of the tasks heretofore handled by a central bureaucracy. Far from being hidden, they would be highly visible as they perform administrative functions while acting as teachers, lending advice and counsel to people who have been products of the leadership that has emerged from Office of Economic Opportunity, Community Action Agency, and Model Cities programs. These poverty programs identified local, indigenous leadership when and where the nation needed it, but the characteristics we are seeking in leaders have changed also; and the people who served as leaders in earlier poverty programs would be meshed into the new system as a vital part of increasing citizen involvement in government activities.

The two kinds of students Dr. Banovetz lists as seeking fellowships do exist in small percentages throughout the country on our college campuses, but how we perceive them may be bound into how we perceive the entire system. Dr. Banovetz has one explanation. But perhaps we would do better to consider what influences are motivating our young people.

Young people are seeking education and growth, and they use a variety of methods to get to their goals. They do not see schools and colleges as the only possible institutions to supply education. They tend to stay uncommitted, they do not decide hastily on formal careers, and they do not give themselves fixed goals to pursue. The new breed recognizes the need for change, feel their individuality, and choose to guard it carefully. They are sophisticated and outgoing; they possess talents that should be cultivated.

Some young people are trying to make the changes in the system that would bring it in line with the new awareness. They have chosen the fellowship programs as a means of acquiring the skill necessary to do the job. Because they have a different yardstick for measuring education, it is hard to agree with Dr. Banovetz that they are not excellent students. Most fellowship programs require that young people compete vigorously for the available spots, as I have said of the National Urban Fellows Program.

For the present administrator, the change is one of awareness. It is necessary to be aware of the social influences that create shortages in the profession and to be keenly alert to the potential of young people, nonprofessional and paraprofessional employees in the system, and community leaders that may be developed to provide a bank of talent to wipe out the shortages. Present administrators should be aware that the degree of interest they demonstrate helps increase the visibility of the profession. The very fact that they are visible and dealing with the complex problems of today in fresh, imaginative ways will attract larger numbers of the new generation.

We must be about changing systems and making them work to solve problems as expeditiously as possible. The greatest challenge to us all—public administrators, and poor, middleclass, and affluent persons—is change and our adaptiveness to that change. And adaptiveness would be our greatest asset in attracting and stimulating a new generation of urban administrators.

Commentary on the Banovetz Paper

By Robert B. Weiss

ABSTRACT: Much of what is stated by Dr. Banovetz elicits a nod of the head in agreement. The points of dispute are relatively few. His emphasis on the urban generalist does not adequately consider the role of retread functional professionals who have broadened their careers, or are interested in doing so. There is demand for retraining and programs to satisfy these needs. The urban administrator is rarely impartial or neutral—a fact that deserves recognition in academic programs. The well-stated discussion of minority students excluded a significant group—women. Despite these remarks, Professor Banovetz's development of the theme that urban administration is not a sufficiently visible career to stimulate student interest is well stated and a point well taken.

Robert B. Weiss is town manager in Manchester, Connecticut and previously served in Windsor, Connecticut and South Berwick, Maine. He has a B.A. degree in government from Boston Universty and earned an M.G.A. degree from the University of Pennsylvania where he held a Graduate Scholarship in the Fels Institute of Local and State Government. He is a past vice president of the International City Management Association and served as president, Fels Institute Graduate Associates 1971–72.

IN RESPONDING to a scholarly paper such as that presented by Dr. Banovetz, the articulation of controversy is much more interesting and stimulating than is assent. Regrettably, perhaps much of what is stated by Dr. Banovetz elicits a nod of the head in agreement. As a result of this personal response, I decided to broaden my own reactions by soliciting responses from five other people: an assistant manager out of graduate training five years; a recent graduate now receiving her master's degree; a professor of public administration and political science; a member of a government institute associated with a state university; and a former president of the International City Management Association (ICMA) with several decades in public service, now associated with a university public administration training program. The comments that follow then, reflect not only my own prejudices developed during my twenty-four years as a town manager but the varied thoughts of others as well.

Most of us react subjectively to external stimuli and this no doubt is my reaction to Dr. Banovetz's paper. My own interest in entering the field of public administration was the result of a combination of factors: the stimulus of a mind-stretching professor of political science in undergraduate school, an English assignment to read Lincoln Steffens' autobiography, and public turmoil over scandal in a nearby city leading to the adoption of council-manager government coincident to the above. The push toward the Fels Program by a professor familiar with their then new approach set me in the right direction. The Fels pattern for graduate training developed over thirty years ago still provides a viable program combining generalist academic courses along with an emphasis on field work in governmental offices during the university matriculation, as well as an off-campus internship program. This program was highly successful and probably was responsible for training more members of the city manager profession than any other graduate program.

Regrettably, the Fels Program has now taken on a new perspective and apparently is concentrating on training urban theorists rather than urban administrators. Hopefully this monograph will provide the blueprint for many institutions searching for improved public service career programs.

In developing his theme, Professor Banovetz appears to have made the basic assumption that most administrators would follow some kind of career ladder from college through a responsible administrative position and his emphasis is therefore on the attraction of young people to the field as generalists. The term urban administrator is an extremely limited one in Dr. Banovetz's mind—a city or county manager. Within this definition, the potential career market is limited, but it seems to me that the vast majority of urban administrators as opposed to generalist managers evolve into such careers as a result of specialized careers or training in limited governmental functions: police, fire, finance, planning, electronic data processing, recreation, engineering, and so on. The more responsible the position and the greater their experience, the more professionals are called upon to be urban administrators rather than functional specialists.

When an urban administrator is defined in broad terms, we can recognize that the majority of critical urban programs are administered by retread functional professionals who are interested in broadening their careers. Add to this the countless numbers who gain access to key administrative positions through political or experiential routes—not professional careers—then we can perceive that we are generally faced with the problem of how to retrain a large number of urban professionals so that they are equipped with the necessary skills to become urban administrators.

Some of my thoughts on this type of retraining include:

1. Creation of career development centers in the major geographic areas of the country where middle management personnel can receive adjunct degrees in urban administration as they are working their way up in a department.

2. Support for the recently established National Training and Development Service, founded under Ford Foundation and Intergovernmental Personnel Act grants. As I understand it, the programs offered here will be what amounts to a residential staff college where administrators can receive refresher training on a four- or five-year cyclic basis with a two- or three-month stay at the training center.

3. Creation of a system of sabbaticals to encourage administrators to spend an academic semester at a university as an instructor. At the same time, the individual could be taking courses leading to an advanced degree. In addition to broadening the individual so placed, this type of program would have other beneficial spin-offs—the exposure to undergraduates of career opportunities and the exposure of political scientists to the real world of government.

4. Encouragement by universities and community colleges of the use of practitioners in the classroom either as invitees for special lectures or for the teaching of a full course.

If we take Professor Banovetz's more limited definition of an urban administrator, one cannot find too much to dispute as to the value of financial incentive, internships, and aggressive public relations programs to stimulate interest in the profession. I take exception, however, to the implication that an urban administrator is impartial and neutral. This is a myth dating back to Leonard White's passion for anonymity. The many statements emanating from the manager profession over the past two decades clearly show the profession's recognition of the policy role played by the manager and the need for commitment to more than the community's physical development by any successful professional. Reflective of the scholarly discussions of whether administration is an art or a science, I might state that the effective manager practices the art of policy involvement in such a way that he can avoid the type of political involvement that can lead toward his being forced to seek a position elsewhere.

More and more communities are involved in the process of goal setting. Hard looks are being taken at various policy alternatives and the design of strategies to achieve desired results. These are exciting concepts definitely involving value judgments. Concerned students interested in reform should be made aware of this trend and be disabused of the mythology of urban administrators' pure neutrality. Instead they should be made aware of the real difficulties involved in changing long-standing patterns and approaches to solving local problems. They should be made aware of the real world of policy determinants and the kind of dedication and effort required if local government is going to serve the needs of people. They should be made aware of the constraints under which elected officials operate in making policies and the boundaries within which administrators operate in affecting policy. They should also be made aware of the exciting role professionals in local government can play and that they can have a measurable effect on what happens because local government is truly government at the grass roots.

My personal experience with minority students has been too limited to permit me to comment intelligently on what Professor Banovetz has written. I suspect, however, that greater effort is required in stimulating minority students to enter governmental careers. ICMA has been making efforts in this direction; however, job placement remains a problem. A broader perspective of career opportunities is probably necessary—directing more minority students toward fields such as planning, police, finance, public works, and so on—rather than purely generalist training.

In this treatment of minority students, Professor Banovetz did not concern himself with women, a minority group where potential for high-level administrative service has not been effectively utilized up to the present. While many women are interested in public service administrative careers, opportunities for clear-cut career advancement are still severely limited. I suspect that government has been slower than the private sector in recognizing the potential for talent in the weaker sex but I suspect that the women's liberation movement will catch up with us.

Professor Banovetz's development of the theme that urban administration is not a sufficiently visible career to stimulate student interest is well stated and a point well taken. I feel that working professionals must intensify their efforts at creating an awareness of the career potential in urban administration. It is too late to inject this thinking when a student has reached the third of fourth year of undergraduate school. Programs should be developed to create the interest in high school students. This means that we who are professionals must get information into the hands of guidance counselors in the high schools and also develop programs in the classrooms. We must also develop better rapport with the professors of political science who have a considerable influence on college students at a critical point when students are exploring various careers.

Summary of the Discussion of the Banovetz Paper

By Frederic N. Cleaveland

RUNNING through the discussion of this paper was the belief widely shared among symposium participants that there is now and will continue to be for the indefinite future a substantial shortage of qualified, trained administrators for urban governments in the United States. State and local government has been a major growth industry in this country for the last two decades and there is ample evidence that this situation will continue. Yet despite what should be a very favorable market situation for the graduates of university programs to prepare urban administrators, paradoxically the demand for trained administrative manpower for local government does not appear to be very strong. A participant with long experience in both academia and government observed that one major problem was the lack of appreciation among local government officials of the value to the city of hiring persons with professional training in urban administration. Most of the schools involved in educating urban administrators are doing a poor job of interpreting to government officials the need for more professionally trained urban managers. The public interest groups and professional associations are making some effort to correct this lack of understanding, but their efforts are minimal and relatively ineffective in changing attitudes. The problem becomes worse because it is difficult to generate and maintain adequate university support for schools of public affairs when the appreciation for and demand for their graduates are uncertain. A university administrator among the participants observed: "If our governmental clients were aware of the need for more trained people of this kind [urban administrators], that would be reflected in all kinds of ways which would make the response by universities a little easier than it is now. It will continue to be difficult for the university to gather together the resources we all want for educating urban administrators until the governmental clients show us that they are interested. Governments have shown very little direct interest in the kind of enterprise we are talking about here [public affairs professional education, especially of urban administrators]."

Symposium participants noted that a second major problem is the poorly organized market for urban administrators, and indeed the absence of a national market for such professional manpower. It is difficult to identify job openings with significant professional growth potential, and placement efforts on the part of universities training people for careers in urban administration tend, too often, to be unsystematic and ineffective. The noteworthy exceptions to this gloomy picture are likely to be those schools where faculty members maintain continuing relationships with alumni of the school in the world of urban government practice. These are also likely to be the same schools where there is regular interaction between the faculty and local government officials working in cities in the region generally served by the institution. Where practitioners are regularly involved in seminars and field work projects and the students are exposed frequently to city hall and county executive offices during their academic programs, placement efforts flow naturally from these continuing relationships. One experienced practitioner made this point eloquently: "If there is a well-established, productive working relationship between a graduate public affairs program and people who are practicing public affairs out in the field, then placement will not be the problem that it now seems to be. My experience in the last six to eight years is that there is a massive inability to develop meaningful productive relationships between the school of public affairs and the work-a-day world in city hall. Professors seeking to develop graduate projects will write or call on the city manager. He has his conception of what will meet the academic requirements of the project and the city manager has his conception of what needs to be done. It is virtually impossible to meld these two levels of expectation into anything that is going to be mutually productive. Mechanics are lacking that provide the kind of interchange required to bridge the gap we are focusing on here."

Looking at the market from another perspective—the availability of trained urban administrators to take on important responsibilities in a city trying to raise the professional quality of its staff—there are problems here too. Some practitioners reported that they were receiving two or three inquiries every week from generally well-qualified people looking for positions in urban administration. But, in sharp contrast, one experienced practitioner cautioned: "We ought to talk to the people in the core cities where the problems are before we come to any conclusion on this business of whether or not jobs are scarce." His experience has suggested that positions in some of the more difficult urban settings are going unfilled because those coming out of the public affairs schools prepared for urban administration are not interested in these jobs. Yet often such positions offer a real opportunity for personal growth and development.

Another important question raised in the discussion of this paper concerned the relative strengths of the comprehensive, independent school of public affairs, on the one hand, and the smaller, limited focus, program in urban administration, perhaps independent or more often organized within one or another academic department (usually political science) or professional school (usually a school of business administration). This discussion also reflected the unresolved issue of how the career of an urban administrator should be defined, an issue first raised by the participants in considering the paper by Watt, Parker, and Cantine on "The Roles of the Urban Administrator in the 1970s. . . ." Those participants who assigned an important role to the smaller, limited focus program often carried on within a department of political science tended to define the urban administrator as the generalist and the desired career pattern that epitomized by the city manager. They readily conceded that the large comprehensive schools of public affairs would continue to train a large number, perhaps a majority, of those pursuing careers in urban administration. Nevertheless, these participants asserted that the smaller more limited training programs located in many colleges and universities throughout the country are also very important because they serve a more limited market both for attracting young people into professional training and for serving the needs of small and middle-size urban communities for professionally trained urban administrators. This market requires the generalist administrator.

Participants who tended to emphasize the overriding importance of the large, comprehensive schools reflected a quite different conception of the career in urban administration. To them this career field includes more than the generalist urban administrator (city manager). Quite specifically, in their view, it includes the functional specialist managers in city government responsible for administering large and important programs within the structure of city government. Thus heads of departments of public works, school superintendents, managers in departments of welfare and of public health are all urban administrators. Accordingly, participants sharing this view believe that the university aspiring to provide professional training for urban administrators must also prepare public health doctors, welfare workers, city planners, public works engineers, and so forth to perform effectively in positions of managerial leadership. They see the large, comprehensive school of public affairs as the necessary instrument for accomplishing this objective, and they define the responsibility of these schools to include developing effective bridges linking the school of public affairs to the school of education, the school of public health, the school of engineering—indeed linking the school of public affairs to every part of the university involved in training professionals required by urban government for the performance of its multiple tasks.

These somewhat different perspectives about urban administrators and their professional training marked discussions throughout the Symposium. Both practitioners and academic participants represented each perspective. While the differences were never fully reconciled, in most instances the group reached a position accommodating both perspectives as relevant and important. Thus in this instance participants acknowledged a continuing role for both the comprehensive, independent school of public affairs and the more limited professional training programs. Some of the flavor of the discussion of these complex issues may be gleaned from the following quotations: One of the educator participants said:

"To make careers in urban public administration visible and attractive we must talk about careers in a whole range of functional fields as well as about careers as generalist administrators. After all, the bulk of the urban public service is in these fields:

public education, health, welfare, law enforcement, and so forth. The real contribution of the independent school of public affairs is in its capacity to build bridges to other relevant professional schools."

From the other perspective, a practitioner stated: "I am concerned myself with the education, pre-service and post-entry, of those who will assume responsible roles of leadership in local government functions in a general administrative kind of position. I do not accept the fact that in the context of this discussion we must include public health physicians, police chiefs, directors of public works, and so forth. I do not think that they are per se urban administrators. They are first of all qualified in their own profession, and they happen to be working in government. I think we have got to look more at who is going to manage the administrators in programs like Model Cities, than to concern ourselves with how the school of public affairs extends its wisdom and knowledge into the school of engineering, public health, and so forth.

Finally, there was a third theme given attention in the discussion of this paper, namely, the problem of attracting, stimulating, and retaining students for careers in urban administration. One academic participant put the issue this way: "We are losing good students every day to law schools and other clearly identifiable professional schools. We have a terrible time convincing people that there is a career field in public administration. How do we reach the people out there who might have gone into our programs but who have gone elsewhere? I see this as a job for the public service professional associations and the public interest groups to come up with some definition of careers in urban administration." Another academic member of the group brought the subject even closer to home: "The real problem is that we can't tell the students what we are preparing them for because we really do not know ourselves." He went on to assert that schools engaged in professional education for urban administration need to know who and what they are and what they are trying to do. Then they must get this across to students, illustrating how the admission process and patterns of student admission, and the curriculum, and the placement process are all organized and conducted to reflect these goals, that is, the school's conception of what it is trying to do. Once students begin to develop some understanding of what is involved in a career in urban public administration, then their professors must work with them individually to help them formulate their own career development plans. This is an important part of the initial process of socializing students into this career field—imparting to them a realistic conception of the career and an understanding of the nature and scope of the profession. Too often the situation arises where a young person is excited and stimulated by a generally inaccurate view of the career field of urban administration and then when he begins his pre-entry educational program he soon becomes disenchanted with the experience. We must find ways to build on his enthusiasm and interest, to develop in him a realistic conception of the profession and both the attractions and the handicaps involved, and then to relate his educational experience effectively to his growing understanding of the career field.

Part of the problem of attracting young people into this career field is its low visibility. Except for city managers, urban administrators are not a very visible career group. Even in the case of city managers, where there may still be a lingering aura of mystique, for young people of the 1970s this city manager image may actually be disfunctional, "turning off" more young people than it attracts. Certainly, public service professional associations and public interest groups can assist in efforts to promote higher visibility and a more positive image. Academicians among the participants also made a good case for the usefulness of undergraduate courses in urban problems and urban government administration as recruiting devices encouraging students to enter professional graduate degree programs. In a similar way opportunities for students to interact with practitioners through undergraduate internship programs, field work courses, and programs bringing practitioners to the campus can help significantly to improve the understanding students have of this career field. Participants agreed that as a career field urban administration is inherently attractive, especially to socially concerned young people. The challenge is how to do a better job of interpretation and image building.

"End-Product" Objectives of Pre-Entry Professional Education for Urban Administrators and Their Implications for Curriculum Focus

By Frederick C. Mosher

ABSTRACT: The term urban administrators connotes a broad swath of occupational roles. A vast number of specialties are required to deal with urban matters, and we are dealing with a rapidly growing public industry which is unusual in its composition of educated people. The number of graduates of schools of public or urban affairs is only a trickle in relation to these demands. Those in the public service will fall into two categories: Specialists with a generalism, including engineers, lawyers, and doctors, and Generalists with a specialism. There is need both for specialists—or professionals—with a broad understanding of urban problems and for generalists in public-urban problems with some competence in one or more specialized fields. The universities of the sixties tended to discourage or totally exclude broader studies of social problems. The seventies have seen a movement toward relevance and openness in academic institutions, which promises to result in universities capable of providing an effective crosswalk between academia and the public, urban world.

Frederick C. Mosher is Doherty Professor of Government and Foreign Affairs, University of Virginia. He has an M.S. degree from Syracuse University and a D.P.A. from Harvard. He served on the faculties of Syracuse University, the University of California, Berkeley, and the University of Bologna, Italy, and in advisory roles to various governmental and public service agencies including U.S. Department of State, UNRRA, Los Angeles City Civil Service Commission, Public Administration Clearing House, CED, National Institute of Public Affairs, and Inter-University Case Program.

IT SHOULD be made clear at the outset that the term urban administrators as used in this paper connotes a much broader swath of occupational roles than its earlier definition which comprehended city and county managers and staff specialists in finance, budgeting, personnel, and others. As described by Thomas J. Davy, the roles of urban administrators include as well: "Positions of substantial policy-making and directive responsibility" both in governments and in organizations related to governmental action; department heads, planners, leaders and senior staff of regional councils, research and service organizations, community action agencies, public service-oriented groups, and community service programs in industry; and "key officials in state and federal programs directed to urban problems."[1] The enormous diversity of urban administrators is magnified by the realization that most federal and state programs have some impact upon urban problems—even those which are directed toward different ends, such as defense and agriculture. When one speaks of end products of pre-entry education, he is referring to some fraction—from a tiny proportion to 100 percent—of almost every major field offered in higher education. Because of this diversity, the question of pre-entry education of urban administrators raises these questions. What features, patterns, and ingredients of such education are common and desirable? What should be the content of programs specifically designed for urban administration? How can those who will become urban administrators but whose primary focus of study, graduate or undergraduate, is something else, be properly prepared?

DEMAND AND SUPPLY

More than one in six of all employed persons are on public payrolls. This proportion is expected to increase between 1970 and 1980 to nearly one in five.[2] Virtually none of this growth will derive from the federal government because of an anticipated decline in military and defense employment. On the other hand,

1. Thomas J. Davy, "Education of Urban Administrators: Considerations in Planning and Organizing Graduate Degree Programs," *Public Management*, vol. 54, no. 2 (February, 1972), p. 5.

2. *Manpower Report of the President* (Washington, D.C.: Government Printing Office, 1971), pp. 162–163.

state and local employment grew from about 6 million in 1960 to 9.7 million in 1970 and is expected to rise to 13.5 million in 1980.[3] "Far more new jobs are anticipated in state and local government during the 1970s than in any major branch of private industry."[4] This is in spite of anticipated declines in the growth rates in education and highways. Principal fields of expected growth include: redevelopment of central cities; public housing; urban transit; public health, hospitals and sanitation; natural resource development; and environmental protection.

The 1970 Census on employment is not yet published, but unless there have been rapid and unexpected changes in trends, it will confirm that governments are heavily peopled by professionals, scientists, and technicians—to a far higher degree than the private sector. In 1960, thirty-six percent of all professional, technical, and kindred employees in the United States were employed by governments. This figure is considerably skewed by school teachers, but even after omitting them, nearly one-fifth of all public employees were in these categories, two and one-half times the comparable proportion in the private sector.

Data of these kinds are obviously rough and global. They do make it clear, however, that we are dealing with a rapidly growing public industry which is unusual in its composition of educated people. There has been no overall estimate of the numbers needed to direct and manage the vast array of public enterprises, but it must surely run in the hundreds of thousands. To these must be added a growing number of urban administrators who do not work directly for government, as suggested above. And to the thousands of new administrative positions which will be established every year must be added the replacements of many individuals, initially appointed in the thirties and early postwar years, who are currently retiring.

The number of graduates of schools of public or urban affairs is only a trickle in relation to these potential demands. In the mid-1960s, the organization now known as the National Association of Schools of Public Affairs and Administration conducted a census of the graduates of the programs of its member universities—all at the graduate level. The total number in the entire

3. Ibid.
4. Ibid.

country was on the order of 500 per year, the majority coming from a handful of the larger institutions. A comparable survey is being conducted this year, and preliminary indications are that it will reflect rapid current growth—though upon a tiny base. The number of joint degrees and joint programs with other professional schools is undoubtedly still so small as to be statistically inconsequential.

Compared with other professional degree programs, the output in public and urban affairs is miniscule. The most recent report on *Earned Degrees Conferred* of the Office of Education (for 1966–67) showed a ratio between degrees in public affairs or administration and business administration or commerce including accounting, of not one to five or one to ten but one to fifty.[5] And while we are producing surpluses in graduate degrees in a great many academic and some professional fields, the demand for graduates in public administration and public policy is growing and far beyond the supply.

Specialists with a Generalism

It has long been appreciated—and by some, deplored—that much of the administration of public affairs in this country has been dominated by specialists in particular functional fields. Parochialism of function rests upon and reinforces parochialism of occupation. The extent to which the horizontal structure of American governments—the definition of departments and divisions—parallels the occupational specialisms in society is not widely appreciated. Most units of government below the very top are led and in substantial part staffed by specialists in occupations recognized as matching the functions. Most public administrators are or were first of all specialists in some occupational endeavor appropriate to the governmental function they are currently directing, and this includes a very substantial number of the political appointees. This means, among other things, that they bring to their administrative jobs the world-view, the methodology, the think-ways, and work-ways of their occupation.

5. The actual figures were: for business and commerce (general and accounting)—42,620 bachelors, 8,783 masters, and 229 doctors for a total of 51,632; for public administration—382 bachelors, 704 masters, 42 doctors for a total of 1,128.

Most of these leaders have been trained and oriented for their specialism at the undergraduate and/or graduate levels in universities and colleges. In fact, there is a surprising parallelism between the organizations of colleges, schools, and departments of the universities and the organizations of governments. Note, for example, the university divisions and subdivisions of engineering, health, medicine, social welfare, law, economics, psychology, and the hard sciences. This is no doubt in part a response of universities to governmental demands in specialized fields, in part a response of governments in shaping their programs to take advantage of the university products. In either case, the universities are significantly involved in nurturing, supporting, and extending occupational—and therefore functional—specialism. The functional parochialism of public agencies begins with education. The faculties of the schools and departments of the universities pretty largely define what each profession is through their teaching programs, their books, and the influence of the professors upon the neophytes. They determine the skills and knowledges required, the boundaries, values, and objectives. Because of their intense preoccupation with the expansion as well as the transmittal of knowledge, the tendency is toward deeper and deeper penetration, that is, greater specialism, in the specific areas of their study. Further, in some fields, there is increasing emphasis upon research and knowledge for its own sake to the sacrifice of knowledge for use, knowledge-oriented to social problems.

The old saw that we can't afford to leave military policy to the generals is now echoed in relation to a vast number of social areas. Thus we can't afford to leave: health delivery to the doctors; education to the teachers; social welfare to the social workers; regulation to the lawyers; streets and highways to the engineers; housing to the builders; mental health to the psychiatrists; science policy to the scientists; financial management to the accountants; lending and investment to the bankers; crime control to the police; drug control to the narcotics agents; or even higher education to the professors.

Until quite recently, only a tiny minority of the schools and departments which produce these professional specialists addressed themselves to the social, political, managerial, and public aspects and implications of their professional activities. Such approaches have been inhibited by a number of factors, including: historic professional parochialism; limitations of faculty knowledge and perspectives; time limitations of curriculums; also the myth that most real professionals are paid on a fee basis. The drive toward pure truth and science in much professional teaching, the aversion to politics, except for lawyers, and the aversion to organization and its management, except in business administration, have also been inhibiting factors.

During the last few years, there have been movements away from professional parochialism in a number of schools, a growing interest and concern about social consequences, attacks on social problems, interdisciplinary and interprofessional studies. The yeast for these developments I think has been provided mainly by the younger people, students and faculty, seeking ways to improve the society and seeking more relevance in their study. And one of the most likely ways of achieving these goals is through linkage of professional training in an established field with study in public and especially urban administration and affairs. In the newer programs in public affairs around the country, the clientele are increasingly lawyers, engineers, doctors, and economists—decreasingly political scientists. They will be "specialists with a (degree of) generalism." Most are headed for public service concerned with local problems, a few toward public affairs research. In the light of this growing concern among professional faculty and students, it is not surprising that the most enthusiastic recent endorsement of schools of public affairs has come from professional schools like education, engineering, law, and medicine.

GENERALISTS WITH A SPECIALISM

It seems unlikely that more than a minority of urban administrators will or should be prepared solely as generalists in the foreseeable future. The underlying structure of our education, our occupations, and our organizations is too functionally oriented to permit dominant reliance upon non-specialized officials. Yet, as there is deepening of specialization in government and in education, there is geometrically increasing growth in the need for people capable of visualizing longer and broader goals, of identifying the interconnections of different specialized activities, and of coordinating and integrating specialized activities towards those goals. Schools and programs and professors of public and urban affairs have long sought to inject a generalizing and synthesizing approach to public policy and administration. Although I am aware of no adequate quantitative supporting data, it appears to me that the accomplishments of urban administrators who have had generalist administrative training have been impressive, this despite the alleged thinness of their managerial training, their relatively small numbers, and their lack of professional credentials.

In order to gain a foothold in the occupational fields of urban administration, the graduates of generalized public or urban affairs programs must usually acquire a specialized field of competence from which to grow. This might be one of the older fields like personnel or budgeting or organizational analysis, or one of the newer fields like quantitative policy analysis or computer technology or collective bargaining. It may be acquired on the campus or in early work experience or both. But the main target should be the preparation of urban administrators for a broad-gauged, constructive career of dealing, in whatever capacity, with a variety of complex urban problems.

In short, there is need both for specialists, or professionals, with a broad understanding of urban problems and for generalists in public-urban problems with some competence in one or more specialized fields. At the universities, the generalists provide a desirable organizational base for both. But the specialists, to date widely neglected, may, in the longer run, be the more important in the effective response to urban problems.

THE CONTENT OF EDUCATIONAL PROGRAMS FOR URBAN ADMINISTRATORS

The core of urban affairs programs—or of public affairs programs for urban areas—may be described as the processes involved in:

1. the identification and definition of problems facing urban areas;

2. the analysis of these problems and of alternative actions responsive to them;

3. the reaching of the best feasible programs and decisions (including all the negotiation and persuasion involved with decision-makers beyond one's self);

4. the translation of decisions into effective action through organizations (which might be called administration, narrowly defined);

5. the assessment of results and feedback to new analysis and decision.

To these may be added the traditional and on-going processes involved in managing and conserving existing plant, other resources, services, and organizations. The latter sentence describes the more traditional and indeed once almost exclusive orientation of city management. It is still essential. But in our times, the dreaming, planning, and executing of change in response to problems is the more difficult and the crucial challenge.

It would be impossible, and not particularly useful, to enumerate all the desirable attributes of urban administrators. But some to which university programs in public or urban affairs might significantly contribute include:

1. appreciation and better understanding of the values, objectives, and ethics sought or involved in public decisions and actions;

2. basic understanding of the institutions, processes, and politics of American government with emphasis upon urban government, intergovernmental relations, and public-private relations;

3. acquaintance with the American city and the environment of urban administration: social, economic, physical, political, legal, technological;

4. acquaintance with the various techniques of problem and policy analysis and assessment and mastery of at least one: systems, economic, sociological, psychological, legal, and others;

5. understanding of the implications, uses, and dangers of scientific and technological development for urban policy and administration;

6. understanding of the socio-psychological elements in planned social and administrative change, including organization development and community relations;

7. understanding of the basic processes and problems of program management in the public setting, including program planning, organization, procedures, budgeting, personnel (including collective bargaining), communication, data processing, and assessment;

8. understanding of the sources of conflicts and roadblocks in public decision-making and execution, and the ways to overcome them.

Obviously, it would be impossible even for a genius to master all of the above subject matter—and some would add others— all the knowledges and skills of a *compleat* urban administrator— in a year or two or even a lifetime of study. More important, and more feasible, are the ways of defining goals, ways of perceiving situations, ways of working with and through people. Jencks and Riesman, in discussing professional education generally, broached the hypothesis that

the function of a professional school is not primarily to teach a narrowly defined set of skills of the kind measured by examinations, but to define a set of general criteria that recruits to the profession ought to meet and to screen out those who do not measure up. . . . Whether he [the novice] actually learns the details of anatomy, court procedure, or sewer design may indeed be irrelevant, or nearly so, since if he gains entry to the profession he can fill in the gaps in his technical knowledge later. *The primary role of the professional school may thus be socialization, not training.*[6] [Emphasis added.]

Among the elements of socialization for urban administration, I would emphasize:

1. A continuing concern about and quest for ultimate values and goals of social action which would overpass the values and goals of any single profession, discipline, or other specialism. (Item No. 1 above)

2. An approach to situations and problems that is *synthesizing,* that is, bringing relevant information and ideas together in the search for feasible solutions, all things considered, rather than compartmentalizing and reducing.

6. Christopher Jencks and David Riesman, *The Academic Revolution* (Garden City, N.Y.: Doubleday & Co., Inc., 1968), p. 206.

3. An orientation to decision and action rather than the accumulation and development of theoretic knowledge, rather than the search for truth. The urban administrator must seek the most promising feasible courses of action on the basis of information which is always imperfect. That means, among other things, he needs a considerable tolerance of ambiguity.

4. A primary orientation to whole people rather than things, as in engineering and the hard sciences, or to parts of people, as in medicine, or to particular aspects of people, as in economics and political science. The people orientation should comprise: an overriding concern for the quality of the lives of people as individuals and in groups or categories; a sympathetic curiosity about people's problems; an ability to communicate with, and particularly listen to, people whatever may be the color of their skin, their sex, their social and economic status, their points of view, their strengths and frailties.

5. A ceaseless and restless striving for change of conditions, institutions, methods, organizations in directions conducive to the achievement of social values, rather than an instinctive fear and resistance to change or the tendency to accept all the difficulties one finds in urban administration as givens within which he must work.

6. A capacity to perceive, define, and attack problems as problems and an accompanying ability and desire to move from problem to problem, that is, problem-oriented mobility.

7. A sympathy for open politics and open political processes and for the ideals of self-government, whatever may be their difficulties, inconveniences, and delays.

8. An underlying optimism about human beings and more particularly about the capacity of mankind to control or influence the conditions confronting them for the better.

The Record to the Sixties

I think that a fair review of the development of higher education in the professions and in the social and physical sciences during the first two-thirds of this century would indicate that, with some exceptions, most of it has not been conducive to these elements of socialization, and much of it has been in opposite

directions.[7]   Thus, there has been ever-increasing compartmentalization, reductionism, and specialization in narrower subsegments
of segments of disciplines and professions which, by their nature,
tend to discourage or totally exclude broader studies of social
problems.   There has been growing scientism and emphasis upon
abstract, rather than operational, theory.   There was an explosive
growth in the numbers of professionals concerned with external
matters and things in contrast to those involving services to individuals or groups as people.   For example, in 1900 the engineers
were a minor profession.   There were more than three times as
many doctors, three times as many clergymen, nearly three times
as many lawyers.   With the dentists and architects, these traditional professions in toto outnumbered the engineers by more
than ten to one.   By 1960 there were more than 100,00 more
engineers than the total of all doctors, clergymen, lawyers, dentists, and architects together.   During the fifties and sixties, there
was a comparably explosive growth of physical scientists.   Even
those fields traditionally conceived as people-oriented, such as
medicine, law, the social sciences, even social welfare, became
more and more dehumanized because of their growing specialization, growing scientism, growing reliance upon categorization and
quantification.

Perhaps more important was the tendency of individual professions or sciences, including the educators thereof, to minimize
the interrelationships and mutual dependencies of themselves and
the society and the polity within which and for which they presumably worked.   Until very recently, there were very few if any
courses in the professions and the sciences which treated the
history of the field in the society or its implications, values and
dangers today—social, ecological, political.   There was a general
and widespread effort to exclude the individual profession from

7. There have been a few general studies and critiques of the development
of higher education and innumerable studies of the development of individual
academic or professional fields.   Only a tiny fraction, however, have addressed the relationship of these developments to public or urban problems
and administration.   For a preliminary effort to summarize and synthesize
this relationship, see Frederick C. Mosher, *Professional Education and the
Public Service: An Exploratory Study* (Berkeley, Calif.: Center for Research
and Development in Higher Education, University of California, April 1968).

open politics and to win official sanction for self-regulation, self-government, and self-determination of goals and projects—even with public funds. Harold Seidman quipped that: "Scientific research is said to be the only pork barrel for which the pigs determine who gets the pork." [8] And I recently heard a doctor describe the medical profession as a culturally underprivileged minority group, primarily because of its ignorance of social problems even in the health field and its disdain for open politics and government. I think that it is fair to generalize that with scattered exceptions the education and practice of the professions and hard sciences were characterized by an ignoring of social affairs, an active aversion to politics and government, except intraprofessional politics, and indeed an opposition to organization generally as a threat to individual professional autonomy.

Behaviorism in psychology and more recently behavioralism in all of the social sciences, generally, though not exclusively, worked against most of the kinds of socialization recommended above. Explicitly or implicitly, they argued for neutrality as to values and goals, for scientific reductionism against synthesis, for objectivity against involvement, decision, and action, for determinism (and pessimism) about man's ability to control and influence his own future. The recent movement labelled new public administration is, in considerable part, a revival of the old public administration. Both were, or are, dominantly oriented to values and goals, to effective decision and action, to change, and to open politics and administration. And both reflect a fundamental confidence and optimism that people can shape their own destinies for the better.

But the study and the teaching of public, including urban, administration did not escape the depersonalizing influence that accompanied the growth of scientism and specialism in other fields. Until at least World War II, its central themes concerned organization structure, the streamlining and standardization of procedures, the planning and control of dollars through budgets, the planning, construction, and operation of physical structures. Even the field of personnel was effectively depersonalized through

8. Harold Seidman, *Politics, Position, and Power: The Dynamics of Federal Organization* (New York: Oxford University Press, 1970), p. 15.

the classification of positions apart from the people who did or would occupy them, the reliance upon objective, faceless tests of aptitudes and performance in selection and advancement. The target of most urban administration training in its early years was the city manager, a professional who should see to it that the government performed its appointed tasks efficiently and who, in doing so, should be protected from, and should resist, the ugly game of politics. There was remarkably little concern about the end results of those tasks upon the people for whom they were presumably performed.

REORIENTATION IN THE NINETEEN-SIXTIES

The redefinition of public administration was foreshadowed soon after World War II by the remarriage of politics and policy with administration, by the rapid growth and popularity of the movement then known as human relations, and by growing concern, kindled by the Supreme Court, about civil rights. But the new and vastly enlarged role of public administration did not truly emerge until the 1960s with the growing realization of the disastrous plight particularly of the cities and the tendency of citizens to turn to governments at all levels for corrective action. The sixties will be remembered not alone for Vietnam but also for: the Great Society programs and the dismal achievements of many of them; the demands for, and growing provision of, citizen participation in public policy and administration; the in-migration of the minority poor and the flight of the well-to-do to the suburbs; the failures in crime control, public welfare, education, health delivery, pollution; the near-bankruptcy of many urban governments; strikes and collective bargaining with public employees; the increasing interlocking of all levels of government on local—and mostly urban—problems. Public administration became public affairs. And its main focus returned to the place where it had started—the cities.

The principal parent of the current resurgence of urban affairs and education for urban administrators was the failures of the sixties—failures that were conspicuous, painful, and tragic. Those failures contributed to student complaints (and revolts) that what they were forced to learn on the campuses was not relevant to the problems of society nor to their own satisfaction. This sense of frustration was shared by many, though certainly not all, faculty members, and gradually the academic icebergs began to move. Many schools and departments began a serious re-examination of their curriculums and research activities that they might be made more relevant to the public problems of today and tomorrow: the lawyers to family law, legal protection and services for the poor, desegregation, law enforcement administration; the engineers to human acceptance and human impact of technological change in a great variety of fields; the educators to new means of reaching, retaining, and educating the poor and underprivileged, the economics and even politics (!) of education, and the social and political implications of integration; the doctors to the problems of delivering health services, especially to the poor, comprehensive health planning, community health and mental health centers, the economics of health; the natural sciences to the social consequences of scientific developments and to environmental problems; the economists to the analysis of the costs and benefits of various social programs and the measurement of results—Program, Planning, Budgeting Systems (PPBS).

These are but a small sample of what is now happening in what may properly be termed a new academic revolution, but I think they are representative. They have certain elements in common: they are all public affairs in that governmental decision and action is a central element; they are all in substantial if not dominant part urban affairs because a large proportion of our population lives in urban areas; they all have a heavy ingredient of social and human factors and objectives; no single profession or discipline is equipped, by its own self-definition, to handle all aspects of the problems by itself; all are interdisciplinary, inter-professional; and the separate fields of specialization increasingly appreciate this; they are all addressed to real and current problems.

Emerging Opportunities in Urban Affairs

If these new interests of faculty and students in other fields, in new courses, new programs, and new research projects continue to grow, as seems likely, they will open new vistas for those interested in improving and broadening education for budding urban administrators.   They offer opportunities for reaching students previously compartmentalized in functional specialties, and many of these new graduates will surely go on to careers in urban administration.   There are multiple possibilities of cross-filtration of materials and attitudes like those described earlier in this paper through jointly credited courses, multidisciplinary seminars, mixed faculty-student research on urban problems, internships, and joint degrees.   In all of this, schools or institutes, or centers of public or urban affairs could play a significant role as organizational foci, catalysts, and coordinators.   In the process they should greatly enrich their programs for their own, less specialized graduate students.   Probably the best way to acquire a problem orientation is to work on real problems; probably the best way to learn to communicate and work with persons with different perspectives and backgrounds is to communicate and work with them; probably the best way to acquire a broad philosophic view about social values and goals is to synthesize one's own view with those of others with different points of departure.

An incidental though not inconsiderable potential benefit of this kind of development could be the beginning of reform of the universities themselves.   Perhaps the greatest curse of university organization has been the compartmentalization of disciplines and subdisciplines, professions and subprofessions and the building of tall iron walls separating each knowledge enclave from all the others.   The spreading concern about public affairs may provide one instrument to drive some holes through some of those walls and possibly even cut through some doorways.   It might contribute, in a small or a major way, to move the *multi*versity back in the direction of the *uni*versity.   Possibly it might encourage the achievement of the aspiration expressed by Thomas Jefferson when, as head of the University of Virginia a century and a half ago, he wrote: "A man is not qualified as a professor, knowing nothing but merely his own profession." [9]

OPTIONS AND IMPERATIVES

This paper undertakes no single blueprint as to the most desirable content and curriculums for pre-entry programs for

9. In a letter to Albert Gallatin in 1822.

future urban administrators. I doubt that such a blueprint at this stage of history is either desirable or possible. The field, if it is a field, is moving in many directions at once, and perhaps that is how it should be. It seems to me that higher education and perhaps especially higher education in public affairs should be regarded as basically experimental, and this may be true for a very long time. Depending upon faculty and student interests and capacities and upon the job market and needs, some schools will lay stress upon policy analysis, some on the tools of management, some on politics, some on organizational development, some on financial administration, some on collective bargaining, some on managerial tools, some on one or another functional field. It would be useful if we had, or now began to establish, better longitudinal assessment of the products of different kinds of programs. But I would be skeptical of any single formula for the training of urban administrators.

I do think, however, that there should be underlying concern in any program about the ways in which we are trying to socialize our students. The elements of socialization suggested earlier may be contested or enlarged upon, but at this level of generalization, one might hope for a degree of consensus. I think too that any program for urban administrators needs a substantial organizational base with a considerable autonomy from other disciplines. This is not that it may become but another academic enclave but for precisely opposite reasons. It should be an open institution, capable of working freely with and through other organizations, faculties, and students on the campus and capable of providing an effective crosswalk between academia and the public, urban world.

This quality of openness will not be easy to achieve on the campuses of most universities. Given the history and the virulence of disciplinary and professional separatism, there will be fear of encroachment and competition in many related departments and schools. One may anticipate the charges that public, or urban, administration is not a science or a discipline or a profession; and that it threatens the traditional academic standards of admission, of prerequisite courses, of scholarship in its teaching and applied research, and of credentials. There will be pressure in some departments and schools to bar non-majors from courses that may be relevant to urban affairs and to discourage or refuse credit to their own students for courses taken in a program for urban affairs.

There is another danger which must be overpassed: that the schools and programs in public or urban affairs will seek to build walls around themselves as so many other disciplines and professions have done. In their quest for autonomy and a favorable academic image, they will be tempted to bar students and faculty and courses from many other fields and to concentrate their offerings exclusively on scientifically sanitized, academically respectable studies, such as organization theory, decision-making theory, or quantitative analysis.

These roadblocks can be overcome, though it may be a slow and difficult process. Those who educate urban administrators of the future must keep their eyes on the main target: to better equip people to cope with the main besetting problems of our times, from whatever field of specialism they may come. Brooks Adams wrote a long time ago:

Administration is the capacity of coordinating many, and often conflicting, social energies in a single organism, so adroitly that they shall operate as a unity. This presupposes the power of recognizing a series of relations between numerous special social interests, with all of which no man can be intimately acquainted. Probably no very highly specialized class can be strong in this intellectual quality because of the intellectual isolation incident to specialization; and yet *administration or generalization is not only the faculty upon which social stability rests, but is, possibly, the highest faculty of the human mind.*[10] [Emphasis added.]

Administration today can hardly be any simpler than it was in 1913. And the most crucial and difficult current need of it lies in the urban areas of America and other countries.

10. Brooks Adams, *The Theory of Social Revolutions* (New York: The Macmillan Company, 1913), pp. 207–208.

Commentary on the Mosher Paper

BY CORNELIUS BODINE, JR.

ABTRACT: Dr. Mosher's conclusion that specialists may be more important in the effective response to urban problems is surprising, and if accurate, it carries significant implications. Programs for public and private sector managers must be full scope—aiming at the integration or correlation of all the specialisms involved. Urban administrators must be akin to local statesmen—technically skilled, socially sensitive, psychologically mature, and philosophically detached. They need to be both black and varied white, but especially black. Both the rigid structure of universities and narrow professionalism can retard the production of urban managers who meet these qualifications.

Cornelius Bodine, Jr., business administration of the City of Newark, New Jersey, is a graduate of Amherst and has an M.G.A. degree from the University of Pennsylvania where he held a Graduate Scholarship in the Fels Institute of Local and State Government. He has been in private business, has served in the federal government in several capacities, and was city manager in Florida, Alabama, Kentucky, Illinois, Iowa municipalities.

THE subject of the paper by Frederick C. Mosher is part of the general theme on objectives of universities in educating urban administrators. As might be expected, he faced a logical difficulty in distinguishing nice boundaries between this topic and the two other main themes of this monograph, namely, "What Are We Educating For" (including knowledges and skills needed in the role of urban administrator), and "Strategies in Building Educational Programs."

To the typical urban practitioner, I suspect that the term end-product objective may be either a tautology or an ambiguity or both. In an educational program the end product must be the turned-out student which the university helped to mold in a certain way at a particular point in time, and at a critical point in the student's development. There is ambiguity in describing the desired end product partly because of the very broad definition given the term urban administrator. In addition, the preferred end product may be perceived differently from different standpoints. For example, there are the immediate job needs and aspirations of the graduating student, and the practical demands of his first employer, as well as the long-range societal needs of urban areas as may be viewed by the faculty and others. Although Dr. Mosher notes that there are many kinds of urban administrators and many occupational paths that may be taken to attain this uncertain status, his paper tends to skirt the practical problems at point of entry and of career development from that point forward.

It is surmised in the symposium outline that if the issues about end-product objectives can be resolved, then the content and strategies for building effective educational programs can be determined. I do not see it that simply myself, and Dr. Mosher certainly uses a wider lens and broader brush. He appears to be saying that the central considerations bearing on the appropriate focus of a curriculum pertain to the urban administrator's ultimate role, his desirable attributes (which appear to be categories of knowledge and understanding) and developing his socialization, the elements of which are well enunciated in his paper. However, the compleat urban administrator is not attainable even in a lifetime of study, and the question of what specifically should be taught to what kinds of normal human beings is left unanswered.

GENERALIST-SPECIALIST

Dr. Mosher touches this matter obliquely in his observations on specialists with a generalism and generalists with a specialism. In doing so, an old question about educating general managers is implied which I thought the schools had answered differently, that is, is it more productive to try to convert specialists to be generalists or to train generalists in what they need to know about the varied specialties they administer?

Dr. Mosher notes that while we are producing surpluses in graduate degrees in a great many academic and some professional fields, the demand for graduates in public administration and public policy is growing and far beyond the supply. Possibly as a consequence, most public administrators are or were first of all specialists in some occupational endeavor appropriate to the governmental function they are currently directing. And even now, he points out, in the newer programs in public affairs around the country, the clientele are increasingly lawyers, engineers, doctors and economists—decreasingly political scientists. Dr. Mosher estimates that it is unlikely that more than a minority of urban administrators will or should be prepared solely as generalists in the foreseeable future. He concludes that there is need both for specialists, or professionals, with a broad understanding of urban problems and for generalists in public-urban problems with some competence in one or more specialized fields . . . But the specialists . . . may, in the longer run, be the more important in the effective response to urban problems.

To me this conclusion is surprising, and if accurate, it carries significant implications with respect to curriculum content and focus as well as the selection of recruits. The reasoning seems to be that specialists are in relatively good supply and that their expertise is essential. Thus, if they can be given a good overall course in public policy, they may respond to urban problems more effectively than persons trained as generalists or general urban managers. I have difficulty agreeing with this proposition.

Surely, a specialist in engineering or medicine or finance will be more effective in his specialty if he better grasps the public consequences of his decision-making and if he sees more clearly the impingement of his area of knowledge on other specialties. That's all to the good. But I do question whether this approach is likely to develop urban administrators who typically can untangle and creatively resolve urban conflicts where they are most problematic. It is hard enough to train a specialist in management of a unit comprised of persons working in fields kindred to his own profession, to say nothing of deepening his awareness of wide-ranging political and social interactions on the urban scene. Dr. Mosher points out that the old saw that we can't afford to leave military policy to the generals is now echoed in relation to a vast number of social areas. Increasingly we witness the triumph of technique over purpose, and the outcome of such struggles is not likely to be reversed by trying to recondition specialists who are dedicated to walking down narrow corridors. Their professional associations will continue to claim their paramount loyalties.

The need is clearly for a greater supply of broad-gauged generalists who understand management and a wide assortment of other things which Dr. Mosher ably describes. The administrators needed occupy a great many more positions than city managers, administrative assistants, and aides to the Mayor. My experience is that in larger cities department heads in both line and staff functions will be more effective in the long run when educated as generalists in urban administration in contrast to specialists who have been promoted from within a professional hierarchy and subsequently given an exposure to public policy.

The design of curriculums for education of managers in the private sector at many long-established, graduate business schools should provide useful parallels to needs faced at the same stage of development by would-be urban administrators. Programs for both must embrace the basic functional and operational activities peculiar to the two categories of institutions, and both must deal with the pertinent external environment affecting each. But the perspective of students in both programs must be full scope— aiming at the integration or correlation of all the specialisms involved. Another approach to the exploration of the relationship of academic input to subsequent performance might be an analysis of the systems for educating urban administrators in the technically advanced foreign countries.

THE ACADEMIC ICEBERG

There seems to be more insight among both professors and practitioners as to the suitable characteristics of good urban administrators and what they do than on how and where to produce them.

Dr. Mosher traces an apparent twenty to twenty-five year cycle of attention or concern by students in the field of urban administration. I tend to concur with him that the recent movement labelled new public administration is, in considerable part, a revival of the old public administration. This current concentration is said to have its counterpart in the new academic revolution resulting in new emphases keyed to current relevance.

At the same time, I get the impression from Dr. Mosher, as well as from others, that the gradual movement of the academic icebergs lacks a sense of positive urgency that the times require. He does not appear to be optimistic that the compartmentalization of disciplines in universities will be readily modified. It is stated that any program for urban administrators needs a substantial organizational base with a considerable autonomy from other diciplines . . . capable of working freely with and through other organizations, faculties, and students on the campus . . . . Yet Dr. Mosher concludes that this quality of openness will not be easy to achieve on the campuses of most universities. Overcoming the academic roadblocks may be a slow and difficult process.

With regard to curriculum, although the options are many and the imperatives are compelling, Dr. Mosher states that higher education in public affairs should be regarded as basically experimental, and this may be true for a very long time. He sees no single blueprint as to the most desirable content and curriculums for pre-entry programs for future urban administrators, and he doubts that such a blueprint at this stage of history is either desirable or possible. He is skeptical of any single formula for the training of urban administrators.

When Sputnik went up in 1957, many academic programs made a major shift. It appears to me that the Sputnik of urban calamity is on the launching pad, and if the universities don't shift to muster their forces and vast resources promptly, other organized entities are going to have to do so, and some are already in motion. It is to be expected that no single blueprint or formula will be forthcoming. At the same time, the feasible options are not altogether obscure. In fact, the current effort to identify particular academic ingredients along with teaching strategies is encouragingly specific. In any event, it is not acceptable to conclude that our choices must be curtailed in any significant way because of the rigid internal structure of the university.

It is believed by many that federal revenue sharing with few strings will be the panacea for urban areas. This may be true for many cities and counties. But for some others, probably some in which the need is greatest, it could prompt a political or social disaster, unless seasoned urban administrators are readily available and providing insight, direction, and control.

POWER STRUCTURE

Dr. Mosher avers that the principal parent of the current resurgence of urban affairs and education for urban administrators was the failures of the sixties . . . Those failures contributed to student complaints (and revolts) that what they were forced to learn on the campuses was not relevant to the problems of society nor to their own satisfaction.

I tend to think that the issues of the sixties would have been quite different were it not for the catalytic effect of the civil rights challenge by blacks and Vietnam. These upheavals, among other things, were moral confrontations in the consciences of many, especially youth, but not only youth. The psychological fallout drifted in many directions influencing in time the rising expectations of many varieties of minorities and the demands of many categories of individuals, not only the disadvantaged, to have more effective voice in the decision-making processes of many institutions. Great waves of questioning now pound the beaches of many established orders. The feeling of meaningful participation in the system is regarded in some localities as an important social value, almost regardless of the soundness of decisions made.

With respect to the government of many central cities, the power base is rapidly shifting. The current rhetoric on institutional change seems to relate less to matters of administrative organization, program, and procedure than to the structure of power—its control, redistribution, and access to it. Urban administrators have always been observers of the dynamics and mechanics of political activity. I suspect that in the future in many cities they will have to understand even better the condition and psychology as well as the organizational drives of minorities and the disadvantaged, and the political implications.

LOCAL STATESMEN

The claim of minority status is close to becoming a political vogue. Other distinct ethnic and religious groups are likely to seek the same kind of special attention now presumably given to the blacks, Spanish-speaking (ex-Puerto Rican and ex-Mexican), and Indians. It is not clear whether the traditional melting pot concept in America will temporarily run to more or less fusion.

In any event, whether one's outlook is political, sentimental, moral, or legal, the shifting power realities, in urban areas especially, must be reflected in educational programs for urban administrators. I am referring not only to the process of selecting or seeking a cultural cross section of students, but also to an attitudinal indoctrination of all students with respect to the need for greater objectivity toward race, culture, and creed.

In describing socialization for urban administrators, Dr. Mosher points out that their people orientation should include an ability to communicate with, and particularly listen to, people whatever may be the color of their skin, their sex, their social and economic status, their points of view, their strengths and frailties. This kind of generality applies to many occupations and does not go anywhere near far enough when speaking of urban administrators or of their education.

In larger central cities, the blacks constitute the minority group of special significance due to their proportionate numbers, resulting largely from the two accelerated phenomena of the flight from agriculture and a different flight to the suburbs. By 1980 a major fraction of the population in dozens of American cities will be blacks, and the balance of power can be expected to follow suit. In January 1972, two out of 2,400 city managers were blacks, and the ratio among other kinds of urban administrators in decision-making roles was probably not significantly better. In short, thousands of blacks will be appointed, willy-nilly, to positions of administrative responsibility relatively soon in key urban areas. The only questions are, how will they have been educated, and will they have had an opportunity to learn how to govern.

In the ebb and flow of power groupings, it must be assumed that the behavior of a political, ethnic, or religious minority will tend to be somewhat different with respect to the balance of society once it has attained ascendancy. This is the norm. The best that can be hoped is that any narrow instincts or impetuosity of any new prevailing authority can be reasonably subdued and guided by the influence of professionalism in the public interest.

It is unfortunate that some white majorities, such as those in a number of the cities in northern New Jersey, where I am presently located, have not provided a more promising model.

In short, the times demand a large infusion of local statesmen, technically skilled, socially sensitive, psychologically mature, and philosophically detached. They need to be both black and varied white, but especially black. The only way that this can happen soon enough is for universities to recruit and develop such young men and women with the clear end-product objective of creating potential local statemen. In addition, the International City Management Association (ICMA), and the other professional associations of the so-called Big Six, must greatly expand their present tardy programs (ICMA led the way in 1968) to induce existing urban administrators to employ and develop the neglected minorities.

MOTIVATION

When a student graduates from a school for urban administrators he should be motivated realistically to do and be something. He should have a clear idea of the alternative paths he might take and of the seemingly menial tasks and confusing environments that he must endure as a team worker before he makes decisions out front. Only a few will start as city managers in small towns and be in the driver's seat right off.

I think that one of the essential elements in the graduate's belief pattern affecting his positive motivation is a feeling that his chosen line of endeavor is important—that the revitalization and wise governance of cities is vital to the welfare of the country. In this context it may be that the most sick and troubled cities will have the greatest challenge and need for him. This is where most of the action is. I doubt that the schools now do a stellar job in creating this sense of mission, and Dr. Mosher does not dwell on this aspect.

Before I decided to enter the field, while still in school, I attended an ICMA annual conference. This kind of motivating exposure should be more encouraged than it is by ICMA as well as by many other professional public service associations. An urban administrator is a human being too. He is likely to want to see in the flesh some sample of those who have preceded him and achieved distinction and of who his spiritual colleagues will be in the urban arena.

City managers don't write books, just reports, articles, and case studies. Managers in the private sector seem to do much better. I can't think of a good autobiography by a city manager since Louis Brownlow (ICMA President in 1923) told us about his passion for politics and anonymity in 1955, and he was a journalist and editor before tackling city hall. In thinking about how to generate potential local statesmen, the schools may have overlooked an important extra-intellectual ingredient, namely, biographical treatment of the careers of some exemplary local performers. It might pay to commission a few city managers to write their autobiographies between jobs.

Representatives of the many public service professions must take the lead in initiating visitations to institutions of higher learning, both undergraduate and graduate, in order to strengthen the awareness of both faculty and students of the importance and nature of local public administration. ICMA has encouraged this approach among its members for years. The urgency to maintain ongoing intimacy between universities and the full range of urban administrators has never been greater.

Commentary on the Mosher Paper

By S. Kenneth Howard

ABSTRACT: This commentary focuses on the objectives of pre-entry professional education for generalist urban administrators. Mosher may have overestimated the effectiveness of pre-entry instruction in administration for potential specialist administrators. It is far easier to learn a specialization after formal pre-entry training, than to acquire a broad view of interrelationships among problems and activities. The importance of pre-entry professional training in laying the foundation for a career in the public service should not be overlooked. Additionally, if pre-entry professional training can help universities focus on urban problems and can play a part in shifting institutions from multi- to universities, the results will exceed our wildest dreams and go far beyond providing individual foundations for future urban generalist administrators.

S. Kenneth Howard is professor of political science, Institute of Government and director of the M.P.A. program, University of North Carolina at Chapel Hill. He received his B.A. from Northwestern, his M.P.A. and Ph.D. from Cornell. He has taught at the University of New Hampshire and was a government consultant in New Jersey. His major publications have been in the field of state budgeting.

THIS commentary will focus on the objectives of pre-entry professional education for generalist urban administrators. This definition of turf narrows the considerations broached in the excellent paper on which it comments. Mosher spoke about specialist and generalist administrators. Only the latter will be emphasized here. Both Mosher's paper and this one are concerned about pre-entry education, but Mosher may have overestimated the effectiveness of pre-entry instruction in administration for potential specialist administrators.

PRE-ENTRY SPECIALIST TRAINING

Pre-entry education is taken here to mean professional training before any extended full-time contact with or actual practice of a given profession. Mosher stresses the desirability of more synthesizing and generalizing administrative content in the pre-entry training of all kinds of professionals, engineers, doctors, lawyers, social workers and the like, and this paper will not take exception to that notion. But it may well be questioned how effective such training will be on a pre-entry basis.

In such fields as engineering, social work, nursing, and teaching, a lot of pre-entry professional education goes on at the undergraduate level. But many of the most talented students who want careers in these various professions seek graduate training almost immediately after they finish undergraduate work. In other fields, such as law and medicine, graduate work is pre-entry training. It is assumed here that most pre-entry professional training will be at the graduate level. During this period of graduate professional education, the students strain increasingly to enter the practicing world of their profession, and generally resist attempts to extend this training much beyond its present limits. In addition, academic members of many professions feel, with some justification, that already too little time is available to provide a fully adequate education for practice in a rapidly changing profession. Training in administration gets a lower priority than further exposure within the profession's specialities. In short, laudable as the objective may be, adding administrative content to existing pre-entry professional programs may be resisted by many specialists in those fields and may well be directed toward an audience that is psychologically tuned out.

Mosher's emphasis upon the importance of professional socialization is well placed and leads to another comment about pre-entry training. In many professions, particularly health and engineering, the mores of the profession tend to place a rather low priority on administrative work. When one becomes a program administrator, one is seen as leaving the profession, joining the enemy or generally turning his back on what he was actually trained to do. This denigration of administrative work as unimportant or useless as a route by which to make a substantial professional contribution is not lost on students, particularly those at the pre-entry level. Individuals who have made their break with the mores by assuming some initial administrative responsibility within a profession seem more aware of the validity of administrative training and seem more willing to absorb it than do students who have not yet entered a profession's daily workings.

GENERALIST FOCUS

Mosher speaks of specialists with a generalism and generalists with a specialism. This paper contends that the latter are more needed, although the former are also desirable. Its conviction is that generalists are better prepared and better able to bolster some of the greatest weaknesses at the urban level: seeing a problem or situation as a whole, choosing between and administering unlike programs and doing strategic as contrasted with operational and program planning.

It is far easier to learn a specialization after formal pre-entry training, the power of professional socialization being what it is, than to acquire a broad view of interrelationships among problems and activities, the power of professional socialization being what it is. Pre-entry education should take advantage of the training potential inherent in subsequent professional socialization while seeking to alleviate the latter's most inhibiting tendencies. How a problem is defined and who sits down to work out a solution to that problem depends very much upon the competence, sensitivity, understanding insight, and personal security of whoever holds responsibility for dealing with the problem. But how a problem is defined depends upon who participates in resolving it. Indeed, deciding who sits around the table may have more to do with shaping whatever results than any other single factor. The broader the perspective of the person making the "who" decision, the wider the spectrum of "who" is likely to be. Thus we cannot leave health delivery policy to doctors, education to teachers, regulation to lawyers, and so forth. The foundations for generalizing and synthesizing should be laid early, and it appears that this result will more likely stem from pre- rather post-entry education, the power of professional socialization being what it is. Unfortunately, the problem of getting young pre-entry specialists to listen remains unresolved.

OBJECTIVES

What objectives should be sought in the pre-entry education of generalist urban administrators? Increasingly careers in urban administration entail six P's: solving *p*roblems by working through *p*eople in *p*rocesses that entail plenty of *p*articipation, *p*aper, and *p*olitics. Frederick Mosher has enumerated very well the desirable attributes of an urban administrator. These qualities cannot all be learned in a given pre-entry education program of any reasonable length, and indeed some of them probably cannot be learned at all in any traditional formal education sense.

Recruitment brochures sometimes speak of preparing students for lifelong careers in the public service. On its face, such an objective is nonsensical. All the skills, insights, understanding, and information that will be needed over a lifetime career simply cannot be provided on a pre-entry basis. A good administrator must continuously be learning. Continuing education is the focus of other papers in this collection, but one word of caution should be given because it underscores the importance of pre-entry education. There is virtually no assurance that the very best people will return or obtain continuing education through formal programs designed for this purpose. In the first place, the very best people are usually the ones that organizations do not want to release because they are so important to the successful operations right where they are. Second, these people are usually doing well and getting ahead with the help of whatever continuous learning mechanisms they have devised on their own. Probably the best people will come back only in the context of a job change, so perhaps continuing education activities should be built around mobility. Although outstanding urban administrators never stop learning, pre-entry professional training may well be the last extended time they spend in an unharried contemplative environment. Its importance in laying the foundation for a career in public service should not be overlooked.

This line of argument provides the basis for dismissing a second possible objective: preparing pre-entry professionals for their first job. The time is simply too valuable and too important in terms of its long-range significance to be wasted on so short-sighted and transient an objective. As now constituted, most pre-entry programs preparing generalist urban administrators could not actually produce people equipped to deal immediately with all the requirements of a first job. Some things simply cannot be learned except on the job. Most faculty members are not equipped to teach those initial things that can be taught. Furthermore, the specific and detailed knowledge required would be so diverse that the key element of learning to generalize and see situations as a whole would itself be lost.

EDUCATIONAL CONTENT

Pre-entry professional education for generalist urban administrators should provide the basic skills and insights that an individual needs as a foundation for continuing his own education and building a career in an environment of problems, people, processes, participation, paper, and politics. The foundation appears to have at least four aspects.

The first deals with the individual administrator himself and focuses on his own self-awareness, sense of security, and personal values. The life of the urban administrator is filled with conflict and change. The only variable that he will always encounter in each new situation is himself. The more everything else changes, the more he is thrown back upon his own wellsprings for guidance, support, and security. Crisis frequently forces one to face fundamental conceptions about his fellow man and himself. Cultivation, self-awareness, and insight should begin early in the hope that crisis, when it comes, will be navigated more successfully than it might otherwise be.

The administrator must also know something of human behavior in organizations. He must appreciate the affective-emotional side of life as well as the intellectual-analytical side. He needs to know how work affects people; how individuals develop the psychological constructs through which they view the world; also, how to deal with problems of motivation; and how to work successfully in, with, and through small groups.

At the same time, the analytical side of administration cannot be ignored. A basic analytical frame of mind, which is much more fundamental than skills in specific techniques, should be acquired. The urban administrator probably must look at virtually everything analytically, while understanding that intellectual and analytical arguments may not win the day or alleviate the problem, especially in an environment that includes emotional and political variables as well.

Finally, the urban administrator should seek to understand how governance is done in the society in which he expects to work. He must know something about political power: who has it, how it is mobilized, and how it shifts with the passage of time and changes in the issues at hand. He must have a sense of the intergovernmental context in which he operates. He must develop an appreciation for the role and fundamental importance of politics in the process of governing.

To get that first job following pre-entry education, the urban generalist will need at least primer knowledge of some substantive field or process—health, housing, budgeting, and so forth. But more important, pre-entry education begins to socialize urban administrators in terms of the elements that Mosher has so well stressed:

1. concern about values and goals,
2. a synthesizing approach to problems,
3. orientation to decision and action,
4. orientation to whole people,
5. striving for and induction of change,
6. capacity to attack problems as problems,
7. sympathy for open politics,
8. underlying optimism about human beings.

The Role of Universities

Mosher is hopeful that by focusing on urban problems, universities will alleviate some of the worst problems of overspecialization to which they are subject. Emphasis on urban problems could have a significant impact on intrauniversity priorities and on a wide spectrum of university teaching and research activities. The simple-minded cry for relevance ought not obscure the significance of free inquiry into dissemination of knowledge about the basic ideas and processes at work in all aspects of human endeavor. But such inquiry is not free in an economic sense, and the importance of public support, especially financial, for all kinds of pre-entry professional training is mounting rapidly. Urban problems like crime, pollution, transportation, drugs, and mental health interrelate with each other, and their alleviation will require insights from many different perspectives. These problems challenge even the most brillant intellect, and there is no apparent reason why attention to them cannot lead to and necessitate basic research just as much as present academic disciplinary approaches do. We cannot afford a process of specialization that tells us more and more about less and less and does so in isolation from the implications of that knowledge for a host of other activities and processes. If pre-entry professional training can help universities focus on urban problems and can play a part in shifting institutions from multi- to universities, the results of pre-entry professional education will exceed our wildest dreams and go far beyond providing individual foundations for future urban generalist administrators.

Commentary on the Mosher Paper

By James T. Jones

ABSTRACT: The general status and needs in the public service set forth by Professor Mosher cannot be disputed. But the greater need now is for more generalists, and curriculum planning should reflect this need. There is a need for functional specialization in our society but the continued production of specialists is insured through existing structure in higher education. Graduate programs should focus on generalist training and give very special concern to the recruitment of blacks and other minorities. It also seems reasonable that a curriculum developed for educating urban administrators ought to emphasize the development of applied techniques and skills without impairing the value of the theoretical content of that curriculum. Yet, as difficult as the task is, the future looks encouraging.

James T. Jones is associate professor and chairman of the Department of Public Administration at Howard University. He has served as associate director of the Center for Community Studies at Howard University. He taught previously at Indiana University, Gary, and served as lecturer in political science at the University of Illinois, Urbana. He was director of operations of the United Planning Organization of the National Capital Area, 1969–70. He was active in local politics in Gary, Indiana from 1964–1968.

THE renewed emphasis on administering urban America is long overdue, and I welcome this opportunity to participate in the renewed concern by commenting on the paper prepared by Professor Frederick C. Mosher. The general status and needs in the public service set forth by Professor Mosher cannot be disputed. His summation of the content of educational programs for urban administrators, his list of their desirable attributes, and the elements of socialization he specified for them are significant factors to be considered in any attempt to produce urban administrators equal to the task. However, contrary to Professor Mosher, I am prepared to hazard the risk of recommending that the greater need now is for more generalists, and that curriculum planning should reflect this need.

The Training of Specialists Is Assured

The fact that structures in government and higher education parallel each other and thus influence the nature of training in higher education is better understood when one adds to these the general characteristics of our society, with particular analysis of the prevailing economic system. The growth, development, and maintenance of an industrialized society such as ours, with its focus on acquisition of the profits from goods and services by the dominant economic elites must be viewed as a major factor encouraging specialism in the training of people. The logical consequence of the demand for specialists by dominants of the economic system is to influence their continued development in both the private and public sectors.

In the private sector specialism in skills and tasks supports the efficiency ethos in the production of goods and the performance of services. In government specialization may be viewed from the perspective of the efficiency ethos, but in an even more positive fashion specialists in government are engaged directly and indirectly in the development of policies which affect the lives of people, as well as the conduct of business and industry.

Obviously, with the unevenness of the influence of dominant economic elites in both the private and public sectors, together with the continuing growth of knowledge and technology, emphasis on the training of specialists will continue. The existence of this high degree of specialization cannot be denied or questioned; the effects of its expansiveness in face of the diversity and magnitude of problems facing the urban administrator in like manner cannot be questioned.

Further, prospective urban administrators will come from undergraduate programs which were developed around specialties. Consequently, the majority of individuals entering graduate programs designed to train them for the public service have acquired specialties, or a foundation upon which to develop specialties, in the form of a major and a minor field. These areas of specialization will gain them initial employment in a public agency, and/or admission to a graduate program training urban administrators.

EMPHASIS SHOULD BE PLACED ON TRAINING GENERALISTS

Acknowledging the fact that there is a need for functional specialization in our society and that the continued production of specialists is insured through existing structures in higher education, I support the view that in the immediate future graduate school programs should focus on the training of generalists. By the training of generalists it is expected that individuals will emerge with a broader view of the complex urban spectrum than is usually attributed to the specialist. Generalists should be more whole-people oriented, and much more capable of coordinating and synthesizing the multifaceted functions of the specialists. Both greater efficiency and improved quality in the overall performance of governmental units should result.

Assuming the general validity of this view, it seems plausible that a degree of flexibility in the curriculum and increased cooperation between the disciplines will permit the training of generalists, and at the same time accommodate refinement of individual specializations.

Admittedly, the level of flexibility and interdisciplinary cooperation necessary to achieve the kind of arrangement suggested above requires an alteration of structures and of attitudes within the institutions of higher education. Fortunately at this time of increasing budgetary constraints some universities, professional associations, foundations, and—to a much too limited degree—agencies of the federal government are giving increased support to the development of flexible, interdisciplinary training programs for public-urban administrators.

Professors of public administration and others concerned with urban affairs must take a leadership role in planning curriculums for urban administration generalists, as well as expanded interdisciplinary approaches to implement the content of those curriculums. Perhaps the greatest deterrent to a vigorous pursuit in the direction of extended interface between the disciplines is the lack of courageous actions toward this end on the part of those who most recognize the need. In sum, those of us trained in public administration, political science, and related fields must use all the skills of our professions to guarantee the emergence of interdisciplinary structures and cooperating arrangements that are crucial to the steady production of qualified urban administration generalists.

If institutions of public affairs and administration fail to begin now to train persons skilled in the art of integrating and coordinating specialized urban activities, this will be a critical negative variable in any effort to improve urban life. If fragmented, piecemeal management and planning in urban centers continue, aided and abetted by loyalty of specialists to their respective crafts, then we can expect a further decline in the quality of urban life. We must be willing to go beyond the liberal tendency of moving from problem to problem, leaving unsolved problems in our wake. I believe any problem created by man can be solved by man if man is willing. Too often he is not. The great emphasis on scientism so ably described by Professor Mosher was in great measure a response to Sputnik, and here the challenge to supremacy in outer space by the Soviet Union was met and surpassed. The challenge to improve the quality of life in urban America must begin with the training of men and women capable of solving the urgent interrelated urban problems of race relations, finance, employment, housing, transportation, environmental pollution, educational quality, and so forth.

THE SELECTION OF BLACKS AND OTHER MINORITIES FOR TRAINING MUST BE EMPHASIZED

The root causes of the urban condition in our country are manifold—economics, politics, racism, poor planning, and many others. Although it is not our task here to focus on causes, the particular position of blacks and other minorities as objects of at least one cause for the urban condition gives rise to their unique position in considering both end-product objectives and curriculum focus for educating urban administrators. Blacks and other minorities are at once victims of racism and denial of access to higher education, especially education for the public service. Therefore, very special concern needs to be given to the recruitment of blacks and other minorities as plans are drawn for meeting the demand and planning the curriculum for urban administrators.

I am referring here to the fact that great numbers of blacks, ethnic minorities, and poor people are now locked in the great urban centers of this nation. The specific point is that these blacks, ethnic minorities, and poor people are continuing to swell their numbers. As this occurs, masses of the white majority abandon the interiors of urban centers, leaving innumerable problems behind, not the least of which is the administering of public affairs of those centers.

Simultaneous with this changing composition of the urban populations is an increasing awareness of their numbers by blacks and ethnic minorities, and of their political strength. This increasing awareness is accompanied by parallel demands by these minority groups for representation at all levels of the governing and administering bodies of the central cities. These groups seek to head departments, administer programs, and determine the content and character of all functions of the governments of their respective cities. Wherever their efforts to gain access to positions are frustrated, they complicate the tasks of the heads of those units, thus adding to the growing list of problems confronting the urban administrator.

As this trend continues in all of its dimensions, and as more and more blacks and other minorities gain administrative posts in urban centers, they, too, need the benefit of education for effective management of urban affairs, as do all others who have historically held these posts. It is likewise probable that efforts to socialize members of these groups along the lines suggested by Dr. Mosher will be a less strenuous task.

THEORY MUST NOT BE ABANDONED, BUT APPLIED TECHNIQUES MUST BE EMPHASIZED IN THE CURRICULUM

The problems of administering the affairs of urban America are so profound that understandably one becomes ambivalent over what the curriculum content for educating urban administrators should include. Accordingly, I do not propose to venture into that unsettled territory, for it is fraught with interrelated considerations of such scope and magnitude as to defy any chance of acceptance in the foreseeable future. If one takes a view, however, of the availability of technological apparatus and the capability to sustain the production of required specialists to aid in the solution of urban problems—given the fiscal resources to obtain both—what is most called for is applied skills in purposeful use of the two. Consequently, it seems reasonable that a curriculum developed for educating urban administrators ought to emphasize the development of applied techniques and skills without impairing the value of the theoretical content of that curriculum.

My specific view of the place for theory in the curriculum for educating urban administrators is to recognize the value that theory holds in the context of its function in helping to explain, orient, conceptualize, and aid the individual in classification of information. And, in parallel fashion, it has the potential for pointing up gaps as well as sharpening the relationships between assembled facts. In an even more enlarged context, the application of theory in the ways suggested above can be a practical activity in contemplation of action related to making sense of conflicting and disturbing situations. Thus used, theory becomes functional as a device for interpreting, criticizing, and unifying valid learned principles in developing processes and procedures in the resolution of problems and achievement of goals.

Further, it seems to me that a kind of modified application of theory as set out above correlates with the development of mechanisms and methodologies and increases the precision in clarification of goals, effecting change and intervention into the conduct of social relations. In sum, if it is the purpose of education to inform and socialize the individual, both will be based on data about the objects of that training for a specific set of reasons. In the case of the urban administrator those are the management of the organizations of urban centers. He must, therefore, be taught skills applicable to the task.

Finally, it is doubtful that the extensive use of abstract, esoteric, recondite language which characterizes the literature of theory building and theoretical methods will be useful, or indeed appreciated, by today's student in preparation for urban administration.

THE FUTURE LOOKS ENCOURAGING

As difficult as the task is for deciding what the scope, objectives, and strategies for educating urban administrators ought to be, there are now some encouraging signs that must not be overlooked. First, and perhaps the most important indicator of a new awareness and concern for revision of the models and methods used in the preparation of urban administrators is the work undertaken by Professor Stephen B. Sweeney and alumni of the Fels Institute of Local and State Government of the University of Pennsylvania. These efforts have culminated in the organizing of this Symposium following two workshops attended by practitioners and intellectuals of highly regarded caliber. The significance of these events suggests a state of readiness to move forward in the direction of constructive change.

A second and equally important category of activity was the Delphi Exercise conducted by the National Academy of Public Administration,[1] and the survey conducted by John K. Parker and Robert R. Cantine.[2] In each instance one can glean an overwhelming desire for change and an implicit willingness of educators and practitioners to join together and chart a course for new directions in education for urban administrators.

Finally, the article by John F. Fischbach in the February, 1972 issue of *Public Management*[3] set forth a challenge to practitioners and educators to join hands in creating interchanges by providing opportunities for training and participating in the process together through dialogue on curriculum, sharing of views in seminars for students, and developing meaningful internships.

As all of these suggestions and emerging views converge, as they are doing in some places now, the many cogent issues raised by Professor Mosher will surely be addressed and hopefully they will come to fruition in the education of capable urban administrators.

1. National Academy of Public Administration, "Developments of the Public Service 1971–1980." (Unpublished mimeographed report).

2. John K. Parker and Robert R. Cantine, "What Are We Educating For?", *Public Management*, vol. 54, no. 2 (February, 1972), pp. 14–19.

3. John F. Fischbach, "Evolving Roles: ICMA, State Associations, Individual Members," *Public Management*, vol. 54, no. 2 (February, 1972), pp. 20–23.

Summary of the Discussion of the Mosher Paper*

By Frederic N. Cleaveland

FOR discussion of this paper, symposium participants were divided into three smaller groups which met simultaneously. This commentary draws liberally from the reported discussion in each of these smaller groups.

The central question with which all three groups wrestled concerned where the principal emphasis should be placed in pre-entry professional education of urban administrators. Should the primary goal be to equip the aspirant urban administrator with a solid foundation for a lifelong career? Or should the first task be to equip him with skills essential for effective performance in his first job in the profession? It is hardly surprising that participants all agreed pre-entry professional education must give attention to both. Such educational programs should be flexible and adaptive because there is likely to be considerable variety in the particular needs of pre-entry students. They are not by any means a homogeneous group, but vary considerably in age, background, experience, and so on. Several institutions represented at the Symposium reported that increasing numbers of pre-entry students in their public affairs programs are in fact seeking a second career after retiring early from one of the military services or other career employment. Such students clearly have quite different needs from those of younger students who enter upon professional education in public affairs directly after completing their baccalaureate degrees.

There was widespread agreement that one major objective of pre-entry education in this case is to instill into students the norms and values of the professional field of urban administration, thus helping to socialize them into the profession. As one ex-

---

* Unfortunately, due to illness, Professor Mosher was unable to attend the Symposium. However, he has read the critiques and this summary, and has nothing to add to his original statement.

perienced practitioner expressed it, "What we've got to achieve is the situation where the product [of pre-entry education for urban administration] won't jump out of the pool when the water gets cold!" This kind of socialization really serves both the long term individual goals of providing the foundation on which to build a career and the short range goal of equipping the professional to survive on his first job. This commitment to the profession will help to sustain the inexperienced professional through the difficulties often experienced in that first job. An observation made in discussion of the Watt, Parker, Cantine paper was repeated because of its pointed relevance—"the city manager does not really feel that he has earned his spurs as a professional until he has been fired at least once." When the city manager, after being dismissed by a city council, then turns up somewhere else managing another city, he has passed an important professional test: he stayed in the pool after the water became cold!

Focusing more specifically upon the career preparation function, it was noted that the products of pre-entry education for urban administration should be prepared to move into any one of a wide variety of positions concerned with problems of urban areas, ready and eager to pursue personal growth and development on the job. This orientation to personal development through his own efforts and through continuing education and training is essential for the professional in this rapidly changing career field if he is to avoid early obsolescence. Pre-entry education should provide students the foundation on which to build and instill in them the commitment to further learning and self-development. The pre-entry educational experience should also provide the student career guidance about the types of professional positions which can contribute to his growth. One participant called this "a kind of rough road map to the top of the profession [of urban administration]," showing the sorts of positions and experience which would best serve to equip a person for leadership in this profession.

One group of participants felt that the role of pre-entry education in producing urban executives could be fully understood only by first defining the role of continuing education in this process. It was generally agreed that pre-entry educational programs could not be expected to anticipate in the 1970s the particular skills, techniques, and essential knowledge base which will be required ten and twenty years hence to manage urban areas effectively in the 1980s and 1990s. Yet to rely entirely on continuing education (in-service training, mid-career training, and so on) to provide this updating of skills, techniques, and knowledge could lead to serious problems. A number of participants were concerned that the most able professionals who were advancing most rapidly in their careers would be the very ones least likely to be spared from day-to-day pressures in order to participate in organized continuing education programs. Those who would be given time off to join in such mid-career refresher training to upgrade their skills, techniques, and knowledge would in all probability be those who could most readily be spared.

Without trying to resolve these dilemmas concerning the appropriate division of labor between pre-entry and continuing education, participants did reaffirm their earlier conclusion that pre-entry education must give significant emphasis to developing certain basic skills in the students. It was generally agreed that products of pre-entry education must acquire enough of these core skills—interpersonal skills, working with figures (statistical analysis), and so forth—to perform in acceptable fashion on their first jobs. As one experienced educator observed: "If, because of their emphasis on socialization, the schools of public affairs came to neglect the teaching of techniques of administration, then this is a bad trade-off. If the young professional does a bad job of budget analysis on his first assignment bcause the school of public affairs neglected the technical aspects of administration, then the school has done a great disservice."

In elaborating further on the function of pre-entry education, symposium participants gave major attention to the internship or clinical field experience, seeing it as probably the principal means to prepare incipient professional urban administrators for their first job. Acknowledging that effective internship programs are extremely difficult to organize and conduct, nevertheless, participants felt that the direct involvement of the student in the real world of urban administration is probably the most important part of readying him for his first professional assignment. One group of participants analyzed in some detail the problems and difficulties of mounting effective internships. They concluded that, for an internship program to be successful, it requires several essential components: (1) heavy investment of faculty time and of the time and energies of practitioners in the jurisdictions where the interns serve; (2) close and continuing collaboration among faculty members, practitioners serving as intern supervisors, and student interns working together to define development objectives of the program and to monitor progress towards achieving these objectives; (3) adequate benefits to the city (namely, to the practitioners), as well as to the university (that is, the faculty members and students), so that all concerned recognize that full return is received for the heavy investments made. The latter requirement is particularly difficult to build into internship programs, for frequently faculty members and practitioners are unable to identify a project appropriate for interns to work on which the city values highly and which also provides useful work experience for interns. Effective internship activities are more likely to occur in a setting where there are regular and continuing relationships between those carrying on a professional education program and the alumni of that program who are out functioning as professional urban executives. These alumni may be involved with the university's continuing education program for urban administrators, as well as serving as intern supervisors in the internship program for pre-entry students. In such a setting of frequent interaction among faculty, practitioner-alumni, and students in progress, the opportunities are significantly enhanced for overcoming normal problems in mounting an effective program to provide clinical field experience for pre-entry students.

Finally, participants also looked briefly at the relationship between pre-entry professional education, continuing education, and the objective of preparing urban administrators for specialized functional fields central to urban areas, for example, education, public health, criminal justice, and so forth. Some felt that these needs should be met through continuing education efforts. In addition, it was suggested that public affairs schools concerned with pre-entry education were probably the best instrument available for working towards some form of collaboration with those professional schools which train functional specialists—schools of education, engineering, law, public health and medicine, and social work, for example. The goal of such collaborative efforts would be to weaken or offset the drive towards "guildism" within such professions by bringing students and faculty of these specialized professional schools into regular interaction with faculty and students of the school of public affairs, both groups committed to upgrading administrative performance across the board throughout urban government. Participants were not overly sanguine about such efforts, but agreed that it is essential to find some way to build bridges linking these specialized professions on the urban scene with the broad profession of urban management. At this point in time those attending the Symposium tended to feel that the schools of public affairs engaged in educating urban administrators offered perhaps the best lever available to build better relationships with the professional schools educating functional specialists for city governments.

The University and Pre-Entry Professional Education for Urban Administrators: What Should We Teach? How Should We Teach?

By Thomas J. Davy

ABSTRACT: The workshops of urban administrators preceding this Symposium suggest certain assumptions regarding the probable roles of urban administrators in the foreseeable future. Important aspects of the urban administrator's job were suggested which should be taken into account in planning programs of professional education for this significant career field. The important thing is that these programs focus on the future. There are a number of specific issues which must be considered in the design of a curriculum, including length of program; types and levels of courses; prerequisites; sequence; a problem-focused integrating learning experience; clinical experience and classroom instruction; and definition of the role of the public administration school. Of these issues, two demand special emphasis: first, learning experience should challenge students to integrate their specialized knowledge and skills to focus upon significant problems; and second, curriculum planning should be a cooperative effort of educators, administrators, and professional associations in the field.

Thomas J. Davy is director of the Public Service Institute of the State of New Jersey. He was assistant dean, University of Pittsburgh's School of Public and International Affairs from 1968–1972. A graduate of Seton Hall University, he received his M.G.A. and Ph.D. from the University of Pennsylvania and held a Graduate Scholarship in the Fels Institute of Local and State Government. From 1947 to 1968 he was associated with the Fels Institute as instructor, associate professor, and assistant director. He has served on the National Council of the American Society for Public Administration and as adviser on public administration training to the United States Civil Service Commission and the Council on Graduate Education for Public Administration.

THE workshops of urban administrators preceding this Symposium suggest certain assumptions regarding the probable roles of urban administrators in the foreseeable future. Representing a broad range of positions, the workshop participants depict the urban administrator of the future as having the following characteristics.

THE FUTURE URBAN ADMINISTRATOR

1. He is primarily a problem-solver and policy-maker. He and his staff play key roles in identifying, defining, and analyzing community problems; devising strategies for coping with them; and formulating the policies and programs to carry these strategies into effect. In the process, they utilize sophisticated techniques of problem analysis and choose among alternative approaches and methodologies of problem-solving.

2. He is responsible, broadly speaking, for guiding and directing the development of the community. This responsibility requires the urban administrator to work continually to build a consensus around policies and programs which reflect clear community values about the quality of urban life. He must take on an advocacy role, promoting these defined community values in such diverse areas of civic life as maintaining public order and safety, protecting public health, facilitating personal development and fulfillment of individual citizens, alleviating the effects of economic and social maladjustments, planning and promoting economic development, protecting the consumer, equalizing opportunities, planning and controlling land use allocations, preserving and renewing the community, and so on.

3. The urban administrator is also directly responsible for organizational development, that is, for managing organizational performance. These managerial responsibilities involve building and maintaining a creative team capable of performing effectively in designing and carrying on programs to achieve community development objectives.

4. He functions in a very complex environment, which may be thought of in terms of social systems, economic systems, ecological systems, political systems, governmental systems. His community is changing very rapidly, both horizontally and vertically. His problems are subsets of a network of interrelated problems the foci of which range from the individual, the family, the neighborhood, and the political jurisdiction, through the region to the nation as a whole, and indeed in many problem areas to international communities. The significant challenge to the urban administrator is the challenge to relate his organization, his program, his community creatively to the larger system or network of systems of which it is a part. Paul Appleby's mesh has become even more difficult to achieve, yet the urban administrator recognizes its necessity; hence, he tends to be preoccupied with coordination and integration, at whatever level of the governmental system he functions.

5. He is conscious of, and deeply involved in, the value assumptions, and conflicts relating to them, that underlie the decisions for which he is responsible. He recognizes that for almost any decision these value assumptions range from fundamental philosophical orientations, such as those concerned with the nature of man, the organization of power, due process of law in all its ramifications, to specific instrumental values, such as those underlying particular processes for citizen participation, the delivery of specific public services, ensuring security of information, providing welfare payments, relocating persons displaced by land development, and so on. In terms of professional behavior those value assumptions represent ethical issues to the administrator and his staff. Whereas formerly his concepts of ethics and the codes derived from them were limited to a restricted set of moral issues dealing mostly with dishonesty or graft, his concept of ethics now encompasses behavioral norms associated with a broad range of values underlying the decisions in which he participates. He is, in other words, consciously seeking a comprehensive, operational philosophy of governance as a rationale for functional, equitable, and consistent decisions.

6. The urban administrator today is more involved than he was even a decade ago in the political process of the community. He shares with other agencies in the political system responsi-

bilities for building coalitions, bargaining and effecting compromises, resolving conflicts, and, in general, evoking and identifying consensus on objectives and viable courses of action for the community. The old controversy regarding the community leadership role of the urban administrator has largely subsided; he is now widely accepted as a community leader in the fullest sense of leadership.

These characteristics reflect the thinking of practicing urban administrators who joined in the two workshops which set the stage for this Symposium. They were not trying to predict the future but rather, on the basis of their current experience, to suggest important aspects of the complex job of the urban administrator which should be taken into account in planning programs of professional education for this significant career field.

AN APPROACH TO CURRICULUM PLANNING

This workshop-symposium project has been designed to raise a number of the essential questions for public administration educators to answer in laying the foundation for a professional graduate curriculum to educate urban administrators in the 1970s. First, it is important for curriculum planners to make explicit assumptions about the probable shape of the future regarding urban life and urban areas. Their foresight may prove only partially accurate and unexpected events may profoundly affect the urban scene calling for unanticipated adjustments in programs of professional education for urban administrators. Such changes are inevitable; indeed educational programs training for a dynamic career field such as urban administration cannot do the job if they become static and inflexible. The important thing is that these programs focus on the future and reflect expectations about the nature of the job of the urban administrator in the decade ahead. If such curriculums are based primarily upon accepted notions about what these positions have demanded in the past, then those of us engaged in conducting these programs run the dangerous risk of producing graduates for careers in the urban field who are largely obsolete their first day on the job, or at least unprepared for the new demands of tomorrow.

One useful way to approach the challenging assignment of thinking systematically about the future in this field of urban administration is to focus directly upon changes currently under way in the roles of urban administrators and then to project these trends into the decade ahead. Next, it is important to try to translate this changing pattern of demands into a set of assumptions about the particular kinds of knowledge and skills required for the trained administrator to cope effectively with the requirements of his job. This Symposium has directed our attention to these significant topics.

Curriculum planning also should reflect some reasonably concrete notions about the kinds of students to be educated, including ideas about their level of maturity, their motivation, their interests, and the values which characterize their life styles. This subject, too, has received appropriate emphasis in this Symposium. Now in this paper we are at the point of considering directly a number of more specific issues important in designing a curriculum for educating urban administrators. The following seven questions are especially worthy of attention; each is considered briefly below.

1. How long should a professional master's degree program be?

2. What types and levels of courses should be included? What is the appropriate mix of generalist and specialist preparation?

3. What prerequisite education, if any, should be expected?

4. Is there an optimal sequencing of the learning experiences?

5. What is the best way to provide a problem-focused, integrating learning experience?

6. What is the appropriate mix of clinical field experience and classroom instruction?

7. What is the special role of those responsible for the urban administration program in the educational process? How should they relate to the social science disciplines and other professional schools?

In this discussion the author has drawn heavily upon his recent experience serving as chairman of an interdepartmental committee of the Graduate School of Public and International Affairs

(GSPIA), University of Pittsburgh, charged with responsibility for making a comprehensive evaluation and undertaking a reorganization of the School's Master of Public Administration (M.P.A.) degree program in Urban Executive Management (UEM). This committee wrestled with a number of the questions listed above, and the following discussion of these issues reflects much of the findings reached and conclusions drawn by the committee.

LENGTH OF PROGRAM

In many fields of professional education strong pressure on educators is leading to a steady increase in the length of programs and the numbers of courses and credit hours required for master's degrees. This pressure reflects accelerated growth of knowledge in all fields, expanded perceptions of professional responsibilities, and recognition of the increasing complexity of the problems associated with professional practice. Public administration is no exception, and over the last several years there has been a mounting trend toward two-year programs, especially among recently established programs. The results of the survey and practitioner discussions in the workshops tend to support the desirability of this trend.

But there are counter pressures also at work imposing constraints upon the tendency to lengthen degree programs to two years. These pressures stem directly from such factors as: faculty resources available to the programs; competition among schools for students; costs to the students; imbalances in financials awards to students if a school offers several degrees with different credit requirements. There is also a growing conviction among educators in this field that pedagogical efficiency can be greatly improved, thereby enabling students to learn more within existing time limits without adding additional terms to the program.

Also related to the issue of length of program are questions of the number of courses a student should be engaged in concurrently and the place of internships or other clinical experience and theses or research requirements. If the professional degree program is rigorous in its demands upon students challenging them to think and to develop skills in applying analytical techniques to real problems, then adding more courses per term can prove counterproductive, leading to lower quality of performance across the board. Clearly, the program should be demanding and should press students intellectually. Yet the demands should not be so impossible to meet that the program encourages superficiality.

Internships or other clinical experience requirements can be worked into a two-year program, as can a thesis or research requirement. Certainly both are desirable, if not essential. Yet such enrichment elements should be added to the total range of degree requirements in a manner to avoid imposing impossible hurdles upon students seeking to complete the degree within the normal time period of two years.

TYPES AND LEVELS OF COURSES

Without attempting to discuss program content in detail, it is appropriate to consider the broad categories of knowledge and skill which the aspiring urban administrator will require to perform effectively on his first professional assignment and around which he will build his professional career. Six categories merit our attention.

Urban public policy—problems, policies, and programs, both existing and possible

Treatment of this broad subject might appropriately include attention to perceived social needs of urban communities; determinants and trends with respect to these needs; public policies and programs for coping with these needs; technological considerations associated with such policies and programs, including both new approaches made possible by technology and the constraints technology imposes; and the nature and style of operation of the particular social and political structures responsible for planning and administering policies identified with each set of urban community needs.

Problem analysis—approaches and methodologies

This category is concerned wtih developing in the student an analytic, problem-solving capability. Some understanding is required of such fields and methods as statistics, economic analysis, cost-benefit analysis, and operations research. Treatment should also focus attention on problem definition and on the application of these various analytic approaches to real problems which include value elements, policy considerations, and dimensions subject to cost-benefit analysis and to the utilization of systems perspectives.

Values and ethics

The aspiring urban administrator needs to understand the role of values in the policy process and to grasp how value systems are related to urban issues and how value conflicts lie beneath many of the controversies which confound contemporary urban communities. This category would also include attention to values associated with political and social institutions and processes, and the ethical and value content of the American constitutional system, judicial processes, and the structure of administrative law.

Conflict resolution and consensus building

This subject category covers theories and practices of democratic systems of governance, especially with respect to representation and participation. It would also encompass interest group and coalition theories, bargaining theory and practice, and game theory.

Public executive systems and their management

The focus of this category is on the institutions of the executive branch in urban government and the management processes involved in building an effective team and directing its efforts towards the implementation of policies and programs. Appropriate attention would be given to such areas as theories of organization, theories of decision-making, administrative processes, executive-legislative relationships in the urban context, interpersonal relations, and to contemporary developments including such phenomena as employee unionism, advocacy roles of the urban administrator, and participative management.

Urban community systems—the urban administrator's environment

Within the category attention would be directed to the institutional setting of the urban community. Thus the community and its region would be examined as an economy, an environmental or ecological system, a political system, a sociological system, a cultural system, and a governmental system. Emphasis would also be placed on intergovernmental and intersystems relationships, and upon community organization. The student would also be exposed to contemporary developments in citizen involvement in community decision-making and to the emergence of new patterns of interest group and clientele group organization.

In addition to these six broad categories of subject matter appropriate in preparing a professional urban administrator, it is essential that the student develop his capacity to integrate diverse subject matter and methodologies. The integrative dimension is a critically important part of the administrator's decision-making responsibility. Every major problem with which he is concerned has economic, political, social, cultural, and technological aspects. Courses he takes in his graduate program will usually have emphasized one or more of these points of view. In the field, he interrelates his knowledges and skills in dealing with any given problem. Learning experiences that help him develop this integrative capacity should, therefore, be an important element of his professional education. Experience suggests that a small research seminar organized around real policy problems affords opportunity for students to develop this integrating skill. Such a problem-focused seminar or practicum can provide a fitting capstone to a student's program developed around basic courses in each of the six broad categories and some opportunity for more advanced courses in at least two or three of these categories.

Another issue worthy of brief comment is the question of balance between breadth of program and depth of program, or to put it another way, the balance in emphasis between training generalist urban administrators and training specialists. In many programs students are urged, if not required, to take basic courses in every one of the categories suggested above and then to select one or perhaps two areas of concentration to insure some depth. The expansion of knowledge in all these categories of knowledge and skill reinforce the demand for students to be brought to some minimum level of capability through specialization by the time they have completed their formal pre-entry professional education. Moreover, the growing expectations of employers that newly appointed M.P.A. graduates will be able to perform on their first regular job assignment with reasonable sophistication strengthens the pull towards specialization.

On the other side of the issue other public administration educators stress that the first objective of a professional degree program to educate urban administrators is to provide the foundation for career development. Those sharing this perspective stress that to lay such a foundation requires breadth in the program, emphasizing such elements as underlying values, and some exposure to the whole range of relevant analytical approaches to urban problems and policies. They assert that career opportunities in urban administration are quite diverse, and that often a student's choice of areas of specialization at the time he is engaged in pre-entry education may not point in the direction of his later opportunities for career development.

For curriculum planners to find a sound answer to this issue of the mix between breadth and depth of a degree program requires that they make some assumptions about the respective roles of pre-entry education and continuing (post-entry) education in preparing urban administrators to meet the demands of their complex, changing roles. Post-entry continuing education is the subject of another paper prepared for this Symposium and is beyond the assignment of this author. A realistic assessment of the need for professional education in the field of urban administration today, however, will clearly indicate the urgency of creating expanded opportunities for continuing education to enable people already performing the roles of urban administrators to develop new skills or upgrade old ones. Moreover, the greater flexibility possible within a program of continuing education—flexibility to permit a direct focus upon filling the particular training needs of a defined group of urban administrators—suggests that beyond a certain point we can rely upon continuing education to provide the fine tuning preparation of specialists. The appropriate division of labor would then be to look to pre-entry education as the primary means of building the solid foundation on which to build a career in urban administration. This will permit more attention to those categories of knowledge and skills which are highly relevant across the multiple roles and tasks of urban administrators.

PREREQUISITES

Many academic institutions have a long tradition of admitting to graduate professional degree programs only those students who have taken a particular group of courses or completed a major in particular disciplines in their undergraduate education. Students entering a professional degree program for urban administration are likely to perform more effectively if they have had courses in such subject matter areas as logic, descriptive and inferential statistics, calculus, accounting, urban politics, urban sociology, urban economics, public administration, political philosophy, and English composition. Nevertheless, to set any particular set of prerequisites will almost certainly discourage some well-qualified students from entering the programs. Is there not a higher value in attracting into the career field of urban administration people from diverse educational backgrounds? Are any of these bodies of knowledge so central that all students must have acquired proficiency before entering? Or in those few cases where specific skills are required, for example, preparation in calculus in order to cope with required methodological courses in quantitative analysis, is it not sounder policy to admit students with a noted deficiency which must be corrected before particular courses in the program may be taken? In that way we can hope to attract into urban administration English majors and scientists, engineering students and those trained in philosophy, as well as political science and economics majors.

SEQUENCING OF COURSES

The question of sequencing centers primarily on the problem-solving category. Some public administration educators believe that a student should first develop competence in problem-solving approaches and techniques in order for him to gain the greatest benefit from courses in substantive fields. Therefore, they would have students concentrate their first term in courses dealing with statistics, systems analysis, policy analysis, computers, research design, reporting, or other methodological areas in which they may lack competence.

Others believe that, although general courses in methodology are desirable for acquiring basic knowledge and skill, the student should and will acquire his most valuable operational competence in methodology through applying these methods in substantive courses and problem-focused seminars. They assume, for example, that in a course in urban politics, pertinent techniques of political and statistical analysis will be emphasized; in a seminar dealing with problems of, say, regional waste management, relevant techniques of systems analysis will be taught and analyzed. Perhaps an approach to resolution of this issue can be found in a careful division of labor between basic courses in analytical approaches to develop insights and perspectives in students, and more substantive courses to develop student capacity to apply these analytic approaches to real problems and data drawn from urban settings.

PROBLEM-FOCUSED INTEGRATING LEARNING EXPERIENCES

As noted previously, the administrator brings to bear all of his knowledge and skills in defining a particular problem and developing strategies to cope with it. In doing so, he should, ideally, perceive and interrelate the economic, political, social, cultural, ethical, managerial, and technological aspects of the situation. Learning experiences should, therefore, be included in the graduate program that will challenge the students to integrate the knowledge and skills they are acquiring in their specialized courses and focus upon significant problems that urban administrators now face, or are likely to face.

Several types of learning experiences may be used for this purpose: problem seminars; role playing exercises; case studies; problem-oriented study projects; and computer-based games. The further development of computer-based urban games is especially promising. The games have special advantages: they require rigorous thinking; they force decisions and provide feedback on them; depending on their structure, they can acquaint students in progressive stages with the complexities of problems; they tend to point up the probabilistic nature of decisions. It can be expected that games will become more sophisticated and will include political, cultural, managerial, and ethical aspects of the problems they deal with, which some of the games available in this field now tend to neglect.

These problem-oriented integrating courses are difficult to design and to teach. To develop them in the urban field requires the cooperation of several professional schools and disciplines and the participation of responsible officials from the policy field with which the course is concerned. So often the problems of the real world, in this case the urban world, cut sharply across the existing patterns of university and departmental organization. Universities and departments are organized in terms of knowledge specializations and such groupings as social or behavioral sciences, biological sciences, and so on . In planning a curriculum, we tend to group courses providing specialized knowledge and skills that we think are relevant to the purpose we have in mind. Specializations, in other words, tend to be our primary focus; training in integrating specialized knowledges and skills in relation to problems is much more likely to be a secondary consideration. Integration of knowledge in relation to a problem is the principal intellectual challenge to the urban administrator. Does this perhaps suggest that in educating urban administrators we should make the integrating learning experience the primary focus? What might a professional degree program based upon this integrating principle look like?

A possible program based upon the integrating principle might be as follows. A student would take no specialized courses. His program would be composed of four three-term problem-oriented seminars, each in a major policy area in which urban administrators are involved. The school might offer ten or a dozen such three-term seminars, from which each student would choose perhaps four. Problem areas for the three-term seminars could be, for example, human services, environmental protection, law enforcement and justice, and so forth. In each of the three terms of a given seminar, the students would deal with problems of increasing complexity. For example, in the human services seminar, the students might address themselves in the first term to devising viable models for coordinating the delivery of social services through multiservice neighborhood centers or programs; the second term might address the problem of integrating, city or region-wide, the funding and management of public and voluntary health and welfare programs, as the models developed in the first term may require; the third term might explore the impediments to effecting the models of coordination and integration in the state and federal legal and administrative systems, and develop proposals for their reorganization. In each term, the student would acquire the substantive knowledge and analytical skills needed for dealing with the level of problem being considered. He would also study the economic, political, social, managerial, and technological elements of the problem. The group would be required each term to interrelate these elements in a proposed policy and strategy for carrying it out. Preferably each seminar set would deal with an actual situation and involve responsible administrators.

Such a hypothetical program would offer a number of special advantages. First, the seminars would stimulate the actual decision-making situation faced by the administrator, thus affording students a vicarious experience in problem definition, policy analysis, and program formulation.

Interacting together over three terms, the faculty group, students, and practitioners could become an effective team. Dealing with the same problem set, each member of the group could become a teacher of the other members; in other words, the group could become a community of scholars in the true sense. In this setting, with the emphasis on integrating varied subject matter, the difficulty of relating disciplinary knowledge acquired in specialized courses to applied problems would largely disappear.

Finally, the student would acquire comprehensive, in depth knowledge, analytical skills, and perhaps operational skills in major areas of urban administration.

Such a program would also pose some interesting questions:

1. Can learning about administration, politics, economics, statistics, and so on, take place more efficiently in a problem-centered context, or in courses that treat such subjects generically?

2. How broadly should the problem areas be defined? We should define them broadly enough to anticipate the problem perceptions that are likely to evolve in the foreseeable future, yet narrowly enough so that the students and faculty can cope with the level of problem considered each term.

3. What is the mix and number of faculty most appropriate for each problem set and how can they best organize? Since an

appropriate faculty grouping may involve members of various professional schools and departments, how are the interschool and interdepartmental arrangements best effected?

4. How can and should practitioners relate to the seminars?

5. Should we, perhaps, look forward toward consortia of public administration programs as an approach to developing such a curriculum built around sets of problem-oriented seminars? It would appear that most schools in this field have limited capacities individually to develop curriculums sufficiently comprehensive to offer students an adequate professional graduate education.

The type of program outlined represents a different approach to educational planning than most of us have been taking. But the administrators' workshops pointed up the tension between the principles of specialization and integration. Certainly we should explore the possibilities and problems of innovation along the lines suggested.

Clinical Experience and Classroom Instruction

A carefully planned and supervised internship with an experienced urban administrator is an essential learning experience for the student who has not had such an exposure. His courses and simulated experiences provide the student with sets of questions and with techniques for interrelating them with respect to typical problems. Facts pertinent to an actual problem in the field are peculiar to the particular political situation and the student can acquire operational knowledge only by experience in live situations. In addition to this operational knowledge, such attributes as political and interpersonal sensitivity, style, command, and other personal characteristics are probably best nurtured through the tutelage and example of people who manifest them. One point about internships should be emphasized: they require cooperative and substantial involvement of the student, the faculty, and the sponsoring administrator if the student is to derive the full benefits expected from the experience.

Practices of granting degree credit for internships vary. Some schools encourage or require an internship but give no credit. Some give credit not for the internship itself, but rather for one or more substantial, substantive reports on problems on which the student has worked during the internship. Others give regular course credit.

ROLE OF THE PUBLIC ADMINISTRATION SCHOOL

As noted previously, the professional education of urban administrators can be viewed as a function of the entire university, in that relevant courses are offered in many schools and departments. Cooperation among schools and departments is essential, we believe, if the university is to provide a comprehensive program of professional education for urban administrators, in the inclusive sense of urban administrator that has been used in the workshops and this Symposium.

It is especially important for the public administration faculty to establish close working relationships with the social science disciplines, particularly political science and economics, and with other professional schools, such as business, public health, social work, engineering, education, and law. Schools of public health, social work, and education have much in common in their graduate professional degree programs for they are all deeply involved in educating urban administrators; the schools tend to differ in terms of technical specializations.

Even where a university has several professional schools engaged in educating different kinds of urban administrators, however, the public administration faculty must play a primary and central role. The dimensions of this role include the following:

1. Serving as the focal point in the university for public service education;

2. Identifying the foundation knowledge and skills for professional education for urban administration; consulting with other schools and departments on courses and other types of learning experiences that will provide these basic knowledges and skills;

3. Offering courses, both basic and specialized, that are considered pertinent to such education and that are not adequately provided by other university units;

4. Providing the leadership in developing, in cooperation with other schools and departments, the problem-oriented integrating seminars;

5. Providing career counseling services for all students in the university who are interested in careers in urban administration, serving as an informational function about civil service requirements, and developing a placement service to refer graduates to employing agencies;

6. Maintaining relationships with urban administrators in the field; arranging for their participation, as appropriate, in the programs of the school; arranging internships and other forms of educationally related field experiences;

7. Recruiting students for the educational programs;

8. Developing with other schools and departments joint degree programs, cooperative research programs, and other forms of activities that will help upgrade education for urban administration;

9. Maintaining relationships with professional associations in the field.

CONCLUSION

There are many other questions pertinent to the subject of this paper; those we have discussed, all too briefly, are some of the principal questions. There is great diversity among universities throughout the country in regard to policies and practices with respect to these questions. Thus, much can be gained for all by more regular discussion of such issues and a continuing sharing of ideas and experience.

Perhaps the major concluding point of emphasis should be upon the principal assumptions which undergird this entire project:

1. Programs of professional education for urban administrators should be planned in terms of our best judgments regarding the kinds of responsibilities our graduates will probably be expected to carry out when they become urban administrators;

2. Curriculum planning should be a cooperative effort of educators, administrators, and professional associations in the field.

Commentary on the Davy Paper

By John P. Crecine

ABSTRACT: The educational plan contained in the paper by Davy for training urban administrators is based on what he refers to as the integrating principle. I have two general areas of comment on the proposed curricular format. One relates to the preferred pedagogical approach to the acquisition of more sophisticated analytic skills than has characterized public administration programs in the past. A second set of concerns has to do with the institutional and intellectual problems of communication and organization implied by the student-faculty-practitioner seminar team proposed. A comment on the specialist-generalist controversy is in order first. This is increasingly a nonissue. The urban administrator must possess specialist skills of a high order. If one is training administrators of the future, it seems far more sensible to train them to be well-versed, not in the technology currently used for decision-making in urban governments, but in the technology likely to be adopted in the next decade or two. Davy advocates a pedagogical approach to the acquisition of the various disciplinary perspectives and analytic approaches that derives the list of perspectives and approaches to be learned from the characteristics of the problem. But who in the group would determine what must be learned to approach a particular problem? Next, I would argue that if the objective is to provide students with an appropriate mix of disciplinary knowledge and methodological skills, the seminar process is extremely inefficient. My position is that there must first be a common set of perspectives and skills to be integrated before efforts at integration make a great deal of sense. In summary, I find the Davy proposal constitutes a superb set of objectives, but not a particularly viable plan for achieving those objectives. One has to pay considerably more attention to the hard work of implementation and the reality of current incentive systems if one is to make progress toward that goal.

John P. Crecine is director, Institute of Public Policy Studies and professor of political science and sociology, University of Michigan. His Ph.D. is in Industrial Administration from the Carnegie-Mellon University. He has been a consultant to the Rand Corporation, United States Bureau of the Budget, United States Departments of Transportation and Commerce; and he has served on Ann Arbor's Planning Commission and the Governor's Commission on Local Government, State of Michigan. He is the author of numerous articles on municipal resources allocation, urban research, and public policy.

THE educational plan contained in the paper by Thomas Davy for training urban administrators is based on what Davy refers to as the integrating principle. Basically, the curriculum deriving from the integrating principle consists of a series of year-long problem seminars involving a team of students, faculty, and practitioners who would come together as a community of scholars to study, in depth, a major policy area or to address a major problem of concern to urban administrators. Although Davy is not clear as to whether this year of seminars in students' educational programs (roughly four per student) is preceded by a year in which analytical skills are acquired,[1] he does propose that the student would acquire the substantive knowledge and analytical

1. For example, "A possible program based upon the integrating principle might be as follows. A student would take no specialized courses. His program would be composed of four three-term problem-oriented seminars. . . . In each term, the student would acquire the substantive knowledge and analytical skills needed for dealing with the level of problem being considered." (Davy, pp. 203–204) as contrasted with an earlier recommendation of ". . . an approach to resolution of this issue (learning methodology in specialized courses vs. acquiring methodological competence through applying methods in substantive and problem-oriented courses) can be found in a careful division of labor between basic courses in analytical approaches to develop insights and perspectives in students, and more substantive courses to develop student capacity to apply these analytic approaches to real problems and data drawn from urban settings." (Davy, p. 202.)

skills needed for dealing with the level of problem being considered in the context of and during the problem seminar itself. I have two general areas of comment on the proposed curricular format. One relates to the pedagogical approach taken to the acquisition of more sophisticated analytic skills than has characterized public administration programs in the past.[2] A second set of concerns has to do with the institutional and intellectual problems of communication and organization implied by the proposed student-faculty-practioner seminar team.

COMMENTS ON SPECIFIC CURRICULAR ISSUES

The curricular plan based on the integrating principle versus the specialization principle is consistent with Professor Davy's comments on seven specific issues deemed of fundamental importance in designing a program for urban administrators. A comment on one of these issues is in order before addressing the specific curriculum plan put forth by Davy and his colleagues at the University of Pittsburgh [3]: What is the appropriate mix of generalist and specialist preparation? Increasingly this is a non-issue. By 1990 I strongly suspect that a general urban administrator, that is, a department head in a large city, a city manager in a moderately large community, or a state or federal official having urban governments or citizens as clients, will find himself in a very vulnerable position if he does not know enough operations research, for example, to seek out a mathematical programming expert to address a transport-flow or refuse collection routing problem or enough to discount a consultant's promise that a linear programming algorithm will solve the city's annual budgeting problem.[4] In the 1990s it is likely to be the case that an urban administrator, to be effective, must possess a host of skills, all currently labeled as specialties. The point is

2. I take it as axiomatic that such analytic skills and methods as statistics, economic analysis, cost-benefit analysis, operations research, and computer methods will form an integral part of any graduate program for urban administrators expected to practice in the 1990s.

3. My comments on the remaining six issues are readily inferred from the discussion of the integrating principle curricular plan, below.

4. On the basis of the relative difficulty (impossibility) of specifying technical relationships and objective functions.

simple. The specialist-generalist controversy relates to relative points on a continuum. The labels attached to points on that continuum also change over time. An administrator who can execute a reasonably competent cost-benefit analysis is currently labeled a specialist in most urban governments. Five or ten years from now, the generalist urban administrator, especially those entering the field, will more than likely be expected to possess cost-benefit analytic skills. If one is training administrators of the future, it seems far more sensible to train them to be well-versed, not in the technology currently used for decision-making in urban governments, but in the technology likely to be adopted in the next decade or two. In addition, possession of specialized skills has always served as an entree to general management positions for many; if these specialist skills also prove useful as part of a general manager's repertoire of skills, so much the better.

COMMENTS ON THE PITTSBURGH-DAVY CURRICULAR PLAN

The integrative principle emphasized by Davy addresses the problem of integrating seemingly diverse bodies of knowledge, organized around the academic disciplines (that is, economics, political sciences, sociology, operations research, psychology, and so on), the problem of developing appropriate methodological skills, and the problem of applying these skills and knowledge to real questions. Integration is to be accomplished by focusing on a particular, substantive policy question. The real world, with its cross-disciplinary problems, is to perform the integrating function and is to motivate students to develop appropriate analytical and applications skills. The particular insights generated by individual disciplinary perspectives and particular analytic approaches somehow are to be brought together in the context of a real problem. In the absence of a unified social and management science, the general approach of letting problems serve as ad hoc organizing devices for the component disciplinary knowledge and skills makes a great deal of sense. Note, however, either there is an assumption that particular disciplinary perspectives and analytic approaches already have been internalized by students and that these must then be integrated or that such perspectives and approaches are acquired simultaneously with the integration of component skills and knowledge.

Davy and his colleagues advocate a pedagogical approach to the acquisition of the various disciplinary perspectives and analytic approaches that derives the list of perspectives and approaches to be learned from the characteristics of the particular problem. Who in a student-faculty-practitioner group would determine what must be learned to approach a particular problem? The generation of a list of knowledge components and methodologies from the requirements of a particular problem seems to constitute a function that few students could perform, given their lack of knowledge and skills, and practitioners may be able to perform to a limited degree in some problem areas and for some skills. The major burden of specifying what it is that should be learned —substantive and disciplinary knowledge and analytic skills— must rest with the members of the faculty involved. Once knowledge and skill gaps are identified, presumably students will be motivated to acquire the requisite knowledge and skills and will do so under the guidance of faculty. Once acquired, these skills would then be put to good use in the analysis of the problem under examination by the seminar until another point is reached in the problem-solving process, where an additional gap in knowledge and skills is identified. Students, faculty, and practitioners will again disengage, learn what must be learned, return to the problem again, and so on. Even if interest in the substantive problem survives as a motivating force long enough to turn relatively naive students (and practitioners from a certain perspective) into reasonably knowledgeable and sophisticated problem-solvers and analysts, I would argue that if the objective is to provide students with an appropriate mix of disciplinary knowledge and methodological skills, the seminar process is extremely inefficient. First, a mix and level problem exists. Are the mix of knowledge and skill for the chosen problem also appropriate for a wider range of problems than those under seminar consideration? Are the levels of sophistication required representative of a wider variety of situations? The implication is that seminar problems ought to be chosen on the basis of how well they reflect an appropriate mix and level of disciplinary knowledge requirements and analytic skills. From experience in trying to select actual problems for teaching purposes according to these general criteria, I can testify as to the difficulty inherent in the selection of one such problem area as opposed to the ten or twelve proposed by Davy. An alternative, of course, is to select, for each student, a combination of seminars which collectively result in the desired mix and level of knowledge and skill; the organizational difficulties of such an approach are obvious.

An equally important defect in the integrative curricular plan is the simple fact that students come to any curriculum with a quite different mix of skills and interests. This means that, should such an integrative curriculum be adopted, each student in each problem-seminar will encounter different deficiencies at different points in the seminar; the deficiency-correction or learning aspects of the seminar would represent a correspondingly complex coordination problem for those faculty-practitioner-student combinations interested in correcting deficiencies for other individuals in the seminar.

Perhaps a telling defect in such a curricular plan is the fact that if skill and knowledge-acquisition involves any generalizable knowledge bases and skill, the needs to acquire such skills and knowledge will arise in many different seminars, at different times during the year, and in different sequences and will imply different levels of sophistication for the particular problems in different seminars. For example, most seminars would undoubtedly require some knowledge of statistics; how and when this knowledge is acquired is the question. The inefficiencies in such a plan—in terms of coordinating the teaching of particular specialized skills across seminars and over the course of the year or in terms of duplicating the teaching efforts in different seminars—are enormous. The inescapable fact of the matter is, knowledge is organized along disciplinary lines and in a somewhat structured fashion. To assume, as the proposed curricular plan seems to, that the way to acquire the general structure of a body of knowledge is to acquire, in piecemeal fashion, only that portion of the structure useful in the context of a particular subproblem is to assume that knowledge is not particularly structured or sequential or that knowledge itself ought to be restructured around problem-oriented themes. Regardless of the utility of restructuring knowledge in a more problem-oriented fashion, this would be a considerably greater undertaking than the construction of a viable curriculum.

The psychology of interpersonal communications suggests that a far more likely outcome of mixing students, practitioners, and faculty, each from different backgrounds, would be that the more diverse the group, the more group discussion would gravitate to a level understandable by all: to a mediocre and superficial level. Rather than raising each other to higher intellectual levels through a transmission to others of each individual's relative expertise, group discussion is more likely to gravitate to the lowest common denominator.

As is becoming increasingly clear, my position is that there must first be a relatively common set of perspectives and skills to be integrated before efforts at integration make a great deal of sense. This is not to say that the acquisition of knowledge and analytic skills should be devoid of applications, cases, and real problems. Rather, for students, the acquisition of analytic and methodological skills and general, that is, disciplinary, perspectives ought to predominate in the beginning of a curriculum gradually giving way to actual applications of skills as and after these skills have been acquired.

Envisioned is a two-part (year) curriculum concentrating on the acquisition of fundamental skills and knowledge in the first portion, perhaps an internship experience between the first and second parts, followed by a second portion of the curriculum featuring problem-oriented seminars of the general type advocated by Davy, with additional courses available for further development of the fundamentals acquired during the first part of the curriculum. The coupling of academic analytic skills and knowledge with the world and problems of the practitioner would be accomplished initially with brief examples used to illustrate methodological and theoretical points. This would be followed by increasingly complex case exercises, giving way to some concentrated attempts, near the end of the first phase of study, at attacking actual policy questions and particular problems, leading, possibly, to the internship and highly concentrated, in depth examination of applied problems in the seminars featured in the second phase of the curriculum. There are certainly other ways of accomplishing the above; for example, devoting ten to twenty percent of the course work in the first phase of a program to an applied problem-solving seminar, where the problems become increasingly demanding as the year progresses and as the student's analytic tool kit grows.

A second general set of concerns generated by the curricular plan contained in the Davy paper deals with the staffing, organization, and composition of the problem seminars. These issues arise regardless of whether the problem seminars comprise the major portion of the curriculum as in the Pittsburgh-Davy plan or occur primarily in the second part of a two-part program as suggested above. As advocated in the Davy proposal, the seminar would consist of a community of scholars: several faculty from various disciplines and professional schools in a university, the students, and practitioners. Information and skills relevant to the accomplishment of the educational goals of a professional program for urban administrators have two main sources. One source is the world of practice. Inputs from the world of practice consist of: information concerning the institutional environment that urban governments find themselves imbedded in; the problems faced by urban administrators; the skills needed; and the techniques and insights that have proven effective in the past. Students of urban administration and faculty involved in the training program must understand much about the world of practice. Information and skills also originate from the social and management sciences that are relevant for and contributing to improvements in the practice of urban administration. The relevant sciences would seem to include portions of at least economics, psychology, sociology, political science, applied mathematics, operations research, computer science, and law.

The way in which an educational program gains access to necessary information and skills is through the people who participate in the educational program. Corresponding to the two main sources of skill and knowledge, above, are two rather diverse social systems: one comprising urban government officials and one comprising academics in the relevant disciplines, usually found in universities. To gain access to the knowledge and information contained in the practical world of urban administration, a professional school must participate in that world either directly or vicariously. Traditionally there are several ways of participating: seeking faculty members with government experience; encouraging consulting practice with government agencies; bringing in urban administrators as occasional lecturers; and offering mid-career training programs and applied research services to various governmental units. Certainly some mix of these means of access is necessary for an urban administration program. For the sake of brevity, let us examine only the option proposed by Davy: welcoming current government officials as participating faculty members on a part-time (presumably) basis. Employing or otherwise involving individuals with substantial experience in urban administration has met with many successes—and an enormous number of failures. Borrowing from an analysis of a similar situation for business schools by Herbert Simon [5] we might reflect on some possible motivations a practitioner might have for substantial involvement in a professional school's teaching program. First, he may see the university experience as representing professional advancement. If the university experience is important for the advancement of an urban administrator, it is probably because the individual has reached a plateau in his career. It is unlikely that such an individual will perform significantly better in an academic setting than in his career as an urban administrator. Second, the prime value of practical experience is when that experience is at a relatively high level. People at relatively high levels are likely to be much too busy to participate in any substantial way in a teaching program. Third, a practitioner might be near retirement and feel he no longer desires to maintain the hectic pace of a practicing urban administrator. The desire for reduced work load has not been shown to make positive contributions to teaching excellence. On the other hand, a particular practitioner may be looking for an entirely new range of experiences, have a strong intellectual bent himself, and wish to participate in the intellectual climate found in a first-rate university. Such individuals are exceedingly rare. Although a program for training urban administrators is probably better able to uncover such people than a business school, given the relative vagaries of the public political process, there is no great supply of practitioners

5. H. A. Simon, "The Business School: A Problem in Organizational Design," mimeographed (September, 1966), pp. 10–11.

available who have the intellectual flexibility, time, desire, and competence required to function effectively in an academic setting. The serious participation of several competent practitioners as advocated in the Pittsburgh-Davy proposal seems highly unlikely for one seminar, let alone participation of sufficient numbers for an entire program consisting (only?) of problem seminars. It would seem prudent in designing curriculums to explore other means of tapping the information and skill base in the world of practice.

The mix of faculty representing the relevant social and management sciences and participants from other professional schools in the university outlined in the Pittsburgh-Davy proposal presents severe difficulties as well. The incentives for wide faculty participation in problem seminars are unclear, especially if the students are basically untrained in the beginning as implied in the proposal. The problems of interdisciplinary communication are well known and would seem to require the more talented and broadly based faculty members from the relevant schools and disciplines to overcome these barriers. This group, of course, comprises individuals with attractive options for other activities. I have discussed the organizational problems surrounding interdisciplinary, public policy activities similar to those represented by the problem seminar curriculums elsewhere [6] and will not repeat the analysis here. Let it suffice to observe that nearly all the incentives for individuals in a university operate in a direction opposite from those that would lead to a meaningful, multi- or interdisciplinary problem seminar as described in the Davy paper. Considerable organizational efforts are required to offset these incentives and these efforts would have to constitute an integral part of any curricular plan such as the Pittsburgh-Davy proposal. A much more fruitful approach [7] would seem to couple a relatively small group of students, already well grounded in much of the requisite methodological and analytic skills and exposed to the

6. J. P. Crecine, "University Centers for the Study of Public Policy: Organizational Viability," *Policy Sciences* Vol. 2 (1971).

7. The experiences with policy seminars in the second year of the Master of Public Policy program, Institute of Public Policy Studies, The University of Michigan, is consistent with the observations which follow.

necessary disciplinary perspectives, with a faculty member having primary responsibility for the seminar. The individual faculty member would determine when and to what limited extent other faculty and practitioners should participate. A prerequisite for the educational success of the seminar seems to lie in choosing a problem or policy question where the individual faculty member has an important stake in the outcome, either through his research interests or through his more general involvement in governmental affairs. Equally important to the success of a policy or problem seminar is ready access to the key features of the problem: participants in the decision process, files and records, and so forth.

In summary, I find the Davy proposal constitutes a superb set of objectives, but not a particularly viable plan for achieving those objectives. Learning methodology, analytic skills, and disciplinary perspectives when there is a need to know has a comfortable ring. So does the concept of a community of scholars composed of students embarking on an exploration into the reaches of urban government and policy, practitioners who have been there before, and academics from a variety of disciplines and substantive backgrounds, all interacting in harmony, communicating effectively and freely with one another, and somehow synthesizing relevant skills and knowledge, arriving at a better solution and integrating the previously unintegrated in the process. I find this scenario appealing and representing an attractive goal; one has to pay considerably more attention to the hard work of implementation and the reality of current incentive systems if one is to make progress toward that goal, however.

Commentary on the Davy Paper

By John L. Taylor

ABSTRACT: Davy's excellent paper is flawed slightly by an interesting omission—recognition of the faculty as a source of inspiration to students. Most in the profession can identify certain individuals who influenced their career development very significantly. In addition to this leadership quality of the faculty, the importance of a group learning experience may be underestimated. Current trends in administration suggest that great benefit will derive from an educational device that gives students an early experience in team building. I would also re-emphasize Davy's observation about internships; they must be a joint endeavor, in which we expect both to teach and to learn.

John L. Taylor has been city manager of Kansas City, Missouri since 1968. He has also been the manager of Fresno, California, Lakewood, New Jersey, and Narberth, Pennsylvania. He is a graduate of Middlebury College and has an M.G.A. degree from the University of Pennsylvania where he held a Graduate Scholarship in the Fels Institute of Local and State Government. He is a former president of the New Jersey Municipal Managers and Administrators Association and has held offices in local chapters of the American Society for Public Administration. In 1971 he received one of the major awards of the International City Management Association for organizational development.

WHENEVER a public administrator, bruised and battered by a few years on the firing line, re-enters the academic world in order to tell competent educators their business, he treads on dangerous ground. Nevertheless, that is my assignment, and I enter upon it taking comfort in knowing that the scholars are an understanding lot and are always gracious in allowing for our shortcomings!

Perhaps the best approach in offering my comments is to jump right into the middle of this excellent paper, and I have chosen to do this by first bringing attention to an interesting omission from the author's list of primary concerns of public administration faculty. In that list I do not find mention of the faculty as a source of inspiration to students. My guess is that most of us who are committed to public administration as a profession can identify certain individuals, often faculty members, who influenced our career development very significantly, who helped shape our concepts of right and wrong, who instilled a sense of the more noble aspirations of this endeavor, who imparted wisdom through their example. So, I submit that a student's opportunity to associate with men of high character is of utmost priority in listing faculty concerns. Perhaps its omission is simply because there is an underlying recognition of this as a given, but I would be more explicit.

This leads me to a second observation about the paper. In addition to the importance to the learning environment of the leadership quality of faculty, I feel that the importance of a group learning experience may be underestimated in the paper. As I understand the author's recommended curriculum, its major thrust is to provide lots of flexibility to meet individual concerns, and I am left with a feeling that the student would proceed through his selected course of studies as sort of an encapsulated unit, too isolated from his peers to develop a close group association. The loss of this opportunity seems fairly serious to me, and I find support for the conclusion in that the author describes an alternative program based upon what is called the integrating principle. I thought it had something to do with low income housing. As noted by the author, an advantage of the alternative is that close interaction among faculty, students, and administrators can result in development of an effective team. Current trends in administration suggest that great benefit will derive from an educational device that gives students an early experience in team building. I would think of this group experience as being the laboratory aspect of the curriculum and therefore extremely valuable.

Closely related to what I have just said, I am pleased with the author's emphasis on case studies, role playing, problem seminars, and computer-based gaming. I surely agree wholeheartedly with the increasing use of these tools to present broad learning opportunities.

I would re-emphasize the author's observations about internships, which provide good insights and important reminders to us that a successful graduate student internship requires as much from us—both faculty and administrator—as from the student. Internships must be a joint endeavor, in which we expect both to teach and to learn. We should accept interns with more than a passing investment of time and energy.

In closing, let me raise three questions which came to mind as I reviewed the Davy paper:

1. The title was "What Should We Teach?" "How Should We Teach?" Are we neglecting a third question, "Who should we teach?"

2. In educating future urban administrators, will the products be sufficiently diverse to provide the public a wide range in choosing their public servants, or are all poured from the same mold?

3. In describing the future urban administrator, we always seem to commit ourselves to a certain omniscient role—no longer the narrow, limited administrator, we become the community leader, policy formulator, community problem-solver, systems integrator, and political philosopher. Indeed, is it true that we public administrators are destined to be those nearest to heaven in the hierarchy of participants in the urban scene?

Commentary on the Davy Paper

By Robert F. Wilcox

ABSTRACT: There is a question whether pre-entry education for the public service should be described, as it is in this paper, as professional. A challenge facing the curriculum planner is to build a system of graduate professional education. Rather than considering a wide range of issues, the curriculum revision process should focus on the two or three most significant questions. Top priority should be given to preparing the student to integrate his skills on a problem-oriented basis. Problems selected for study should be those about which the student feels concern rather than those which are neutral or value-free. Next in priority is the question of appropriate mix of field experience and classroom instruction. The internship is badly in need of reform. Curriculum revision should include construction of new courses rather than reliance on fitting existing courses into a new matrix. In linking curriculum revision to the future needs of urban administration, it is necessary to translate changes in the role of the urban administrator into a set of assumptions about requisite knowledge and skills. We have a long way to go in refining consultative relationship between practitioner and academic. Education for executive posts in the public service is a lifetime process, beginning with pre-entry preparation which in turn is followed by continuing education to update knowledge and introduce new skills. The concept of education for a second career is an essential part of training for executive-level responsibilities.

Robert F. Wilcox became dean, Graduate School of Public Affairs, University of Colorado in 1972. Prior to that he was head, Office of Public Understanding of Science, National Science Foundation, 1971–72 and director, School of Public Administration and Urban Studies and professor

*of public administration and urban studies, California State University,
San Diego, 1968–71. He is a member of the National Academy of Public
Administration. He has been active in civic affairs in California state and
local government and is author of monographs, articles, and technical publications in the fields of public administration and local government.*

TO BEGIN with, I must quarrel with the use of the word professional as a modifier of the noun education in the title of
this paper. If we except a handful of graduate programs, including that of Pittsburgh, we can say with assurance that there has
been very little professional education for urban or any other
kind of public administrators in this country. Recent evidence is
found in the Parker-Cantine analysis of the 1971 surveys and
workshops conducted to gain the practitioner's view of the urban
administrator's job and the knowledge and skill requirements
needed.[1]

Experience on the job outranked graduate professional education by a ratio of more than two to one as the source of skills and
knowledge necessary to successful performance as an urban administrator, according to these practitioners. Can you imagine
engineers or physicians responding in this way when asked about
the utility of their graduate training? Continuing education was
the least important factor among the four listed, ranking even
below undergraduate education. Assuming that the views expressed in this case were representative, how can it be argued that
the bulk of either graduate or continuing education for urban
administration is professional in any meaningful way? The great
challenge facing faculties and practitioners is to build a system of
graduate professional education which will equip students with
knowledge and skills they will begin to utilize as they start on
their careers.

Part of the challenge is to convince specialists who enter or
are in the public service that there is anything particularly difficult or challenging about moving into a position involving major
administrative responsibilities. A recent study of scientists and
engineers in the National Institutes of Health and the National
Aeronautics and Space Administration found that senior manage-

1. John K. Parker and Robert R. Cantine, "What Are We Educating
For?," *Public Management*, vol. 54, no. 2 (February, 1972), p. 14.

ment officials were unaware of or tended to ignore the importance of the process of transition from specialist to administrator, the problems associated with it and the importance of relevant training for managers.[2]   The authors of the study reported:

These data (on performance of management functions) strongly suggest that one of the problems in the transition of scientists and engineers rests in unrealistic opinions and negative attitudes as to the role of management functions in the pool of individuals from which managers will be drawn.[3]

THE FOCUS OF THE PAPER

It is unfortunate, although understandable, that the substance of the Davy paper had to be based primarily on curriculum planning at one university. It would have been desirable to have had comprehensive information about the various policies and practices in graduate education for urban administration throughout the country, for there is little doubt that great diversity exists.

The heavy hand of disciplinary orientation has hampered the growth of professional education for the public service in universities across the land. The fact that data on policies and practices are not readily available reflects the fragmented and highly particularistic nature of education for the public service. The lack of information emphasizes the need for vigorous continuation of the National Academy of Public Administration's study of education in this field.

The Davy paper draws heavily on the work of an interdepartmental committee assigned to evaluate and reorganize the Master of Public Administration (M.P.A.) degree in Urban Executive Management (UEM) at the University of Pittsburgh. In addition to the long experience of the university in education for public affairs, and the talents of the committee's members, the committee had two important resources to guide its curriculum planning effort: (1) a set of questions designed to link the practitioners' findings as to the nature of the urban administrator's emerging role with the curriculum builders' concern for providing

2. James A. Bayton and Richard L. Chapman, *The Transformation of Scientists and Engineers into Managers*, National Aeronautics and Space Administration, SP-291 (Washington, D.C.: U.S. Government Printing Office, 1972), pp. 7–9.

3. Ibid., p. 48.

the kind of professional education necessary to prepare the future administrators to perform effectively in that capacity; (2) the judgment of selected urban administrators on the probable role of this important group of managers in the foreseeable future.

SEVEN ISSUES

Given these resources, some of the seven issues identified in the paper as being especially important in curriculum planning seemed to me to be relatively unimportant. The resolution of some of the less important would appear to be a function of determining answers to the more important. The Davy paper does not rank-order the seven issues. On the basis of the findings of the urban administrators' workshops, I would be inclined to give top priority to the problem of preparing the student to integrate his knowledge and skills on a problem-oriented basis. The acquisition of substantive knowledge and analytic skills would be carried on within the problem-solving context.

Laura Nader, an anthropologist, said recently: "Today we have anthropology students who are indignant about many problems affecting the future of homo sapiens, but they are studying problems about which they have no feelings."[4] Without doubt, the same thing can be said about students in our schools of public affairs and administration. While some anthropologists would defend this feelingless approach as appropriate for a science, who would attempt to justify for an applied field like ours?

If students feel strongly about issues, they are motivated to study them, to ask important questions they would not otherwise ask. We need to ask whether our schools are suppressing the normative impulse and thereby draining the energy from what is inherently an exciting and challenging subject matter.

A sense of concern among graduate students can be an energizing phenomenon. Laura Nader suggests that anthropology should be studied up, in the sense that anthropologists should examine the cultures of power and influence as well as those of the powerless and poverty-stricken, as traditionally has been the

4. Laura Nader, "Up the Anthropologist: Perspectives Gained from Studying Up" (Mimeographed paper delivered at the Annual Meeting of the American Association for the Advancement of Science, Philadelphia, December 1971), p. 2.

case.[5] Perhaps students of public affairs and administration should be challenged by studying down, by focusing on the problems of those who are administered as well as of the administrators, on the recipients as well as the providers of services, on the clients—or victims—of government as well as the governors. For example, interns might help inner city residents cope with city hall or the rural poor with the county courthouse. Their learning assignment would be to take on the task the courts already have begun to face in equalizing the distribution of public services and benefits. This approach might motivate some students by confronting them with the kinds of issues they can become indignant about.

The Public Policy Program at Harvard University utilized for its first-year students a three-week exercise culminating in a formal hearing on a public policy issue. An illustration is an exercise involving a hearing on automotive air pollution. Teams of students representing the Environmental Protection Agency, the automotive industry, and other public and private groups prepare written briefs and oral arguments based on research and analysis. In this case, the exercise was an integral part of a longer range project on automotive air pollution being carried out on an interdisciplinary basis.

The substantive knowledge acquired in this approach is related to the problem to be solved. The student does not spend a considerable part of his period of graduate study acquiring knowledge that may well be obsolete by the time he reaches mid-career.

The issue of the appropriate mix of clinical field experience and classroom instruction is next in importance, in my view. The function and nature of the field experience have been ignored or considered to be of secondary importance too long. If professional education is our aim, we must pay a great deal more attention to what traditionally, and with scant justification, has been called the internship. We must come to an understanding with practitioners that the clinical part of education for urban administration is just as important as the classroom phase. The student needs testing on the firing line, and this is the only way he can get it. If we begin to take the field experience phase seriously, the educational process will become longer and more

5. Ibid., p. 5.

expensive and necessarily will have to become more selective. No graduate program in urban administration should admit a candidate unless provision has been made for him to carry out the duties and assume the responsibilities of a manager on an apprentice or trainee basis under an experienced administrator. Our goal should be to transform the individual from student to practitioner during the field experience.

One of the seven questions asked for consideration of the special role of those responsible for the urban administration program in the educational process. Is this really an issue? Can there be any doubt in our minds that the school of public affairs has primary responsibility for the development of a graduate program integrating its own resources with those of other departments and graduate schools in the university? If the school of public affairs does not take the lead, no one else will, as the Honey report pointed out so long ago. Henry Reining has used the particularly apt term of port of entry to the university's resources to describe the school of public affairs. This school must serve as a liaison agent between the university and the public service, seeking to mobilize the university's various forms of expertise on behalf of the government and the multiple clienteles of government. It is up to us to carry the message to the rest of the university.

Questions pertaining to length of program, sequencing of courses, prerequisites, types and levels of courses and core courses seem to me to be definitely secondary in importance and largely governable by the law of the situation. For example, there can be no general answer to the question of whether courses in methodology should precede substantive courses and problem-focused seminars. For a rigorous policy analysis program, the answer obviously would be yes. But the comprehensive school of public affairs prepares students for a variety of careers. Perhaps those emphasizing management can learn their methodology in problem-oriented courses.

Rather than think in terms of numbers of semesters or quarters, I would prefer to experiment with the student's ability to achieve desired levels of knowledge and skill as determined by examination, performance in field work, and competence in research. This approach would be an effort to achieve the goal mentioned in the paper, ". . . that we can greatly improve our pedagogical efficiency and thereby enable our students to learn more within specified time limits."

Rather than rely on fitting courses and parts of courses currently offered into the desired matrix, I would include the construction of new courses as a mandatory part of the reorganization of an urban administration. Existing courses are based on the diverse interests of instructors in a variety of disciplines and professional schools, with all their inherited inflexibilities. While granting that urban administration is highly eclectic, I would argue for the development of courses for the needs of the new program. The slate would not have to be wiped clean all at once. With adequate study and planning, the curriculum could be recycled in from five to ten years. If we are to become more professional in our approach to graduate education for the public service, we must do what other professional schools have done, that is, develop our own curriculum, making it so relevant that students from other fields will enroll in our courses. This is not to say that certain highly specialized courses should not be taken in other departments or schools by students who have special needs.

Wisely, the paper contained no hard and fast conclusions on sequencing of courses, particularly with regard to the argument that certain methodology courses had to be completed during the first term. Equally sound was the resistance to hard and fast prerequisites.

SKILLS AND KNOWLEDGES

The Davy paper correctly points out that curriculum planning must be based on systematic thinking about the future of urban administration. Changes in the role of the urban administrator must be translated into a set of assumptions about the knowledge and skills which the trained administrator needs to cope with the requirements of his job.

A series of surveys and workshops of urban administrators was conducted during the summer of 1971 as part of a study of future needs. The present Symposium is a second phase of that study. One product of the surveys and workshops was a compilation of assumptions of the probable roles of urban administrators in the foreseeable future. These assumptions are dealt with in the first few pages of the Davy paper by way of background for the treatment of curriculum planning.

Trying to categorize the skills and knowledges required by future urban administrators is risky indeed, but several of the tables in the Parker-Cantine analysis of the results of the surveys and workshops on the future of urban administration invite such a classification.[6] I have classified those skills and knowledges having to do with relationships external to the urban public bureaucracy, that is, elected officials and citizens, as political in nature; those skills and knowledges having to do with relationships within the public bureacracy as managerial.

Table C, Future Importance by Managerial Category,[7] gives top priority to two political functions: involvement with citizens and relationships with other governmental jurisdictions. Other high priority functions are managerial in nature, except for that of maintaining communication with the community. Table E, Importance of Various Categories of Knowledge,[8] suggests that several kinds of knowledge that would help the administrator in providing political leadership outweigh in importance all factors relevant to managing organizations except knowledge of human relations. Table F, Importance of Various Categories of Skills,[9] seems to give the nod to essentially political skills, that is, assessing community needs and consensus-seeking.

We may see evidence in these self-assessments by practitioners of an overreaction to emergent problems for which traditional training and experience had provided little preparation. They may have been expressing resentment over the fact that they have been thrust into new roles quite remote from those formerly expected of an expert in management. Certainly, the change in role has been forced upon urban administrators in a relatively short time.

While making a place for these new roles, the curriculum planners should not forget the fact that the very credibility of public administration rests upon its ability to do the jobs which

6. Parker and Cantine, op. cit., pp. 15–19.
7. Ibid., p. 16.
8. Ibid., p. 17.
9. Ibid., p. 18.

the public expects of it, and to do them in a reasonably competent fashion. The provision of health and other social services, housing, education, transportation, the carrying of the mail, safety on the streets, and a myriad of other functions depends heavily upon management capabilities which, sadly, are all too often lacking. The management of complex organizations is a major challenge in itself for the urban administrator, quite apart from fulfilling a community leadership role.

In their assessment of areas of knowledge, the practitioners whose views were reported by Parker and Cantine gave greatest importance to people-oriented categories. They would have the educator's planner place least importance on knowledge relating to technological innovation, engineering principles, and the specific services rendered by government. There seems to be reflected here a reaction against the efficiency syndrome and technical training for the nuts and bolts of urban administration. However, I would argue that technology must be looked upon in an entirely separate light.

The use of a wide range of technologies in attacking a variety of urban problems suggests that a graduate curriculum in urban administration should include attention to the potential of technology as an instrument for achieving desirable social goals. Public Technology, Incorporated, operating under the wing of the International City Management Association, and the National Science Foundation's Intergovernmental Science Program are making vigorous efforts to familiarize state and local officials with the potential of technology. Can a graduate curriculum in urban administration do less for its students?

THE NAPA DELPHI STUDY AS A YARDSTICK

The National Academy of Public Administration (NAPA) recently completed a Delphi exercise having as its purpose the gathering of the collective views of a group of well-informed leaders in public affairs in the United States regarding the changing character of the public service in the United States during this decade. These collective judgments constitute a valuable resource, according to the authors, "for guiding the assessment and

TABLE 1—Comparison of Delphi Respondents with Workshop Findings

Delphi Likely Developments (in order of likelihood)	% of Delphi Respondents Selecting Certain or Probable	Reflected in Workshop Classification?
Citizen intervention in administration	98	yes
Higher educated work force—more minorities	98	yes
More task forces, project groups	95	?
Nationalization of domestic problems (that is, trend since New Deal)	94	no
Greater emphasis on systems perspective	89	yes
Change generated by new technology	85	no
Unionization, including majority of mid-level management	84	no
Government as employer of last resort	82	?
New evels of government: regional, metro, multi-county	82	?
Substlantial reshaping of public programs	81	yes
Blurring of distinctions between public and private enterprise	75	no

revision of academic programs preparing people for careers in the public service." [10]

The NAPA finding can be used as the basis for a horseback validation exercise of the assumptions of the surveys and workshops on the future role of urban administrators—or vice versa. In any event, I found it interesting to compare as best I could (1) the findings of the workshops as to the general types of knowledges and skills needed by the urban administrators, with (2) the developments seen by the Delphi participants as having the most likelihood of occurring in the next nine years.

The workshop classification places considerable emphasis on urban problems, policies and programs, and urban community systems, as the urban administrator's environment. However, the Delphi respondents see greater reliance on state and local government as particularly unlikely. There seems to be substantial disagreement here, especially in view of the Delphi group's view of the likelihood of nationalization of domestic problems—in other words, power to the center, however undesirable.

10. Frederic Cleaveland and Richard L. Chapman, *A Summary Report on Developments Affecting the Public Service, 1971–1980—A Delphi Exercise,* mimeographed (Washington, D.C.: National Academy of Public Administration, April 1972), p. 1.

The outcome of my tally is four yes, four no, and three un-decided. Which is correct, the Delphi respondents' findings or the UEM Committee's classification, if there is indeed substantial disagreement between them? The answer doesn't matter. The lack of agreement may give us cause for concern. It suggests that we have made the barest start on the very necessary process, in building a professional curriculum, of consultation with our practitioner counterparts. We have a long way to go in refining our consultative relationships.

EDUCATION FOR A SECOND CAREER

I would like to close with a look at the myth and reality of the lifetime guarantee we have become accustomed to offering with our M.P.A. degree. How long should the guarantee be in effect? A lifetime, really? Twenty or even ten years? It has become a shibboleth of the promotional literature on graduate programs in public administration that they are preparing future executives. It is said that we train the leaders of tomorrow. It really would not do for a program to advertise that its aim is to prepare men and women for middle management positions, with the possibility that innate ability, good luck, influential friends, or some other extraneous cause might elevate a few to top posts.

Margaret Mead has said that change is occurring so rapidly that most of us who have not grown to adulthood during the past decade or so cannot possibly comprehend the future. The reason is that we tend to predict the shape of the future on the basis of the past with which we are familiar. Our past, however, no longer has any meaning for the future. It is not a valid base for looking ahead. If there is any truth in the Mead position, it is foolhardy for us to pretend to our students that two or three terms of graduate education can prepare them for positions of executive leadership a third of a lifetime ahead. It is entirely possible that we have grown accustomed to projecting an un-thinking optimism about the future role of the administrator. Perhaps we should think more about the painful possibilities that will confront administration as it becomes more involved in regu-lating conduct in areas about which large numbers of people have strong ethical and moral sensibilities.

FIGURE 1—The Hourglass Model of Executive Career Development

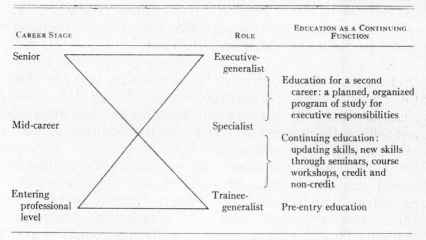

CAREER STAGE	ROLE	EDUCATION AS A CONTINUING FUNCTION
Senior	Executive-generalist	
		Education for a second career: a planned, organized program of study for executive responsibilities
Mid-career	Specialist	
		Continuing education: updating skills, new skills through seminars, course workshops, credit and non-credit
Entering professional level	Trainee-generalist	Pre-entry education

Seymour Berlin, Director of the Bureau of Executive Manpower of the United States Civil Service Commission, has suggested that the career of the federal executive resembles an hourglass in its generalist-specialist-generalist trend. Fresh from his formal education, the entering level professional is a generalist as he moves into the first stages of his career. Whether he has studied a discipline or a profession, he is more up-to-date on the total scope of his chosen field than he ever will be again.

As he moves toward mid-career, the professional tends to become more specialized, even though he may, incidentally, be required to perform some supervisorial duties. Past mid-career, moving into the executive field, his role becomes increasingly that of a generalist rather than a specialist. He becomes more concerned with major policy questions and may assume major managerial responsibilities.

Our pattern of education for the public service fails to recognize the hourglass nature of career development. We think of education in two distinct segments, pre-entry and continuing, and we pay a great deal more attention to the former than the latter. We view pre-entry education as laying the groundwork for the career even up to the executive level, with continuing education providing for a refurbishing of skills and the acquisition of new skills on an ad hoc, as needed basis. A good deal of continuing education is offered by governmental jurisdictions in the form of in-service training. Participation typically is on a self-selection basis, with no particular motivation to participate on the part of those who need it the most.

Rather than looking at education as a process with two distinct stages, it should be regarded as a continuing function. From this viewpoint, pre-entry education can be followed by continuing education to provide the necessary updating and new knowledge and skills as the professional becomes more specialized, as usually he must in a highly specialized public bureaucracy. However, as he approaches mid-career, the upward mobile professional should plan his education for a second career—his career as an executive. The training which permitted him to operate more effectively as a specialist is no longer appropriate. The foundation gained from pre-entry education needs to be strengthened and adapted to a changed world. Now the executive must broaden his perspective to include major segments of the organization and their relationships with the external environment. An appraisal of his educational needs and a blueprint to meet them is needed. A planned, organized program of study is appropriate. This is not to imply that anything like a repetition of pre-entry education is needed. Education for a second career may include a mix of full-time and/or part-time, university or in-service, credit or non-credit, formal or informal learning. The important thing is that it be designed for the goal of effective executive performance.

Commentary on the Davy Paper

By Sherman Wyman

ABSTRACT: Many of my reactions to the Davy paper are warmly empathic. There are, however, at least, two important issues suggested but not treated directly by the essay. What about some evaluation? To date our evaluation measures have been couched largely in terms of such criteria as quality of faculty, some generally accepted notions about appropriate core curriculum, resources for student support, and success of alumni. But little empirical data exists to substantiate which aspects of the content and skill learning featured in these programs is positively linked to the effectiveness of their graduates. We also need a better on-off campus learning mix. Graduate education in urban management need not be limited to distinct blocks of experience which are typically first totally on and then totally off campus. To sum up, if we are going to assist effectively in the development of able executives, we need mazemen and women who can insure appropriate individual and group expression and involvement without equivocating a commitment to their best sense of the communal public interest.

Sherman Wyman, after several years in a variety of local government assistant city manager roles and a Fulbright year studying local government in Norway, completed a Ph.D. in public administration at the University of Southern California. Since then he has served as assistant professor of political science and director of the Bureau of Governmental Research and Training at the University of Denver and assistant professor of political science and director of M.P.A. studies at the University of Kansas. He is currently director of the Institute of Urban Studies, University of Texas at Arlington.

THE Davy paper evokes a mixed Skinnerian response: some pleasure and some pain. But regardless of their nature, many of my reactions are warmly empathic. We have been mutually engaged lately in attempting to seek out one or more appropriate graduate education routes for learning about the management of urban mazes.

The review of the labors of the Urban Executive Management (UEM) program planning group at the University of Pittsburgh suggests they would agree there is yet much to be understood about which rewards initially attract and then best motivate this or that aspirant en route to a graduate degree in urban management. Moreover, they appear to concur that neither academics nor practitioners have a clear understanding of many of the important components of a learning model for the complex art of urban executive mazemanship. The variety of the demands of the urban settings which will be experienced by any given group of urban students defies easy generalization.

My empathy is considerable around the suggestion that the UEM group felt themselves constrained in fact if not spiritually by the realm of the possible within their university environment. In spite of this reality, the group has developed a thoughtful, flexible approach to packaging a master's level experience in urban executive education.

There are, however, at least two important issues suggested but not treated directly by the essay. Both would seem to have implications for every program in urban management and as well, for the entire universe of public affairs education.

WHAT ABOUT SOME EVALUATION?

First and perhaps most concerning is the point that the UEM curriculum planning endeavor at Pitt and similar efforts elsewhere are still largely based on a process not unlike that of the art of searching for water with a willow rod.

Techniques, reputation, and the necessary electricity are passed mystically from generation to generation. Once in the field, if the right vibrations are felt and the rod bends inexorably earthward, a well is sunk. But no accurate scores are kept on the effectiveness of one practitioner of this trade versus another in consistently locating superior sources of water. And little comparative evaluation data exist on such recent innovations as the use of various types of wire and pipe rather than willow.

We are really not much beyond water divining when it comes to evaluation of approach A versus approach B in urban or general public affairs education.[1] To date our evaluation measures have been couched largely in terms of such criteria as quality of faculty, some generally accepted notions about appropriate core curriculum, resources for student support, and success of alumni. Certainly these elements are not irrelevant. They, in part, explain the considerable success during the past two decades of such urban programs as those at Kansas and Pennsylvania.

But little empirical data exists to substantiate which aspects of the content and skill learning featured in these programs is positively linked to the effectiveness of their graduates. Indeed, it is not easy to refute the charge that much of the success of these programs and others like them is largely a function of superior recruitment and placement programs. Both of these activities are seen, in turn, as largely due to the loyalty of many alumni who understandably wish to perpetuate and enhance the image of their alma mater.

It is high time we start to measure with some rigor the efficacy of curriculums now based largely on the intellectual orientations of their faculties. This is not meant to suggest that one curriculum model can or should be universally accepted. It does mean that individual faculties need to work harder at erecting objectives for their own programs and then to develop and consistently apply meaningful evaluation procedures.

There are many benefits which regularized evaluation would generate. Certainly documentation of approaches found more effective would be of measurable benefit to others with similar programmatic interests. Another, perhaps more compelling notion, is that this kind of documentation may be necessary soon in many public systems to effectively defend the privilege of developing and experimenting with unique curriculums and modes of learning. If such patterns do not emerge, it would seem a fair bet that many of both the established and new urban and

1. Appreciation is due to Professor Jeffery Cornog for his persuasive comments on how little is actually known about the impact of graduate public administration education.

public affairs graduate programs will soon be faced with delegated objectives and allowable behaviors for reaching them from their increasingly anxious legislative patrons.

A BETTER ON-OFF CAMPUS LEARNING MIX

A second broad reaction is that the Pittsburgh plan in spite of its innovative packaging is still very much rooted in the traditional ways of configuring university learning: semester-long courses which are of a set duration and take place either on or, in the case of an internship, off campus. The integrating seminar proposal combining educational input from a team of academics and practitioners over an eighteen-month period presents an intriguing exception. But it is unfortunately offered only in brief as a tentative proposition.

Why does our thinking around graduate education in urban management have to be limited to distinct blocks of experience which are typically first totally on and then totally off campus? Does reliable information exist to substantiate that this approach adequately integrates learning from block to block? Like a number of innovative generic and business administration programs, cannot we involve ourselves and our students in some of the excitement and rewards of experiential learning at various points en route to the degree?

One counter response is that sufficient experience is usually brought into the classroom and shared effectively by those fortunate enough to have some. This assumes rather improbably that most programs enjoy a steady and balanced experience profile among their applicants and can afford to stipulate experience for a set percentage of their enrollees. And of greater issue, such a position also implies that a previous tour on the firing line is the only type of experiential referent for learning about how to manage urban places.

Experiential learning, other than the traditional internship, has not swept graduate programs in public administration by storm.[2] Many who teach the trade of public administration shy

2. Data supporting this point from a national survey of master's programs in public administration and some brief notions advocating accelerated experimentation in applied behavioral science-experiential learning can be

from designs which can put the values, knowledge, and skills proffered by the literature into an operational setting for testing and dissection—and concomitant learning.

To pick one example, most Master of Public Administration programs appear to be offering some of the recent change and organization development literature as part of a general course in the theories of organization and management. But few are providing opportunities for their students to throw these concepts up against the reality of functioning public organizations, a process, incidentally, which can provide several second thoughts about the efficacy of some of these concepts, particularly when pursued in the intimate and highly politicized environment of the urban manager.

Admittedly, it may not be easy to find local public agencies who feel they can afford the time and possible risk required to involve one or a team of students in the design and implementation of either an organizational or community-oriented change experience. It is in many ways easier to remain on campus with case studies, simulation exercises, visiting practioner-experts and then drop the student into the total emersion of a traditional internship. But these measures cannot alone provide the unique emotional and intellectual growth potential which is possible in a high intensity mix of classroom communicated content and skills and the alternatively unpredictable, rigid, wearing, pedestrian, sublime world of urban administration.

VALUES AND SKILLS OF PARTICIPATORY LEADERSHIP

I have no serious quarrel with the classification of knowledges and skills which the UEM committee developed as its planning framework. Its scope is a generally inclusive one ranging from such substantive areas as policy and program, management theory, community structure and values and ethics, to analytical and interpersonal skills.

The generalist-specialist mix of forty percent general or base courses and sixty percent specialized also seems reasonable, per-

found in "The Role of Behavioral Science in Graduate Public Administration Programs," by William Eddy and myself, a paper prepared for the 1972 national conference of the American Society for Public Administration.

haps more so than for executive roles at other levels of government. The typical urban executive must have at least a smattering of one or more specialist skills if he is to be able to effectively develop systems where this know-how simply may not exist or be within immediate reach in the form of additional budget for staff specialists.

While a devotee of providing as much flexibility as possible for tailoring programs of study to individual needs, I am somewhat worried by what may be an underemphasis in the Pitt UEM program (and others) to two related areas that increasing numbers of urban-oriented practitioners and academics agree are now critical. Some level of appreciation for, if not commitment to, the values of participatory leadership and at least a modicum of training in related ways of behaving are now as important to many urban roles as the ability to develop a personnel system or design a program budget.

Things may not be changing all that fast within city hall. But the scene around the town today is one of more highly vocalized and organized groups demanding to be in on the action. Brokerage and negotiation are now key components in the urban mazeman's skill kit.

Inside the organization, too, the advent of employee organizations and employment of change-oriented youth who took part in last year's high school demonstration are beginning to impinge on the comfortably paternalistic style of many urban supervisors.

Discussions of the appropriate values for public leadership are legend. There appears no need to unravel this yarn here. However, it might be helpful to quickly note that much of the value core that emerges in such diverse places as the new public administration literature and treatises on citizen participation carries much in common with that of the basic tenets of participatory management. That is, to behave in an open, genuine, other-regarding fashion is equally appropriate to the behavior of an urban executive in a staff meeting, collective bargaining session, or gathering of an action-oriented minority group.

I am optimistic that we can assist measurably in sensitizing aspiring urban executives to participatory values and complementary behaviors. Various configurations of interpersonal skill laboratory and outside experiential exposures appear to be promising means for getting at examination of the behavior of oneself and others and the values that underly it. Ample literature exists which treats both the intraorganizational as well as the political dimensions of the participatory movement.[3]

To sum up, if we are going to assist effectively in the development of able executives for modern large- or small-scale urban places, we need mazemen and women who can insure appropriate individual and group expression and involvement without equivocating a commitment to their best sense of the communal public interest. This group must also exhibit sufficient brokerage and negotiation talent to secure their own as well as their organization's legitimacy. And when so engaged, as Warren Bennis observed after his initial baptism in university macroadministration, they will often have to learn to live with much less than the warm consensus which can derive from an intimate microsystem experience with one's immediate administrative staff or academic colleagues.[4]

But in order to be more certain of what we are about, new curriculums such as Pittsburgh's UEM must be accompanied by some attempt to evaluate impact. In effect, the Pittsburgh proposal represents one articulation of the kind of learning deemed appropriate for urban management. We still need to know how successful this approach and others will be in actually assisting those who so aspire to function more effectively as executives in mazeful, urban places.

3. For a current overview of citizen participation by scholars and practitioners see the fall, 1972, special symposium issue of the *Public Administration Review* which is devoted to this subject. The essays are specifically intended for curriculum development and should have considerable value for programs in urban management.

4. Warren G. Bennis, "A Funny Thing Happened on the Way to the Future," *American Psychologist*, vol. 25, no. 7 (July, 1970), pp. 601–602.

Summary of the Discussion of the Davy Paper

By Frederic N. Cleaveland

PARTICIPANTS in the Symposium were again divided into smaller groups—this time into two groups—to consider this paper and the commentaries prepared in advance. The two groups moved in substantially different directions and this analytical summary draws upon both small groups as well as discussion in plenary session.

One group turned its attention to broad, general issues about the nature of learning. From this beginning the group evolved through discussion a provocative conception of the role of a university as a center of learning. This conception then served as a background against which to examine the more immediate issues of what to teach and how to teach. The general objective in educating potential urban administrators is to go beyond the imparting of specific knowledge and skill to develop in students a sense of the learning process as a continuing experience through life. The essense of such a learning process consists of four distinct components. First, the learning process involves imparting cognitive knowledge—in this case developing in learners increased understanding of substantive matters about government and public affairs on the urban scene. This might include instilling greater awareness of urban areas as complex social systems, the nature of specific problems in particular urban areas, and the social, political, and economic dimensions of urban life.

The second component is skill training to develop in students specific capabilities in identifying and analyzing problems and in formulating alternative policies and choosing among them. Also involved is the sharpening of managerial skills, and developing abilities in areas of continuing importance such as budgetary analysis, personnel administration, and organizational analysis.

A third essential part of the learning process is the "affective" dimension, that is the process of sensitizing aspiring urban administrators to the importance of interpersonal relations and developing in them the capacity to relate effectively to other people. It is crucial that those seeking professional training for careers in administration learn early in their professional education to grasp the dynamics of interpersonal and intergroup relations within a bureaucratic setting. Some symposium members felt that students often gained much understanding about the affective dimension of learning through their personal experiences as members of a cohesive group of students in a defined instructional program. The so-called "bloc program"* in the view of a number of symposium participants has developed strong loyalty and "in-group" identification among students. Also those schools, institutes, and departments which have worked to keep up with their alumni, and have involved students, alumni, and faculty in periodic and frequent interaction about current issues and problems of substance in the urban field have generally succeeded well in providing students a learning experience rich in its affective dimension.

Finally, the fourth essential component of the learning process is to build into students the capacity to move readily and without strain or discontinuity from the concrete to the abstract. This skill involves the ability of an aspiring professional to gain transferable knowledge through his continuing clinical experiences in the real world. He must be able to move from a concrete "happening," through the process of reflection about the full meaning of the concrete event, to the crucial stage of evaluating the event and its importance and placing this concrete reality in the setting of generalizations which can give it broader significance. Finally, this process sets the stage for reexamining the context surrounding the "happening" in order to weigh the alternative courses of action or behavior available and thus illuminate the choice among these alternatives. This capacity to gain transferable knowledge by moving from concrete reality to ab-

---

* A "bloc program" would be one in which all students worked together one course at a time through the year. Thus the first three weeks might be fully devoted to the study of the administrative process; then all students would move together to the course in personnel administration for two and a half weeks; then, the course in fiscal management for four weeks, and so on. This "bloc" or "end-on-end" course program has been offered for many years at the Maxwell School of Syracuse University as one of the alternatives open to students seeking the Master of Public Administration degree.

stract reality is crucial to effective decision-making in a practice
field like urban administration.

From this formulation of the learning process the group moved
readily to discussion of the implications of this conception for
the role of the university. The objective of the university is to
create a climate which facilitates self-learning among all its students and faculty. Regarding students the university's objective
is to develop in each "learner" a clear sense of learning as a
continuing, life-long experience and a clear commitment to self-
learning. The university begins its work with a new student by
helping him to define his own learning needs. This calls for
faculty members to perform the essential role of "learning counselors." From this start, guided by an assessment of the student's
learning needs, the faculty members help the student to identify
the resources of the university which may be able to meet his
defined learning needs. Curriculum in this context becomes the
design of an individualized learning experience. The faculty
guides the student's selection from among the university's resources including courses, alternative methodologies, and approaches, and helps to chart the student's way through the
"learning terrain" which is the university. Such a conception of
the university emphasizes: student self-direction; the provision
of many resources to be fitted together or "packaged" in many
different ways; the student choosing with faculty help from
among these many resources those which fit his learning needs.
But does this model of the university make unwarranted assumptions about student maturity? Is it a model more appropriate to
the description of the university role in continuing education
(see discussion of the Sherwood paper)?

The second group of symposium participants turned their
attention more directly to conclusions about the proposals in the
Davy paper. Their conclusions fit remarkably well with these
general prescriptions set forth above which emanated from the
first group. Top priority, as viewed by members of the second
group, should be given to what Professor Davy calls the "development of integrating skills" through problem-solving seminars.
In planning such seminars, issues to be used as organizing themes
should be chosen because they tap the normative impulses of
students. Too often faculty members select the problems to be

examined without student input, with the unfortunate result that students work on issues outside the core of their central concerns.

Participants agreed in substantial numbers that experiential learning organized around some form of clinical field work is significantly more powerful in its impact on students than vicarious learning. Yet such clinical experience must be integrated into both theory and the systematic literature in relevant disciplines. To permit gaps to occur between library and classroom learning focused on theory and principle and the learning which comes through direct experience is to lose perhaps the best opportunity for developing integrating capabilities in students.

Also, note was taken of the many different forms which clinical experience may take from the widely employed internship in public affairs, to the medical school's intern experience, and the apprenticeship model utilized in a number of professions in earlier generations.

One significant by-product of the clinical experience is likely to be increased interaction between the administrator-trainee and the seasoned practitioner. Other ways to involve practitioners of urban administration in the educational process were also explored. Bringing the skilled city manager into the classroom as a regular faculty member was widely applauded, but participants agreed that it seldom happened. One experienced city manager observed that the best time to attract one of his professional colleagues to the campus for more than a one-shot performance would be when he is between professional assignments. Most agreed that the really skilled urban manager should not be subverted permanently from his active career, but a brief sojourn on campus for a term or two can actually strengthen his professional capacity as an urban administrator. Finally, there was agreement that such an active practitioner should be accorded full academic title and prestige if a university is to expect to attract the best qualified practitioners to participate actively as faculty in its professional training program for urban administration.

Symposium participants observed that requirements associated with effective professional education for urban administration pose significant demands upon the contemporary university. These include in particular demands for increased flexibility, for greater diversity in programs, and for creative new approaches to learning. The requirement that the university find a more effective way to build the skilled practitioner into its instructional program is one illustration. The traditional reward system governing the employment and advancement of the teacher-scholar faculty member is not well suited to the urban administrator-practitioner as faculty member. He is not likely to have a research degree like the Ph.D., nor to have written scholarly books and articles. Yet in a field like urban administration his special knowledge and his rich experience in the real world of urban problems represent an indispensable set of qualifications for conducting seminars for aspiring urban administrators. On the other hand it was readily acknowledged that not all practitioners, no matter how successful they may be as urban managers, prove to be effective in the seminar room. It takes all the knowledge and experience, plus that subtle quality of the great teacher who can turn anecdotes into clear, case-study illustrations, and random experiences into evidence to support generalizations.

Another demand upon the university which works against the traditions of many academic institutions is the requirement for interdisciplinary approaches to problem identification and problem solving. As already noted, symposium participants generally endorsed the Davy proposal for seminars designed to develop integrating skills among students. Yet it was also widely recognized that such seminars to be effective must be interdisciplinary in character, most appropriately conducted by a team representing two or more disciplines or professions, and perhaps also including practitioners as well as academic scholars. To mount this kind of an instructional program is likely to be costly both in instructional dollars and in terms of effort required to overcome school, departmental, and disciplinary separatism.

A number of the participants from universities observed that the separately organized school of public administration would probably have decided advantages in coping with these demands for flexibility and innovation. If the school of public affairs is large enough and strong enough within the university it can develop a truly interdisciplinary faculty and avoid many problems of having to build and maintain tenuous bridges to other component elements within the institution. Moreover, the autonomous school of substantial size can develop its own reward system, according appropriate recognition to the contributions of practitioners and to team teaching and other forms of innovation and experimentation. The professional degree program in urban administration organized as part of a teaching department (like political science) or professional school (like a school of business administration) is much less likely to benefit from an interdisciplinary faculty of its own or a reward system for faculty ideally tailored to the needs of the professional program in urban administration.

Some symposium participants were cautiously optimistic that universities would indeed respond to these demands. They pointed to some of the presently existing schools and programs which are developing interdisciplinary approaches which seem to involve practicing urban administrators effectively, and which generally succeed in producing graduates with integrating skills. Other participants were skeptical that universities would respond to these requirements to become more flexible, innovative, and experimental in this area of public affairs professional education. Even if universities should want to respond, a number of symposium participants expressed doubts about whether these institutions can indeed provide the kind of professional education required to meet the needs of American society for skilled urban administrators. These participants proposed as an alternative the development of professional training institutions outside the higher education university system—non-university institutions like the recently established National Training Development Service. Such institutions can be designed with an interdisciplinary focus, with practitioners built into central roles, and with a concentration upon problem definition, analysis, and solution. Indeed, perhaps one of the best ways to challenge universities to respond more effectively is to develop competitive alternatives to the university for providing professional education for urban administration. Finally, the development of such non-university institutions performing educational functions in providing professional training would enrich the scene, affording new alternatives to those seeking careers in urban administration.

Most symposium participants saw positive value in such pluralism in professional education, pluralism both in the kinds of institutions providing professional training in urban affairs and in the kinds of programs or approaches available to prepare for a career in urban management.

On this issue of program content, structure, and approach the discussion of the Davy paper brought a clear endorsement of program diversity and ample choice for students within programs. Symposium participants found substantial diversity already existing from school to school; they think this wide variety in the nature of programs is likely to continue, and they believe such diversity to be desirable. Finally, participants also favored the practice of flexibility and choice within programs so that students can adapt what is offered to their own particular needs and interests. Such internal flexibility is especially important in a field like urban administration which draws its professionals from a variety of disciplinary backgrounds. Such flexibility can be essential for programs which seek to bring together students at the pre-entry stage with no prior experience, those who have already begun their professional work, and those at mid-career who are established practitioners seeking further education to equip them for top-level positions.

The University and Post-Entry Continuing Education for Urban Administrators

By Frank P. Sherwood

ABSTRACT: The role of the university in providing continuing education for the urban administrator must be assessed in the context of the university's total responsibility for their education. Pre-entry and post-entry education must be viewed on a continuum, where learning is a lifelong process. The individual and the organization must develop a learning commitment which will enable both to assume a proactive stance toward demands of their dynamic environment. Today's philosophy of pre-entry education has not accommodated to the implications of rapid societal change for leadership. Continuing education has been dependent on prevailing philosophies and approaches to pre-entry, degree-oriented education. We need to address ourselves fully to the nature of that relationship and its implications for the total education and development of urban administrators.

Frank P. Sherwood was appointed first director, Federal Executive Institute, United States Civil Service Commission, June 1968. A graduate of Dartmouth, he received his Ph.D. from the University of Southern California where he joined the faculty as lecturer in 1950. In continuous service at the university to 1968, he became full professor in 1957, and served as acting dean and director of the School of Public Administration. His assignments in federal, state, and local governments have been mainly consulting on organization and management issues as well as engaging in a great variety of training activities. He is a member of the National Academy of Public Administration and currently is President of the American Society for Public Administration.

I N A recent article in the *Washington Post,* Alice Rivlin, a
senior researcher at the Brookings Institution, provided the
basic argument of this paper when she declared that it is ". . . less
and less sensible to think of college as a once-in-a-lifetime activity
for the young." [1]

When we consider the role of the university in the education
of the urban administrator, it is appropriate to examine first the
changes that are now occurring in institutions of higher learning
today, and which can only accelerate in the future. Even if it
were determined that this society needs a group of elite urban
mandarins, it is becoming less and less likely that the educational
system of the future will be able to cater to such demands. In
fact, what is happening to our institutions of higher education is
itself a part of the reality with which urban administrators will
have to deal.

In my own lifetime I have seen a marked shift away from
the perception of college as an isolated, wholly preparatory experience to one which is far more a part of the total human experience. One of my old undergraduate college professors, who
later became president of a prestigious liberal arts college, found
it quite incomprehensible that I should have taught university
classes composed of people whose ages ranged from twenty to
fifty-five, who were in some cases preparing for their first jobs
and in others rounding out careers as administrators, and who
were in some cases taking the course for purposes of a credential
and in others simply pursuing their own strong learning needs.

These new kinds of learning situations have occurred first,
very obviously, in the major metropolitan areas of the country.
With few exceptions they are of relatively recent vintage, very
largely occurrences of the post-World War II period. We can
point to many factors that have contributed to these changes.
The move of the nation toward large concentrations of reasonably
dense population is certainly one; urban transportation, even
with its shortcomings, is another. With population concentration
and fairly good transportation, it was possible to put increased
leisure time to many uses. In short, it became feasible to work
and go to school at the same time.

1. *Washington Post,* February 9, 1972.

Further, there have been increased incentives to do so. While more will be said later about the effects of change on learning needs, there is little doubt that increased amounts of knowledge have been put to useful purpose. Rising job opportunities in a mobile and relatively prosperous society have very considerably increased the motivation to engage in learning and relearning. As the nation has become more technocratic and achievement-oriented, visible evidences of skills and knowledges have also become more necessary. New demands that all the human resources of the country be well and fully used, that is, providing equal opportunities to the total population, are rapidly broadening the numbers in the educational system far beyond projections of even a few years ago.

Such changes have inevitably produced their tensions. The costs of education are rising uncomfortably, and we do not have evidence that productivity is increasing. Indeed, in a number of institutions it has probably declined in the past twenty years. One unsettling aspect of the productivity problem has been the general reluctance to change approaches to learning in the colleges and universities. Despite the glut of ideas and information available through the various media, professors tend still to see themselves as transmitters of accumulated wisdom to the great unwashed. They see their role in fairly mechanistic, conveyor belt terms. The product is put on the line by the professor and picked off by the students, in varying amounts, of course. The idea that the professor is really the facilitator of the learning experience of others is still generally unaccepted. In this respect the institutions are facing their own identity crisis, as it becomes clear that information in and of itself has a declining value in a rapidly changing academic market place.

A review of these types of forces operating in higher education has caused Ms. Rivlin to raise the obvious question, "If one could start from scratch today, what kind of system would he design?" The picture she projects is markedly (for some, radically) different. It would have these features:

1. Higher education would be conducted on a part-time, or part-year basis.
2. It would actively involve people of all ages.
3. There would be few colleges in the traditional, Ivy League

sense; there would be many learning centers within easy commuting for most of the population.

4. There would probably still be faculties, but not in the traditional lecturing sense. Because many types of media can effectively impart information, the faculty would spend its time leading small discussions and supervising practical work.

5. General learning today would be inverted. Young persons without experience would be heavily engaged in supervised practice. Older persons with experience would be more involved in theory, in head trips, that would enable them more effectively to integrate their experiences. This approach, clearly, is 180 degrees different from operating philosophies today.

In varying measure, of course, the future is already here. The Minnesota State Metropolitan College, located in St. Paul, has already announced it will carry things further than even the model suggested above. It will not have a set of buildings designated as the university but will be located in the workplaces around the community. And it will follow through on Ms. Rivlin's prediction that the future institution will be characterized by a situation where many professors teach part time and some teach at their place of business, rather than the learning center. Apparently Minnesota State will have very few full-time faculty. Incidentally, the dean of program development of this revolutionary new educational undertaking is the former executive director of the United States Civil Service Commission, Nicholas J. Oganovic.

There are many other evidences of change in our educational institutions. Certainly the entire community college movement should not be overlooked. In the Commonwealth of Virginia, a network of twenty-four of these institutions is being created in only five years.

Partly, the purpose of these introductory comments has been to make a fairly obvious point. Our educational institutions are in at least as high change as any element in the society. In considering their role it is essential that we not freeze them in patterns which have been a part of our own experience and which we can easily assume to be immutable reality.

However, there has been another purpose in beginning this essay with a discussion of ongoing and impending shifts in the educational establishment. It is the concern for mood. Though most will agree this is a time of enormous change, the recitation of the many statistics about its rate frequently does not get to the inner, the visceral man. They tend to be ho-hum items, boiler plate. If we can appreciate what is happening to a center-piece of our stability, good Old Ivy, perhaps we can free ourselves to think more openly and creatively about what lies ahead.

There is another prefatory comment that underlies much of the motivation to write this paper.

There are institutional stakes in charting the university's role in educating urban administrators. It is my personal view that the federal government has moved well ahead of state and local governments in the recruitment, utilization, and development of its human resources. Discrepancies in salary levels are evidence of this; but it also seems apparent that the depth of leadership resources and the facilities for new learning, relearning, and up-dating are all far superior at the federal level.

To the extent that executive leadership does make a differ-ence, we may be experiencing a time when the informal factors affecting the federal balance are heavily tipping toward the cen-ter. Indeed, it appears essential that in a vital, decentralized system of government leadership resources must be shared equally among the parties at interest. It is inconceivable that local leaders can stand up to the power of the central government without a lot of help from the nation's educational institutions.

Thus, while it might be said that the propositions of this paper apply generally to all administrators, the central focus of concern is the leader in urban local government. In the vernacu-lar, that's where the rubber meets the road. It is also the point at which it is undoubtedly hardest to free up resources for the presumed esoteric rewards of training, where the anti-elitist prejudices against top management development are probably most strong, and where the administrator himself has the hardest time trading off short-term gains for long-run investments.

SIGNIFICANCE OF RAPID CHANGE FOR ADMINISTRATIVE BEHAVIOR

In 1946 Princeton University held a conference on education for the public service. It was not the first effort of this kind; but it is quite a useful bench mark. What was said at that conference might be considered to represent the best prewar thinking on the newly emergent problem of the university responsibility for the quality of American public administration. Rowland Egger, Arthur S. Flemming, and Donald Stone contributed pieces, as did the late and much loved John M. Gaus.[2]

While there were many still intriguing ideas in the papers prepared for that conference, it is interesting that the phenomenon of rapid change did not appear to be a matter of central concern. None of the papers were directed toward the problems of preparing people for a future that no one could foresee. Even with World War II, the idea of change and turbulence as a continuing fact of life had not been fully recognized, much less the problem of preparing leaders who could be comfortable with uncertainty and risk.

In a sense the discussants were still seeking the Holy Grail of public leadership, namely a body of knowledge that would best prepare a man early in his career to discharge the mantle of leadership at a later date. The notions were static, namely, that there is a body of knowledge that is valid and durable enough to make a difference twenty years later.

Today we need to raise very hard questions with respect to the viability and essential validity of this assumption.

Not too long ago, perhaps a couple of centuries back, we could transmit knowledge with the full expectation that it would be maximally useful during the lifetime of the recipient. Knowledge remained useful longer than man lived. But that situation has been changing for a very long time. Today it is not stretching reality too much to say that most knowledge has a life expectancy of five years. Man's average longevity is fourteen times that.

Unfortunately, belief in the durability of one's knowledge can have dysfunctional consequences. The knowledge cannot be wrong; and therefore the situation must be tortured to fit the principle or the dictum learned long ago. There is a tendency to universalize, to treat all situations the same. The environmental dimension is almost totally missing; and when it does appear, the tendency is to simplify it to suit the mind's pictures of how the world ought to be.

2. See Joseph E. McLean, ed., *The Public Service and University Education* (Princeton, N. J.: Princeton University Press, 1949), p. 246.

I have the personal feeling that many of the participants in the educational programs for which I had responsibility fifteen or so years ago have been rendered less effective today because of that experience. In some cases they were given tacit support in their desire to believe that education was a terminal event—to be concluded before age twenty-five. In others the 1955 body of knowledge was so deeply ingrained that any experiences or subsequent inputs of a disconforming nature simply could not be accepted. And, of course, there was the sin of omission as well as commission. We simply didn't do much to advance the basic precept that the end of all learning is more learning.

NEW TESTS OF ORGANIZATION EFFECTIVENESS

So much for the past. What is needed today?

The question should be answered first in organization terms. The forces operating on America's traditional institutions of higher education are illustrative of the fundamental point that organizations must always be seen as a part of the larger social system in which they operate. The essential requirement, then, is for the organization to do those things which are consistent with the interests and the demands of the elements in the environment with which it transacts. Increasingly, organization theorists are saying that the key point of analysis should be the transaction between the organization and its environment.

In the ideal sense organizations which do not provide outputs valued by the larger system should find their resources terminated. They would cease to exist because of their insensitivity to environmental demands and inability to move in the directions indicated.

In effect this is quite a dynamic view of organization behavior; and it differs substantially from traditional theory. It rejects the idea that the major part of an organization's behavior is determined by external authority. It does not assume that whatever goals the organization pursues stay in place very long. It discounts the machine model of organization in which the individual and his goals are totally subordinated to a larger organization interest.

It does assume high change in the society, an essential temporariness in the organization and in the way it does its business, and an increasingly complex goal structure in which the many partners at interest—both inside and outside—must bargain collaboratively on activities to be undertaken.

Given these assumptions, there emerges an important and fundamental change in the way we think about organization performance. Previously, when goals have been viewed as givens and fairly enduring, the tests of performance have tended to be instrumental. How close did we come to the target? How well did we do with the resources assigned us? When the organization takes charge of its own changing destinies, the question of what becomes far more important. It may be less consequential, for example, to be efficient than to do the things that need doing. The real test in this concept is the capacity to identify new requirements and to construct a human system that is flexible enough to respond rapidly.

For the student of government these notions of organization effectiveness have a special relevance. How many studies have there been at all levels of government, not only in the United States but in other countries as well, in which outmoded functions and organizations have been identified? Yet none of them is jettisoned. Even with a $30–40 billion budget deficit, President Nixon was not able to abolish the federal tea tasting function.

There are clearly no easy answers to these very perplexing questions, for it has to be said that the environment which demands change also has in it forces that resist change. That is why many people do not like to use terms like coping and adaptation to describe the transactions between an organization and its environment. In substantial degree the organization has responsibility beyond passive response. As some have said, the organization should have a proactive stance.

In this context we would do well to put more emphasis on the organization as a learning entity. What it does at any given time is perhaps less important that that it be conscious of what it is doing. As with individuals, an organization should be using its experience to learn how it can more effectively deal with, and serve, the elements in its environment.

In moving a total organization toward a greater learning commitment, the behavior of the leader is crucial. Again, we must identify change as the culprit which has put these additional burdens on our leaders. While still important in the influence process, authority and command have lost much of their power in today's organizations. The leader's behavior is increasingly influential in setting tones and styles for organizations. The old dictim, Do as I say, not as I do, doesn't work very well either for parents or for organization leaders.

The man at the top in local government, the person with whom this conference is essentially concerned, has to model the kind of behavior he wants from his organization. If he seeks an openness to learning in the organization, he had better be sure to be open to learning himself. Put another way, it is really quite hard to imagine a learning and changing organization led by an unlearning and unchanging leader.

The focus on the continuing development of the urban administrator is not, then, a minor, esoteric matter. It may well have a far more direct effect on the conduct of our urban business than most people have conceived.

SEPARATION OF PRE-ENTRY AND POST-ENTRY EDUCATION: BASIC PROBLEMS

Obviously, the development of motivations and aptitudes to learn as an adult and as an urban leader do not just suddenly occur. Everything depends on what has happened earlier. In this respect it is the whole education that yields the kind of person who can himself model the kind of learning style that is required of the entire organization.

Yet there has been a traditional separation of the pre-entry experience, typically called education because it is associated with degrees, from later learning, often labelled training because it does not provide credentials. It is true, of course, that not all degree-oriented education is restricted to pre-entry students. In the field of public administration, a large share of students are pursuing degrees on a part-time, post-entry basis. Yet the separation persists. Most institutions have maintained their traditional policies and practices by treating the post-entry people as if they were preparing for their first job. The curriculum requirements, the teaching methods, and the general approach is the same for the two groups. Thus all the degree-oriented courses taken by working students may be considered, for the purposes of this discussion, as in the pre-entry category.

The difference between pre-entry education and post-entry training is characteristically sharp in the minds of most academics. Yet it is clear that the separation is far more institutional and artificial than it is natural and organic. Putting education into compartments denies its wholeness and its dynamism. The more static, less developmental aspects of the process are therefore often overemphasized.

Universities have tended, as a result, to concentrate their interests on the preparation of entering personnel, rather than on the development of people on the job. Yet, as was pointed out in a study of New England executive manpower in 1969, the crisis of state and local leadership is not going to be resolved through recruitment. Those who will move into the top jobs are already working in those governments. "The problem of the New England governments in obtaining upper and middle managers is one of *development*." [3]

Predicting Tomorrow's Leaders and the Fallacies Involved

Behind the traditional distinction between pre-entry and post-entry education is, of course, a more basic issue with respect to the nature of career leadership in the public service. Even a casual review of the earlier literature of public administration makes it quite clear that our attitudes and approaches to public service education have been very much influenced by the British concept of the generalist. As a result, a predominant thrust of graduate professional education in United States public administration has been toward the preparation of an all-purpose man. Such a person is expected to possess the innate qualities of leadership, have a feel for the big picture and his place in it, and be sophisticated enough to live in, and move among, complex organizations. Unlike preparation for many other professional disciplines, pre-entry education is not expected to be particularly applicable to the man's work in the early part of his career and is expected to be maximally useful at a later time, as much as two decades hence, when he reaches top management levels.

3. Matteson Associates, *Public Managers for New England: Report to the New England Board of Higher Education*, mimeographed (Bennington, Vt: 1969), p. 23.

It is fair to say that there is now considerable disenchantment with these assumptions. The schools and programs have neither been numerous enough nor large enough to produce many leaders for the governments. Second, the governments don't seem to have gotten the message about whom they should choose as leaders. Third, the products of these schools and programs have not been all that generalist in their behavior and activities. Fourth, the traditional notions of the generalist are meshing less and less well with emerging concepts of leadership.

Any idea that there are traits positively correlated with leadership has now been pretty well abandoned. Research since World War II has agreed quite substantially on this negative conclusion. The successful exercise of leadership, as well as recruitment into the role, seems to be a result of a complex set of factors that include the makeup of the man himself and the demands of the situation in which he is placed. The capacity to influence as a leader comes from many sources, one of which is certainly knowledge of the program and problems being tackled. The belief people have in a leader's ability to navigate in the given territory is another source of influence. Thus the notion that leaders can easily move from one complex milieu to another seems realistic for only a very few fantastically competent, excessively charismatic individuals. Generally, leaders will emerge out of situations they know and in which they have learned to live effectively.

In these terms it is neither rewarding nor wise to seek to predict who will be the leader at the outset of a working career. Since situations vary so much, the risk of a mistaken prediction is high. Instead of emphasizing a job perhaps twenty years up the road, growth and development should be far more incremental. Competence is built over time; and the experience as a whole becomes, quite explicitly, the basis for effective leadership performance. In effect, the process is continuous, not discontinuous.

It is possible that the preceding paragraphs will strike the least responsive chord with those who have invested heavily in the development of urban administrators. The city manager has been the success story of American education in public administration; but, as Professor Frederick Mosher has written, the city managers are really the only generalists (as a group) in United States governments.[4]

Further, relatively few of the city managers become leaders of large, complex systems. They are, for the most part, generalists in fairly small organizational situations. And times are changing. What a manager does today in an urban, economically and socially differentiated community is very considerably different from what he did even ten years ago. It is likely there will be even further specialization in the role of the city manager. His credentials as an urban expert may be more consequential than his general management talents.

PRE-ENTRY METHOD: FOCUS ON THE TEACHER AND CONTENT

As was suggested earlier in this paper, the separation of pre-entry and post-entry education has had substantial implications for educational philosophy and method. It has likely tended to reinforce the idea of the teacher as the central figure, with his resources of knowledge to be tapped by the young and inexperienced pre-entry student. Consequently, many faculty members have a real inability to participate in more interactive, more democratic learning situations. It is not unusual for a faculty member to see almost all his value in his knowledge. Take that away from him and ask his participation as a facilitator of learning, and he will frequently regard the experience as unrewarding and totally alien to his sense of role and personal ability to contribute.

That the separation puts a great deal of emphasis on the content of the pre-entry experience was clearly evidenced in *Public Management* for February, 1972. The issue carried several articles on a major project in examining the education of urban administrators, of which this Symposium is the final piece. John K. Parker and Robert R. Cantine, in a thoughtful and quite careful analysis, attempt to come to some conclusions about the value which present urban administrators feel they received from their various experiences.[5] Fifty-seven of 103 respondents said

4. Frederick C. Mosher, *Democracy and the Public Service* (New York: Oxford University Press, 1968), p. 78.

5. John K. Parker and Robert R. Cantine, "What Are We Educating For?" *Public Management*, vol. 54, no. 2, (February, 1972), pp. 14–19.

the most important contributor to their performance was on-the-job experience; twenty-one felt their graduate professional education was most significant; fifteen their undergraduate work; and ten their continuing, post-entry education.

One obvious question is whether such retrospective evaluations have validity. Can the parts of the whole be neatly separated? Should they? A liberal arts education might seem quite irrelevant to the tasks at hand and be so judged; yet it might have made the man.

Methodological questions aside, the relatively low value assigned to continuing education is of clear significance to this essay. Theoretically, the experiences in continuing education should have had pronounced application to present work responsibilities. This presumes, of course, that continuing education is and has been an important part of the respondents' activities. However, it is more likely this was not the case. The results in the table may therefore indicate only that ninety percent of this sample of urban administrators has not seriously regarded learning as a lifelong process.

Motivation is an important dimension of continuing education. Typically, no union cards are involved. A need to learn is almost the exclusive incentive. As has been observed before, what happened in pre-entry education can have a great bearing on such incentives.

If we were to hypothesize that the respondents in the Parker-Cantine study had indeed had significant continuing education experience, there is a second set of questions with respect to the low evaluations. These involve their skills and dispositions as adult learners on the one hand and the abilities and interests of the trainers to facilitate their learning on the other. Put another way, the respondents might have been provided some very good training and development opportunities with which they were not prepared to deal. Or they might simply have been thrown back into the traditional classroom situation which they found even more abhorrent as experienced and successful adults. In either case these alternative scenarios suggest the scope of the problems we face in facilitating the growth and continuing development of urban administrators.

Undoubtedly much of our problem in bringing continuing education to a more meaningful place in the life of the urban administrator comes from our great difficulty in conceptualizing leadership and its processes. Great man beliefs do persist despite research findings, in which case about everything that is needed for effective performance is assumed to be in place at birth. More recently, there has been a dehumanization in some leadership theory, with the emphasis on role and functions. In this latter case it is not so much who the person is as it is what he does; with this assumption, it is most congenial to speak of a body of skills and knowledges possessed by the administrator. The Parker-Cantine study uses this latter perspective in its attempt to appraise the value of pre-entry education for urban administrators.

The four categories of managerial activities in which the 103 respondents said their pre-entry education benefited them most were these: determine organization structure, determine budget and other financial strategies, administer personnel systems and procedures, and determine policy and program priorities.

It is quite apparent that these are functions of the position. They say little about the human being enacting the role. Yet the higher one rises in an organization and the more complex the demands placed on him, the more important are the individual strengths and competences he brings to the role. Consider the basic abilities and skills the Committee for Economic Development has stated tomorrow's business managers need: objectively seeing and solving problems; understanding people and how to work with them effectively; skill in communicating; ability to organize and use scarce resources; ability to concentrate and apply one's self wholeheartedly; an open and flexible mind which also has a foundation of fundamental convictions and principles; and an ability to keep on learning.[6]

Learning is a personal experience; and its rewards are greatest when it quite clearly enhances individual strengths and competences. We must be very careful to build an awareness of one's self, one's potential, and one's growth needs into understandings

6. Committee for Economic Development, *Educating Tomorrow's Managers: The Business Schools and the Business Community* (New York: 1964), pp. 26–27.

and orientations toward the leadership process, particularly in preparation for leadership.

A GROWTH-ORIENTED MODEL OF LEADERSHIP DEVELOPMENT

Perhaps the best way to conceive of learning which emphasizes the individual is in terms of the human maturation process. Success in life comes as each of us discovers, develops, and uses our full potential. The application of these concepts to administration are particularly evident in the writings of Chris Argyris; but they run through the work of many others as well.[7] More generally, Harry A. Overstreet has received much recognition for his use of the concept of maturity as a basing point for personal development.[8]

Building on Overstreet's concepts, Professor Malcolm Knowles, an adult educator, has identified fifteen dimensions of maturation. Each is stated in terms of a continuum, in which one starts from a position of immaturity, such as dependence, and moves toward the pole of maturity, in this case autonomy. The other dimensions are: from passivity to activity, from subjectivity to objectivity, from ignorance to enlightenment, from small abilities to large abilities, from few responsibilities to many responsibilities, from narrow interests to broad interests, from selfishness to altruism, from self-rejection to self-acceptance, from amorphous self-identity to integrated self-identity, from focus on particulars to focus on principles, from superficial concerns to deep concerns, from imitation to originality, from need for certainty to tolerance for ambiguity, and from impulsiveness to rationality.[9]

Scrutiny of the Knowles list should help to make the point that each of us has growth needs. We need aid and perhaps

7. A personal growth model was suggested by Chris Argyris in his *Personality and Organization* (New York: Harper and Brothers, 1957), pp. 20 ff. It was later refined into his "mix model," a concept of organizational as well as individual maturity, in his *Integrating the Individual and the Organization* (New York: John Wiley & Son, 1964), p. 146 ff.

8. Harry A. Overstreet, *The Mature Mind* (New York: W. W. Norton, 1949).

9. Malcolm S. Knowles, *The Modern Practice of Adult Education: Andragogy versus Pedagogy* (New York: Association Press, 1970), p. 25.

some goading in the persistent pursuance of them. For those who aspire to top level urban jobs, there must also be the continual reminder that leadership is in large measure personal. Performance is not going to be much better than the strengths and commitments of the person in the role.

To employ a now-overdone concept, we need a system view of lifelong learning. Education cannot be compartmentalized in life; and it should not be so in our institutions. The rapid change in our society and the consequent responsibility of the individual, and particularly the urban leader, to take charge of his own learning simply must be recognized in the total education process. Professor Knowles has stated the argument briefly and very well: "It is no longer functional to define education as a process of transmitting what is known; it must now be defined as a lifelong process of discovering what is not known. What children should learn is not what the adult world thinks they ought to know but how to inquire."[10]

As one of my colleagues is fond of saying, "We have got to get away from the business of answering questions that were never asked!"

SUMMARY

The real task now is to deal with the university's total responsibility for the education of our urban administrators. Until we have faced that issue, it seems unwise to dwell on a subordinate part of the whole, such as the place of post-degree activity.

Clearly it is the argument of this paper that the whole has not been satisfactorily addressed.

Educational approaches today do not satisfactorily prepare the urban administrator with skills, aptitudes, and motivations for lifelong learning.

Today's philosophy of pre-entry education has not accommodated to the implications of rapid societal change for leadership.

The premises of pre-entry education can be sharply questioned, particularly in the degree to which they emphasize credentials as evidence of achievement and as they suggest such education is predictive of effective leadership performance later.

10. Ibid., p. 38.

The stress on pre-entry education is further evidence of the institutional problems of change which confront American higher education in moving in the directions identified by Alice Rivlin. The rewards and the resources go to pre-entry education and not to the more suspect public service—continuing education—activities.

In effect, continuing education has been very much dependent on prevailing philosophies and approaches to pre-entry, degree-oriented education. We need to address ourselves fully to the nature of that relationship and its implications for the total education and development of urban administrators; and it has been the purpose of this paper to bring some of its key dimensions to the attention of this conference. Hopefully, these discussions will lead to perspectives which will give more emphasis to learning as the basic means by which both individuals and organizations grow and change to meet rapidly shifting demands and challenges.

Commentary on the Sherwood Paper

By Don L. Bowen

ABSTRACT: Sherwood focuses on the long-run goals of educating urban administrators but has less to say about how we achieve them. Much as we may deplore the prevailing philosophies and approaches to pre-entry, degree-oriented education, the fact is that it does provide a base, something to work with, in dealing with continuing education concerns that is largely nonexistent in the case of public administration. Pre-entry programs are urgently needed in light of the demand caused by the drastic increase in public service employment and the increasing importance being attached to governmental functions. Sherwood's idealism with regard to the value of learning must be tempered by a regard for measurement or evaluation of educational programs. This pressure for measurement must be reckoned with in both producer and consumer dimensions. Perhaps, the best approach is to keep pre-entry and post-entry together and to blend public administration with other speciality endeavors.

Don L. Bowen has been both a professor of government and active in public administration since he received his master's and doctor's degrees from the University of Denver and Syracuse University respectively. He has taught at the University of Oklahoma and the University of Maryland and is now professor of political science and chairman of the public administration program at the University of Arizona. He served with the Oklahoma Legislative Committee, and was executive secretary to Congressman John Jarman of Oklahoma. His association with the American Society for Public Administration from 1956–70 included service as executive director from 1962–70. He is a member of the National Academy of Public Administration.

THE Sherwood paper does justice to his usual knowledgeable reflective, and more than occasionally provocative self. And with most of what is said I would probably be in warm agreement—if he had said more.

266

By this I mean I liked his analysis setting forth what our situation is. And by implication, particularly reference to the Alice Rivlin model, he had a good bit to say about where we should be. But he had a lot less to say about how we get from here to there and what happens in the interim.

This is a loss because clearly much of what he has in mind for the university and post-entry continuing education for urban administrators comes under the heading of long-run goals. But this is one of those instances in which we can't think usefully just in long-run terms. Many of our urban administrator needs are of right now! And what happens now will have a great deal to do with what happens long-run.

Moreover we cannot start from scratch as Ms. Rivlin postulates. In the university system with which we are concerned there are vast institutional, individual, and other commitments that are just not amenable to overnight change. And, even if they were, there are some that probably should not be changed because they are during the interim at least productive. Others that appear to be a drag as things presently stand may in reality provide a base of unexpected but much needed support for some of the changes that I suspect all at this conference would welcome.

The long and short of it is that while we are pursuing strategies such as Sherwood suggests we also will and ought to be doing something else. It is to these intermediate activities, in whatever that time frame is, that my comments on his paper are directed. And in this context the principal culprit in his analysis—pre-entry, degree-oriented education—emerges in a somewhat better light. Not as a hero to be sure, but at least as a modus operandi that offers substantial promise for providing a fuller response to some of the more immediate urban administrator needs in post-entry continuing education, as well as Sherwood's more ultimate goals.

And here it may be well to emphasize that, for me, preparing urban administrators is part and parcel of the larger objective of developing university public administration capacity more generally and an objective to be pursued as much in the interests of the urban administrator as the public administration community more broadly. Government executives are all of the same genus, if not species, and in their development more is to be gained by working with what they have in common than dwelling on differences.

TWO TACTICAL ADVANTAGES OF DEGREE-ORIENTED EDUCATION

In a number of ways, Sherwood sets the stage for my urging that we take a further look at degree-oriented education before it is jettisoned, but perhaps most directly in discussions of its relationship to post-entry continuing education. In the final paragraph of his paper, for example, he says, "In effect, continuing education has been very much dependent on prevailing philosophies and approaches to pre-entry, degree-oriented education. We need to address ourselves fully to the nature of that relationship and its implications for the total education and development of urban administrators."

Before encountering those two sentences, I had read with much approval his argument that learning is a lifelong process. Illuminating, too, was his analysis of some of the current problems of university continuing education including nonteaching-oriented teachers, compartmentalization of disciplines, rising educational costs, and the low value often attached to continuing education, both by individuals and participating organizations including the university itself.

But I was reading what Sherwood had to say in the light in which I think it was intended—as a critique of the total university system and its central and customary thrusts. Specifically, I had in mind, or it seemed to me that what he said was most pertinent in the case of, university programs in engineering, education, business, law, and medicine in terms of professional schools. I saw like application in departmental disciplines such as mathematics, English, psychology, and so on. All of these endeavors have in common that they are a highly visible and firmly established part of the university organization with substantial faculties, student enrollment, and concomitant capacities for research and community service. All also have a full range of programs and degrees, undergraduate through the doctorate.

Referring again to Sherwood's two sentences cited above, there are many ways, both substantively and organizationally, we can direct our attention to the relationship between endeavors of this level of university development and post-entry continuing education. Experience of both great depth and breadth is readily at hand. But to bring urban administration into the picture, even including public administration more generally, greatly alters the character of the conversation. In only a handful of institutions would there be anything like parallel treatment. As one measure of differences, for example, there are probably less than three dozen institutions in the entire country offering an undergraduate degree in public administration and not more than three of these with undergraduate programs offer a doctorate (D.P.A. or Ph.D. with comparable emphasis) in public administration.[1] And regardless of the range of degree offering, few would argue that except in isolated instances do any of these programs have the standing on their campuses characteristic of the professional schools and disciplines cited above.

Much as we may deplore the prevailing philosophies and approaches to pre-entry, degree-oriented education, the fact is that it does provide a base, something to work with, in dealing with continuing education concerns that is largely nonexistent in the case of public administration. Under these circumstances one wonders if perhaps the best bet for university post-entry continuing education for urban administrators isn't first to see to its establishment on university campuses in so-called pre-entry programs.

In addition to its base providing function, I could also argue for the value of this approach on other grounds. It seems to me that degree granting programs, though initially largely designed for pre-entry purposes, are rapidly changing. In any event, they are serving some forms of post-entry continuing education reasonably well in addition to their pre-entry function. A somewhat removed but still relevant beginning is experience with post World War II and current GI bill students who bring with their military interrupted careers a kind of continuing education note to pre-entry programs. More in point are the off-campus

1. Figures based on preliminary findings of 1971–72 National Association of Schools of Public Affairs and Administration survey of public affairs and administration programs at 108 institutions, presumably close to the total number of American senior colleges and universities offering anything called or otherwise resembling a public administration degree in any of its several forms, many of marginal strength at best.

offerings of some institutions in large metropolitan areas—programs staffed, scheduled, and otherwise designed very much with the on-the-job-student in mind. Also relevant are the on-campus, full-time student enrollments composed of military and other early retirees looking to second careers.

Aiding and Abetting Forces

Now let me turn from the working within the system values that so-called pre-entry urban administration degree-oriented programs may have—and the desirability of getting more of them on the books—in behalf of post-entry education to some of the forces at work that are especially pertinent to such considerations. These forces also have profound consequences for further development, both in size and character, for those public administration programs, urban-oriented and otherwise, already in being. This latter category is a drastically different and smaller universe than we'd like. It nonetheless has an urgent relevancy because the continuing development of urban administrators will not wait. And though of a finger-in-the-dike kind of dimension in what these programs can do in post-entry continuing education, they are at least that much a factor. They are also a focal point of interest in terms of the models they may develop as guides for their kindred but still to be born counterparts on other campuses.

One of these forces on the demand side is the sheer weight of numbers. Frederick C. Mosher in the paper he prepared for this Symposium helps make this point with the conclusion that ". . . while we are producing surpluses in graduate degrees in a great many academic and some professional fields the demand for graduates in public administration and public policy is growing far beyond the supply." Figures not available at the time his paper was prepared lend specificity to the magnitude and character of this demand. Estimates released earlier this month indicate that job opportunities in state and city government will increase forty percent before the end of this decade. This is double the growth rate for the labor force as a whole. More than 750,000 positions in state and local government are destined to become a part of the national job market each year. Approximately 250,000 of these are openings for administrative, professional, and technical workers. And while for reporting purposes local and state needs are lumped together, well over two-thirds of those to be employed will likely be working in local, primarily urban, government.[2]

Another consideration might be summed under the heading of increasing regard for those in public service administration. Contributors to this growing esteem range from rapidly increasing public service compensation levels to the fact that the problems urban administrators are called upon to deal with are no longer remote and unimportant or menial. Concern with garbage collection is now escalated into regard for total environmental quality. Learning the three R's is more and more linked with social values such as racial equality, economic opportunity, and integrating the ofttimes separating generations.

This growing importance attached to public administration is reflected by rapid establishment of new and accelerating development of existing public administration programs on the college campus. Until a few years ago institutions with strong programs could be counted on one hand. Within the past decade another handful has been added. Now change without precedent is in the wind. Large-scale public administration curriculum and research adjustments are under way on more than a dozen major campuses over the country including Indiana University and the Universities of Chicago, Georgia, and Colorado all aimed at developing greater capacity in the public administration sector. If smaller institutions were made part of the tabulation the number would rise several fold, for example, University of Massachusetts at Boston, University of Nebraska at Omaha, Sagamon State University, Georgia State University, Drake University, and San Jose College to name just a few that come to mind.

A good bit of this public administration/affairs campus activity is being supported by other professional schools, just as these schools some years ago were helping in the development of programs in business administration. Central in this assist is the growing importance of government at all levels and the new interest of students in other professional schools in the public as well as the private sector. Those responsible for engineering,

2. Figures reported by Sylvia Porter, "The Job Picture—IV," *Arizona Daily Star*, May 11, 1972.

medicine, business, architecture, and other university enterprises with solid professional school standing are looking for a public administration/affairs component that can be made a part of their curriculum options. The combined interests of economy and strength of scale lead increasingly to identification and development of a university-wide center of public administration/ affairs that in addition to contributing in its own right can be used by professional and other academic specialities.

At least one other factor of major import to the establishment of new and further development of existing urban administration programs deserves mention. It stems largely from the growing concern over educational costs. Following a decade of rapid expansion in higher education, the mood of the country is much that a time for some consolidation has come. While there will continue to be some new dollars, the flow, especially from federal sources, will not remotely resemble that of recent years and adjustments and innovations will largely stem from internal realignments and stratagems. Among other things this portends a greater likelihood that an institution will become more itself and look to its own needs and resources rather than to what is happening in the Big Ten or the Ivy League. Hallmark of this development will be a new order of diversity. And it seems fair to say that, to the degree urban power means political power, colleges and universities, especially publicly supported institutions, will become more and more identified with urban problems, including the care and feeding of their administrators.

THE MATTER OF MEASUREMENT

The Sherwood paper makes an ardent and convincing argument in many different ways for the value of learning as a lifelong process and the role in this process that can be played by continuing university education. But little is said by way of measuring that value except by the implication that it will be proved in the crucible of experience. While I greatly admire the idealism of that view, it leaves the matter of education so much in the act of faith realm that it is not likely to generate the kind of participation any place that is required to do the job that needs doing. Measurement in education is now much more an issue than it has ever been before and it takes a number of forms.

Kindred concepts include accountability, accreditation, and degree granting.

The first of these, accountability, is now turning up on many fronts, especially in the halls of state legislatures in the case of publicly supported institutions. Reasons for this new concern for performance are numerous and little would be gained by detailing them here except to say that the motivation to assess performance and fix responsibility is more and more a part of university funding relations.

A related accountability interest is the heightened visibility being given higher education accrediting activities. While university and many other administrators openly resist new accreditation efforts, they at the same time take pride and in a measure feel that their leadership capability has been demonstrated when the accrediting body takes positive action, an action that can range all the way from proclaiming the university's total well-being, as through a Middle States' visitation, to certification by more specialized accrediting bodies in nursing, urban planning, and the whole spectrum of university programs subject to such external scrutiny. No legislator, governor, or university president wants a medical school that is not accredited. Nor does any student want to be a participant in such an enterprise.

At the other end of the continuum are boards of licensing and certification that legitimize or deny the student's entry into the field of endeavor he has looked to university education—continuing and otherwise—to prepare him for. Graduating from an accredited program of higher education is a minimum requirement in most licensing qualifying procedures in occupations with public administration import.

Even in those areas where licensing is not operative, some recognition of educational effort and achievement is often essential, and if not essential almost always warmly sought by the individuals concerned. Likewise many organizations supporting educational activities of individuals also want some minimum assurance that the performance of their participant was satisfactory, even to the point of insisting that agency underwriting of the educational costs is dependent upon satisfactory program completion. In cases where credentialing of individuals is not done by the university it may be taken over for all effective purposes by a professional association, for example, as the American College of Hospital Administrators has done in the case of hospital administrators.

Thus, rightly or wrongly, the pressures for measurement, or something that looks like measurement, have to be reckoned with in both producer and consumer dimensions. In light of these considerations I wonder if Sherwood's disposition against pre-entry curriculums as presently existing, largely on the grounds that they fall into his unacceptable system of degree-oriented education, would nonetheless want to see some form of measurement both of programs and individual performance in those programs as an unavoidable and practical component of the university's role in post-entry continuing education.

SUMMARY

An argument has been made that in any area of learning the relationship between so-called pre-entry degree-oriented and post-entry continuing education is integral, or at least of high dependency. For the most part public administration in its urban or any other form is not established, or at best weakly established, in the university system. This is the first problem to overcome.

One conceivable approach to getting it on the campus would be to ignore pre-entry relationship and attempt establishment in the post-entry dimension only. But I doubt either the feasibility or desirability of such endeavor. Going it alone in post-entry continuing education, even if separation from its pre-entry interests were feasible in terms of campus power structures, would at best make awkward—and likely impossible in many institutions—equally vital relationships. I have reference to urban administration relations to other specialties.

Like public administration more generally, urban administration always happens best in conjunction with some other substantive field. People are usually not just urban administrators. They are urban health administrators, urban transportation administrators, urban police administrators, and so on. More than any other professional endeavor, urban administration is an overlay—some would call it hyphenated—profession. This reality argues forcefully for close ties with other professional schools and academic disciplines. Though the precise mix may vary, keeping it all together—pre-entry and post-entry and blending public administration and other speciality endeavors—has many gains. Few would argue that the university system does not need and is not undergoing change. Perhaps modifications in view are more urgent for urban administration than other higher education enterprises. But from every standpoint being a part of each part of that system is the essential first step in university preparation of urban administrators, both in terms of strategic urgency and long-range significance.

Commentary on the Sherwood Paper

By Morris W. H. Collins, Jr.

ABSTRACT: In his paper, Frank Sherwood proves once again that his knowledge of the problems and needs of continuing education for the public service is unexcelled. There is full agreement that a vastly increased program of continuing education is needed for state and local governments, and on the fallacy of making a sharp distinction between pre-entry and post-entry education for the public service. The primary concern here is that he has failed to grapple with some of the major problem areas faced by the universities in expanding continuing education opportunities for urban administrators. First, attitudes toward continuing education: it is looked upon as a secondary concern of the university; it is a lower order of activity. Second, university structure: the overall organizational structure in most universities is not designed to favor continuing education. Third, dollars: to achieve the radical restructuring along the lines envisaged by Frank Sherwood would involve tremendous sums of money. Fourth, academic rigidity: perhaps more important than money are the rigidities in the universities which operate against expanding continuing education opportunities for urban administrators. Despite these constraints, a prime conclusion is that urban administrators themselves can probably get the kind of continuing education they want from the universities, if they are willing to organize and press their cause.

Morris W. H. Collins, Jr. is director, Institute of Government and professor of political science, University of Georgia, Athens. He is a graduate of the University of Georgia and received his Ph.D. from Harvard. He has served on several state and federal commissions, has been active in the American Society for Public Administration conferences on continuing education, training, and university government research and is president, National Association of Schools of Public Affairs and Administration.

I N HIS paper Frank Sherwood proves once again that his knowledge of the problems and needs of continuing education for the public service is unexcelled. There can be little disagreement with most of what he says; it is with what he does not say that this critique paper will be most concerned. Specifically, this critique will deal more fully with some of the concrete problems faced by universities in providing post-entry continuing education for urban administrators, problems which Sherwood either omits or deals with only casually.

Recognizing, however, that a critique should do more than discuss what the critic thinks are significant omissions, the present discussion will deal first with the Sherwood paper itself, with agreements and disagreements.

Agreements

Sherwood builds an excellent case on the need for continuing education for urban administrators. The stress throughout his paper on change, on the importance of the urban administrator's serving as a change agent, on the deficiency of the education of most current urban administrators in terms of meeting change— these are compelling arguments for vastly increased efforts by the universities in post-entry education for urban administrators. Sherwood also builds a good case for greatly expanding continuing education to provide incremental education throughout a lifetime rather than a one-time intramural educational experience.

There is full agreement here with Sherwood's view that a vastly increased program of continuing education is needed for state and local governments, if this nation is to maintain a viable federal system. There is a tremendous catching up job to be done in terms of the educational competence of state and local officials.

This critic feels, then, that Sherwood has made a good case on the needs for continuing education in the urban administration field. Indeed, the feeling here is that as one looks ahead, the needs will become ever more acute at an accelerating rate, that we are in for real trouble if the universities and public officials do not take bold and imaginative steps to meet these needs.

There is also strong agreement with Sherwood on the fallacy of making such a sharp distinction between pre-entry and post-entry education for the public service. This can be taken a step further to decry also the sharp distinction drawn between credit (degree-oriented) and non-credit education. It is oftentimes difficult to distinguish between such education; and there seems to be a growing number of cases where non-credit continuing education is in many respects indistinguishable from the more prestigious credit instruction.

Finally, Sherwood's indictment of the universities throughout his paper for what they teach and how they teach it, particularly in public administration, will find substantial agreement in many quarters. It is not the indictment but his exaggeration of it which leads to disagreement.

DISAGREEMENTS

For one thing, Sherwood exhibits a rather narrow concept of knowledge. He apparently is speaking of idiographic knowledge—the concrete, the specific, the unique. Knowledge is, of course, much broader than this. He himself speaks of education as embracing skills, aptitudes, and motivations. The truth is that the universities are not doing nearly so bad a job of teaching as Sherwood and many in the public service today are claiming.

Further, it is well known that university schools of public administration and public affairs train only a tiny fraction of urban administrators; most of them come out of other professional schools and colleges; and even the social sciences train only a small fraction of urban administrators. And these other discipline areas of the universities are generally doing a better job of teaching than public administration and the social sciences. Those urban administrators coming out of such fields as engineering, landscape architecture, planning, and public health, to name only a few, are not being taught for the most part by instructors who see their roles in fairly mechanistic, conveyor belt terms. They are acquiring basic professional skills with a heavy dose of practical application. One can decry the fact that they receive so little preparation for subsequent urban management positions; but, under Sherwood's concept, with which there is full agreement here, this incremental part of their education might well come later anyway.

It is ridiculous to say, as Sherwood does, that most knowledge has a life expectancy of five years. This is gross exaggeration! Many have said for a long time that knowledge is becoming obsolete at a very fast rate, but not at this rate. It is probably nearer the truth to say that the half-life of most knowledge today is about ten years.

But why argue degree? What is more important is that much knowledge is timeless—basic knowledge, for example, of the scientific method, knowledge, which might be classed in a very broad sense as a skill or even as an attitude. Knowledge of philosophies would also seem rather timeless, although here again one could argue that the way in which this knowledge might be perceived is changing rapidly. But the wide range of skills which one hopes are being taught in our universities today, particular skills such as written communication, these are timeless.

Problems of universities in expanding continuing education for urban administrators

It can be seen, then, that there is no great disagreement with what Sherwood says. The primary concern here is that he has failed to grapple with some of the major problem areas faced by the universities in expanding continuing education opportunities for urban administrators. Having made as fine a case as he does on the need for post-entry continuing education and having pictured the kind of education needed, it would seem to this critic most important to discuss, at least briefly, some of the problems which universities face in expanding, even in moderate degree, their programs of continuing education.

The remainder of this paper, then, will attempt to delineate some of these problems, to note the prospects of overcoming them, and to set forth possible actions that might be taken toward their solution.

Attitudes

Sherwood alludes to the problems which universities have with attitudes toward continuing education. It is the belief of this critic that this is one of the most fundamental problems faced by the universities in expanding continuing education programs. Continuing education is looked upon as a secondary concern of the university; it is a lower order of activity.

It would be a mistake, however, to treat these attitudes as monolithic within the university community. Top executives and governing boards evidence a considerable desire to respond to pressures from the outside for expanded programs of continuing education for the public service. These executives and board members, particularly those of public universities, recognize that their sustenance derives from some of the very public officials who are demanding increased continuing education, particularly from governors and legislatures. One can predict increasing pressures on top executives and board members of the universities to provide greatly expanded programs of continuing education for the public service, particularly for urban administrators. One can just as confidently predict that these top executives and administrators will respond as best they can to these pressures.

The attitudes of academic administrators, those concerned primarily with residential teaching, are quite different. These deans and department heads are primarily concerned with on-campus, degree-oriented teaching. Unfortunately, in many universities these are the persons who determine promotions and other rewards, not only of academic teaching personnel but of those engaged in continuing education as well. Very often faculty members who engage extensively in continuing education are looked on as second-class citizens; and some of these academic administrators view continuing education as a polluting or corrupting activity within the university.

But these academic administrators are, in the end, subject to control of the top executives and to the boards; they are not a law unto themselves. Though there is admittedly a long way to go, there are signs that these administrators are changing, that they are beginning to give more recognition to the continuing education function. In at least one institution, extensive criteria for promotion have been formulated for those involved primarily in continuing education; and this activity is counted toward the promotion of even those who are engaged primarily in academic teaching.

As to the professors themselves, it probably is not exaggerative to say that the overall majority of liberal arts professors have looked on continuing education as a definitely inferior sort of activity. In many universities, senior faculty members have re-

sisted any expansion in continuing education. Again there are
signs that a new day is dawning. Young professors in the social
sciences, young law professors, and younger teachers in other
disciplines are becoming more socially aware, particularly of the
problems of the cities of this nation. In part due to the influence
of students, they also are becoming more aware of the importance
of practical laboratory experiences for students in the social realm.

In a more crass vein, we also know that financial inducements
are now being offered which are rather compelling for many of
these professors. An important item for the action agenda must
be to make rewards even more attractive, to corrupt these faculty
members even more, if you will. Other rewards must also be
developed for meritorious accomplishments in continuing education, concrete rewards such as faster promotions and larger pay
increases.

Organization

Sherwood speaks of the need for universities to go outside the
walls, for radically restructuring the university to do much of
its teaching on the job, in the organization. Such a radical restructuring is appealing and probably should be the long-range
goal. But this critic is much more interested in taking the next
step, in modifying the present organization of the university to
the extent that a much more effective range of continuing education opportunities can be made available to urban administrators.

In most universities today, the overall organizational structure
is not designed to favor continuing education. As noted above,
this activity often gets secondary consideration, being subjected
to the control of administrators primarily concerned with residential teaching. There are evidences, however, that more and
more universities are organizing extramural education functions as
an independent activity, directly under the university's top
executive—for example, having a vice-president for services.
Such organization assures that the special needs and conditions
of continuing education will receive the special consideration
which they must have.

Another major problem in university organization for continuing education has been how groups of institutions could form
consortia to render more effective continuing education programs

Interinstitutional cooperation is, of course, a difficult and complex matter; but, again, there are signs that progress is being made. The sheer cost of providing effective continuing education opportunities for urban administrators and others will probably bring about a great deal of such multiinstitutional cooperation.

In considering university organization, we must not overlook the rapid growth in recent years of schools of urban affairs and similar programs at colleges throughout the nation. Most of these programs lay heavy stress on post-entry continuing education activities for urban administrators.

Dollars

To achieve the radical restructuring of this nation's higher education system along the lines envisaged by Frank Sherwood would involve tremendous sums of money. Lifelong education is an admirable goal, but to give the people of this country, including urban administrators, this opportunity will involve astronomical sums of money.

It is crystal clear to all who are engaged in continuing education that the lack of dollars has been a real problem. The universities have conceived their prime mission to be the education of degree-oriented students. For the most part, they have taken the stand that continuing education must be, at least largely, self-supporting. It is easy to rant about the waste of higher education dollars. Frank Sherwood's comments on the outputs of organizations are very much to the point here. Certainly most of us would agree that many of our higher education organizations rank poorly on the output scale.

As a practical matter, the most pressing fiscal problem is probably the reallocation of resources, not just the procurement of large additional sums of monies. At least some universities are beginning to institute more effective budgeting procedures, call it program-planning-budgeting systems, zero-based budgeting, or what have you. At the least, some institutions are beginning to ask questions about output and do something in the nature of program planning. In the case of public institutions, governors and legislators are asking ever harder questions about what the public is getting for its tax dollars and about the efficiency and effectiveness of educational practices.

The truth is that the necessary dollars may not be too hard to come by. It is a truism, of course, that what society really wants it will pay for. If we decide that we really want effective continuing education for urban administrators, we probably will see it funded. Then, too, many of us engaged in continuing education in the universities believe that post-entry education for urban administrators can be made at least nearly financially self-sufficient.

We also see in the offing large additional sums for these purposes from the federal government, particularly from the Intergovernmental Personnel Act (IPA) program. The new National Training and Development Service (NTDS) recently launched by the big six public service organizations (the six major organizations of state and local government officials) with Intergovernmental Personnel Act funds and a Ford Foundation grant also offers hope of at least some supplemental funding.

Rigidities

Perhaps more important than money are the rigidities in the universities which operate against expanding continuing education opportunities for urban administrators.

Conventional instructional methodologies have been deplored by one and all, including Sherwood throughout his paper. Likewise, the structuring of practically all higher education teaching to conform to degree requirements and the overwhelming stress on credit education present rigidities that will be difficult to overcome. Finally, the rigidity of where and when instruction is offered has been a real barrier to effective post-entry continuing education for urban administrators. Too often courses have been scheduled on college campuses far removed from where the urban administrators work and live. Too often, also, these courses have been offered at times or in time frames which made them infeasible for most urban administrators to schedule.

There are hopeful signs that each of these rigidities is being relaxed. But teaching methodology is often closely related to the dollars available. Many of the newer methods of teaching require sizable outlays of funds, not only for equipment but for a tremendous amount of preparatory research needed to teach in the more effective manner, for example, programmed instruction.

It can be expected that the increased funds becoming available will help improve instructional methodology.

The considerable growth in recent years of internships and other kinds of field experience for students is probably only a beginning. One can predict that these kinds of educational activities will increase tremendously in the years ahead.

It should be noted that teaching methodology in continuing education has often been considerably ahead of teaching methodology in residential instruction. The continuing education environment has in many cases afforded the flexibility to experiment, to try radically new techniques of instruction. Public officials could do much to foster this by insisting on more effective instructional methodology and rebelling against more traditional modes of instruction.

There are also indications that the degree as the prime award for educational achievement is being supplemented by other kinds of rewards. The current development by national and regional college accrediting associations of the continuing education unit is a hopeful sign. This is an effort to establish credit points for hours of continuing education activity which meet established criteria. These credit points will probably never lead to a degree, but they may well lead to various kinds of certifications and to other recognitions. Indeed the whole program of certification in the public service offers real hope for different kinds of rewards for educational achievement.

There are also hopeful signs that the universities are beginning to meet public officials at least halfway in providing continuing education opportunities. In degree-credit instruction, more credits are being offered through extension at off-campus locations. There are interesting moves to offer credit courses on a drive-in basis. Special courses are also being offered in one- and two-week blocks, for example, meeting intensively for one week then skipping several months and meeting for another intensive week, giving to the participant who completes it credit for a full course on a residential basis. It can be predicted that many other kinds of flexible educational opportunities of this sort, even on a degree-credit basis, will be offered.

The availability of federal funds through a variety of programs, including IPA, gives to the universities and the community colleges opportunities to offer vast new programs of continuing education. The efforts of the NTDS hopefully will do a great deal to improve the quality and effectiveness of the kinds of continuing education that will be offered.

Partnership with public officials

A really effective program of continuing education for urban administrators requires the very closest partnership between the university offering the education and the urban administrators. There has been far too little of this kind of close partnership in the continuing education of the past. Too often academicians have wrapped their mantles about them and rejected as impure the joint planning of education for urban administrators. Too often the attitude has been, here it is, take it or leave it. It seems safe to say that there will never be really effective continuing education for urban administrators until there is the very closest partnership, the most intimate involvement of urban administrators in planning with university personnel for these programs.

Even more important is the failure of public officials to become involved in supporting and fostering public service education by the universities. Other interest groups in society, particularly the professions, have made their influence felt quite strongly in the universities. The foresters, for example, make certain that there is adequate forestry education, including facilities; and they often have a great deal to say about what kind of forestry education will be offered. The same is true of many other professional groups. But the public administration community has exercised scarcely any influence on university education.

Here is a sleeping giant that needs awakening! If public officials organize, even loosely, to exert pressure on the universities to offer more effective programs in public administration, the response would probably be amazing. What is needed is an effective lobbying by public service officials for the kind of education which they want. If urban administrators want effective programs of continuing education, then urban administrators must organize to make known their wishes to the universities.

CONCLUSION

The thrust of the Sherwood paper is that effective continuing education for urban administrators is becoming an increasingly acute need. His paper envisages in bold terms the radical restructuring of the universities to meet this continuing education need.

This critique paper has, in large measure, concurred in all that Sherwood said. The primary focus here has been on some of the immediate problems faced by the universities in moving to meet these post-entry continuing education needs of urban administrators. A prime conclusion is that urban administrators themselves can probably get the kind of continuing education they want from the universities, if they are willing to organize and press their cause upon the universities.

Commentary on the Sherwood Paper

By Frederick E. Fisher

Abstract: The role of the university community in post-entry continuing education for urban administrators is not at all secure. There is currently much interest being expressed in the adult learner and the university will experience increasing competition from other institutions for the urban administrator as a specific client group.

The adult learner has unique characteristics that must be addressed if post-entry continuing education is to be successful. The continuing education system must develop an awareness for the emerging social technologies of training and development, and a capacity to deliver in new ways.

The role dimensions of the public manager are difficult and dynamic. Continuing education must be closely keyed to realities of the administrator's personal world, his organizational situation, and the larger community environment.

Continuing education for urban administration should be a vital function of the university community, but it must be reality-based and in tune with the new technologies of the developmental process.

Frederick E. Fisher is vice president of the National Training and Development Service for State and Local Government, Washington, D.C. He is a graduate of Allegheny College and has an M.G.A. degree from the University of Pennsylvania where he held a Graduate Scholarship in the Fels Institute of Local and State Government. He has previously served as borough manager of both Grove City, Pennsylvania and State College, Pennsylvania and as director, Professional Development Center, International City Management Association.

Prosecuting Attorney Thomas Foran, in a speech after the infamous Chicago conspiracy trial, said, "Our kids don't understand. . . . They just look at us like we were a bunch of dinosaurs." [1] I am haunted by the prospects of a similar response to this Symposium when its results reach the new generation of urban administrators. The list of participants is more indicative of the past than the future. As I sit pondering this response to Frank Sherwood's paper on the The University and Post-Entry Continuing Education for Urban Administrators, I wonder about those of us participating in this Symposium and hazard some guesses about the group as a select community. I'm guessing we are nearly fifty years in average age, ninety-seven percent white, 100 percent male, and a good seventy percent out of touch with reality—reality as seen by today's youth, tomorrow's urban leaders. If we are not careful, this could turn out to be one great big academic ripoff—a grandiose effort in recycling old prejudices and worn out norms.

MODELING BEHAVIOR

Frank Sherwood has stressed the importance of men at the top modeling the type of behavior they want for the organization. Learning and changing organizations require learning and changing leaders. While he says, the development of such people is perhaps most acute in local government, I'm inclined to believe the need is equally as great in our academic institutions, where future urban administrators get selected and nurtured.

I have some real concerns about the ability of the university community to adjust to new challenges, to be open and creative in a world that is in a constant state of dynamic, nervous flux. This is particularly true in the field of continuing education where the post-entry administrator has increasing options from which to draw his strength and renewal, including the private market place. While the university is still considered the primary fountain of new knowledge, it has not kept pace in the new ways of disseminating that knowledge. Even more important, from the practitioner's point of view, the university is too much in agreement with T. S. Eliot's Prufrock, who was able to rationalize his way into a state of do nothingness with the belief that "there will be time . . . time yet for a hundred indecisions and for a hundred visions and revisions. . . ."

1. Tom Hayden, *Trial* (New York: Holt, Rinehart, & Winston, 1970), p. 29.

Donald Bigelow, writing about the dilemma facing teacher education, tells us that the student protest movement is a protest against nineteenth century educational methods being applied to students who will live much of their lives, and whose children will live all of their lives, in the next century. It is a protest against colleges and universities which remain places where the professors' education may continue while the students will not start; it is a protest against the Ph.D. credit card which is validated by scholarly ghosts of the nineteenth century and universally accepted as a criterion of excellence in the twentieth; it is a protest against teachers who go to think tanks, to foreign countries—yes, even to Washington—in order to serve their country while not always serving their students. Finally, it is a protest against those who are unable to unite "the young and the old in the imaginative consideration of learning!"[2]

That's a pretty strong indictment of the formal academic scene. Whether it is true is perhaps not too important. It is perceived as true by too many, and therefore, is true.

A recent American Society for Public Administration Conference panel discussion about post-entry educational programs for the public service found some highly respected public administration professors lamenting the lack of responsiveness by their own university communities to new challenges and rapid change. The question that remained unasked and unanswered was, What are your schools of public administration doing about the problem? After all, most colleges and universities are public institutions, and yet, the academic world concerned with public administration as a discipline has allowed their mother institutions to stutter along untouched by a body of knowledge that was initially tailored to meet the needs of such public service organizations.

PA SCHOOLS—WHITHER THOU GO?

Urban administrators have traditionally looked to schools of public administration to fulfill their personal retooling needs. These schools were the logical places to turn for post-entry training for they offer a familiar face, a bit of nostalgia, and a common theoretical background. Besides, most urban administrators had

2. Donald Bigelow, ed., *The Liberal Arts and Teacher Education* (Lincoln, Nebr.: University of Nebraska Press, 1971), p. XXIX.

never been exposed to other opportunities. But, I sense that times and circumstances have changed. Improved communications, increased mobility, and the intensifying crunch of public office have all brought to the doorstep of the urban manager an increasing understanding of his professional development deficiencies and the delivery system available to meet those needs. With few exceptions, the University of Southern California being the prime one, schools of public administration are not equipped to deliver the kinds of developmental efforts so desperately needed by the urban executive.

Where does the urban administrator turn for continuing education and where will he turn in the near future? Massachusetts Institute of Technology's Sloan School of Management, traditionally concerned only with the private sector, currently offers the only several week-long program in executive development for urban managers. The University of Chicago's Industrial Relations Center has recently been mixing it up with local government types. The International City Management Association has turned to Scientific Methods and Educational Systems and Design (both private training firms), the Menninger Foundation (the psychiatric community), and National Training Laboratories (a nonprofit applied behavioral science network) for its latest training and development offerings to members. The fact is, these resources have much to offer the harassed, slightly out-of-touch public manager. All the time one wonders where the schools of public administration are.

The research done at the front end of this project indicates that the current roles being fulfilled by urban administrators are demanding more sophistication in interpersonal and negotiating skills. Many of the graduate schools for urban administrators are moving in the direction of policy formulation and quantitative analysis. While these areas of concentration might well be appropriate for pre-entry preparation, I wonder about the role of these schools in post-entry education for urban administrators. As the graduate moves up the ladder from a job that has utilized his quantitative skills effectively into a position of leadership requiring skills of a more interpersonal nature, where will he turn for support in his professional development needs? Probably not to his old alma mater if it is still cranking out the analytical types. This is a dilemma that must be faced by many graduate schools if they wish to have continuing influence on their graduates. In addition to the role requirements for professional development, the maturing individual has certain needs for personal growth that are not necessarily tied to his job responsibilities. The Menninger Foundation has had particular success in reaching executives over thirty with a developmental program that calls for a full measure of introspection. Urban administrators have different psychological needs for training and development that are quite apart from the specific job requirements, and yet, fulfillment of these needs often have dramatic effects on the exercise of leadership responsibilities.

Frank Sherwood has raised the issue of the professor as the facilitator of the learning experience of others. In large measure, it is the old bugaboo of process versus content. Too often the professor, in his pursuit of knowledge—put another way, his pursuit of the Ph.D.—is forced to concentrate his efforts on the literature and theory of his particular discipline. This rigorous exercise in self-flagellation too often leaves little room to pursue the process of learning, the development of interpersonal skills, or the basic concepts regarding behavioral change—unless, of course, these areas happen to be covered in his course concentrations.

Since the university community, in large measure, still addresses its educational responsibilities pedagogically, the new emerging art and science of andragogy remains the property of those engaged in relevant adult educational endeavors of a more vocational nature.

The education of adults is a significantly different matter from the teaching of children, and yet, formal educational systems still cling primarily to the traditional classroom format. Mid-career executives have tolerated these traditional approaches to their development in the past, but I suspect their patience grows thin. The future role of the university in post-entry training for urban administrators will depend in large measure on their ability to understand the uniqueness of educating adults and the new social technologies available for facilitating the learning experience of busy executives.

CHARACTERISTICS OF ADULT LEARNERS

Malcolm Knowles, professor of education at Boston University, has identified four crucial assumptions about the characteristics of adult learners that must be taken into consideration by those who assume the role of providing post-entry continuing education. These assumptions are that as a man matures, "(1) his self-concept moves from one of being a dependent personality toward one of being a self-directing human being; (2) he accumulates a growing reservoir of experience that becomes an increasing resource for learning; (3) his readiness to learn becomes oriented increasingly to the developmental tasks of his social roles; and, (4) his time perspective changes from one of postponed application of knowledge to immediacy of application, and, accordingly, his orientation toward learning shifts from one of subject-centeredness to one of problem-centeredness." [3]

These assumptions, if we buy them as valid, create some significant pressures upon the academic world in general, if it is to succeed in responding to post-entry continuing education. It means, among other things, that they must become attuned to the existential concerns of the individual and the institution he serves, and become able to develop learning experiences that will be articulated with these concerns. It calls for program builders and teachers who are people-centered as well as content-oriented.

There are several other dimensions to the issue of university response to post-entry education. One has been mentioned earlier and is the role of modeling behavior, and Dr. Sherwood has stressed it in his paper. All individuals and institutions are teachers in everything they do. Often universities teach opposite lessons in their organizational operation from what they teach in their educational programs. It would be useful if these incongruities could be ultimately wrung out of the system. Furthermore, there is a need to have wider participation in decision-making and a mutuality of responsibility in defining goals, planning and conducting activities, and evaluating. The involve-

3. Malcolm S. Knowles, *The Modern Practice of Adult Education* (New York: Association Press, 1970), p. 39.

ment of outsiders in the determination of these basic issues will not come easily to many university campuses.

The university is not currently in a position to impact significantly on the post-entry continuing education needs of urban administrators. There are several reasons. First, the university has seen its primary function as turning out finished products. Frank Sherwood has spoken forcefully to that dilemma. Secondly, the part of the academic community traditionally concerned with turning out urban administrators, the schools of public administration, are too often weak sisters in the institutions in which they reside. They simply do not command the respect that other schools do in vying for resources. Consequently, they are less able to respond to the demands of external program responsibilities. Thirdly, most public administration schools have not attempted to keep abreast with the newer social technologies of learning.

Finally, the competition for the urban administrator, as an adult learner, has become increasingly keen. A few academics have expressed grave concern over the initiation of the National Training and Development Service (NTDS) by the major public interest groups. They looked for reassurance that the university's role was clearly defined in the NTDS plan of action. This concern suggests an insecurity about their present role in continuing education for the public service. NTDS will take a wide-open attitude about building the network of resources to impact upon local and state governments with training and development. Already state leagues of municipalities, regional councils of government, and academic institutions of a varying nature have taken a proactive stance about their ultimate involvement in NTDS activities. In one university, it is the School of Education that has said to NTDS, "We can serve the needs of your client system exceedingly well—count us in." The NTDS has articulated a philosophy about the role for training and development in state and local government, stating that it must become an integral part of the process of government—a strategy for managing change. Who ultimately responds to that challenge with resources is more the function of the provider of the resource than NTDS. If schools of public administration are ultimately left on a siding as NTDS and its conglomerate of resources take up positions on the main track, who is to blame?

ADMINISTRATOR'S DEVELOPMENT NEEDS

Enough about the universities' problems of vying in the market place for the urban administrator as an adult learner—I would like to spend the remaining space looking at the administrator's continuing education needs. They are quite different from those of the younger, pre-entry student who has been the primary client of the university.

The urban administrator is older—that in itself creates a dynamic; successful, by his standards; out of tune with much of the new knowledge of his profession; and in a role of public leadership for which he has received very little formal academic help or support.

It is the role dimensions of the public manager that need to be addressed in any effective plan for his continuing education. "The role of the manager can be visualized as a dynamic interplay between environmental forces and pressures operating on the manager and forces originating from within the manager, his values, personality, and aspirations. Role conflict is inescapable, for there is really no way that a manager can harmonize perfectly the competing pressures emanating from within and from without." [4]

McGregor went on to say that "for the professional manager, the magnitude of role conflict is likely to increase. . . , for the environment of the modern manager is more dynamic, turbulent, and clogged than that of his counterpart operating in the relatively stable and more certain world of the nineteenth century." [5] Remembering that these remarks were made half a decade ago in the context of the private manager's world, you sense the confoundedness of the public manager's dilemma today. He is torn among his roles as legislative and policy consultant, chief executive of a complex system, public servant, community leader, and private citizen.

4. Douglas McGregor, *The Professional Manager* (New York: McGraw-Hill, 1967), p. 55.
5. Ibid.

City managers have found themselves praised for their organizational leadership acumen, but dismissed from duty because they were not in tune with community needs. Other managers have the community good firmly in command, but the formal organization goes to hell. Still others do great on these two difficult fronts, and yet run amuck with their bosses—the political shakers and movers.

Psychological Needs

It is to these kinds of role pressures and conflicts that continuing education must address itself in assisting the urban administrator meet his responsibilities to self, service, and society. It means more effective ways of assessing his needs than currently are available and a support system that can respond both individually and collectively to the developmental requirements of input, skill development, and behavioral and attitudinal change. But, it also means providing certain services that do not fall easily into the traditional matrix of education. Harry Levinson, in his discussion of the exceptional executive identifies three unique phychological needs of those who exercise leadership roles—ministration needs, maturation needs, and mastery needs. While all are important, it is the ministration needs that may be most difficult to respond to through current continuing education processes. Levinson defines ministration needs as "those which require someone else to do something for the person who has the need. . .needs which cannot be met by the person himself." They include "the need for closeness, for gratification, and for support, protection, and guidance." [6] While the work environment has the primary responsibility to provide these individual ministration needs, too often the leader of the organization has nowhere to turn in having them addressed. This is particularly true of the city manager as he performs in a role that necessarily isolates the man from the institutions and individuals who can best serve in meeting these particular needs. Any continuing education effort must be cognizant of ministration needs and attempt to meet them.

The other two needs identified by Levinson are equally important in executive development and must be pursued in any

6. Harry Levinson, *The Exceptional Executive, A Psychological Conception* (Cambridge, Mass.: Harvard University Press, 1968), p. 147.

comprehensive post-entry continuing education effort for urban administrators. Maturation needs imply that the individual has potential for development and expansion. According to Levinson, the process will unfold naturally, if circumstances are conducive; and conducive circumstances include congenial climate, adequate psychological nourishment, and protection from inhibiting or destructive external focus.

The university community should be working hard in developing public institutions that allow the maturation of their employees to unfold as naturally as possible. The natural tendency of the human organism is toward growth, learning, and problem-solving. Organizations and administrators must learn how to stay out of the way. The continuing education trick is to help institutions create that climate and then respond to the individual needs that are identified to further facilitate that maturation process.

Finally, Levinson talks of mastery needs—those related to integrating the various facets of the administrator's personality and coming to effective terms with his environment. There are three components to mastery needs, according to Levinson, "the need for ambitious striving and realistic achievement; the need for rivalry with affection; and the need for consolidation." [7]

Ministration, maturation, mastery—all of these personal needs must be addressed if the university is to be effective in meeting the post-entry education requirements of the urban administrator. In Poetry and Truth from My Own Life, Goethe wrote: "If you treat a man as he is, he will stay as he is, but if you treat him as if he were what he ought to be, and could be, he will become that bigger and better man." This, it seems to me, is the essence of continuing education for the urban administrator.

7. Ibid., p. 202.

Summary of the Discussion of the Sherwood Paper

By Frederic N. Cleaveland

SYMPOSIUM participants in considering the paper by Frank P. Sherwood were unable to reach a consensus regarding the role universities can or should play in continuing education. All did concur on the crucial importance of effective continuing education to meet the development needs of contemporary government officials especially at the urban level. Moreover, there was also agreement on viewing pre-entry education and continuing education as two points on a "learning" or an "educational" continuum. As noted in the discussion of the Mosher paper, symposium participants saw the primary role of pre-entry education to be the socialization of the aspiring professional into the field of urban management, providing him a foundation for his career and preparation for his first career position. Continuing education in the same way carries primary responsibility for updating knowledge and upgrading skills to overcome risks of obsolescence, and to keep the professional urban administrator continually abreast of new developments in the field, open and alert to new approaches and to changes in emphasis. In addition, continuing education must provide the further preparation required for advancement into a position of broader managerial responsibilities, or for shifting into a related but different career line. This conception focuses attention directly upon the continuing character of post-entry education. For the urban administrator in mid-career it is not a question of a one-shot "refresher" seminar or course, but rather a program of continuing, systematic exposure to the latest developments in his career field or the new knowledge and skills required.

While participants generally agreed that universities are not performing very well in their efforts to meet the needs for continuing education, there was wide divergence when it came to interpreting the agreed-upon facts and drawing conclusions about what to do. One group maintained universities must and indeed would respond to the increasing demands for more attention to continuing education for urban administrators. Another group was convinced that universities would not respond. Still a third group asserted it would be better to forget about universities and pass them by in favor of developing new institutions outside the higher education system to take leadership in continuing education.

An academic participant with long university experience summarized the criticism of the university: "We haven't faced the issues raised by the paper at all. What he [Frank P. Sherwood] proposes would produce a basic change in the way we [the universities] do business. It would require us to be student-centered and process-concerned. It would require us to get rid of grades, lecturing, and so forth—to get into individual contracts with our clients, the students, and to keep score, perhaps, in terms of the degree of success on their part in achieving the goals that have been mutually agreed upon in terms of their personal development. . . . Our faculties will not tolerate these fundamental changes. They insist on continuing with lectures, acting as 'masters of the mysteries' and not as facilitators of learning on the part of students. This is a tremendous stumbling block. . . ." His pessimistic view was reinforced by another participant from the academic side: "I doubt very much that the universities can really develop a comprehensive, responsive, relevant, efficient continuing education program for the reasons given in the papers. The good programs now carried on were developed in a period when circumstances reinforced them; I don't think those circumstances pertain any more. I am not sure NTDS [National Training Development Service] or federal training agencies can do it either; however, they are free of these restraints, and they can innovate. They can put money into technological development of training. They are much closer to the clientele, and can be responsive in that respect. Universities should stretch themselves, but I don't think they will in terms of money and all the things we have talked about."

But others among the participants believed that universities would rise to meet the needs for more effort on continuing education. "If the public really wanted it [expanded programs of continuing education], they could have it. It doesn't take much pressure to make universities do something." The same participant observed at a later point: "I think society will put so much pressure on the public universities [for expanding continuing education programs for urban administrators] that they will not fail to meet the demands."

The third group of symposium participants shared the point of view that universities are not well-equipped to perform effectively in continuing education and, therefore, that they should be by-passed in favor of building new institutions outside the university system to meet the needs. One of the participants from the university world expressed this viewpoint clearly: "If one views this whole question [of continuing education for urban administrators] from the standpoint of a recipient of the service, then I would offer this: post-entry education for urban administrators should not be procured from institutions of higher education as currently organized and operated. One would have a much wider choice of types of education if one took from other institutions. There would be no hang up on the degree question; you would be much more likely to get a thorough interdisciplinary training situation; you could have your program tailored to your specific needs probably much more directly than from an institution of higher education; you would certainly receive the benefit of newer teaching techniques and methodologies for imparting education; you probably would have a better chance of evaluating performance, making whatever evaluation you came up with stick. Indeed, going this way, we may introduce enough competition into the arena that higher education will have to meet the demands that they do not presently meet." Another academic participant put it more bluntly: "I think the government agencies [interested in post-entry training for their administrators] are going to say [to universities] 'to hell with you,' and then proceed to set up their own operations [for continuing education]."

Even on the issue of how great is the demand for continuing education there was not wide agreement among symposium participants. All agreed that the need was great, but some believed the demand is well-mobilized and would soon force a university response while others questioned whether the demand was now or could be made effective. One younger practitioner observed: "If you think urban administrators are going to come to universities and demand from you that you do something, you are wrong for they are not going to do it. If you propose something, they may dispose. If you have something to sell, they may buy. They get their help where they can when they need it. Their overpowering concern is the city. It is not the university. . . . Besides the needs are different in particular areas. Every urban administrator you talk to would articulate his needs in a different way. I am not sure you can get urban administrators to articulate any core of development needs."

There was even some difference of opinion about how much attention is being given to continuing education in this field of urban management. Despite the implications of many statements that little is going on in the way of continuing education, one experienced urban administrator spoke out: "There is probably more [post-entry] training going on than we admit to. Much of it is stimulated by the guilds [urban affairs professional associations like the International City Management Association, the National League of Cities, and so forth] working together with the universities in an area producing well-conducted workshops on an annual basis. I don't think enough is being done for the [city] manager because the managers have not taken the time, themselves, to push for the kind of training they really need."

Another important perspective was introduced, questioning whether the university in the contemporary world enjoys any significant comparative advantage in attempting to play a central role in continuing education. One academic participant developed the thesis of the university as a kind of "information center." Thus the university, through its faculty research and its graduate and professional schools and undergraduate colleges, gathers contextual knowledge and develops analytical technology applicable to the understanding of the nature of man and his world. The university puts together this contextual knowledge and imparts it to students. It also gives them the body of analytical technology and helps to develop their ability to apply this technology. The university can teach and train reasonably well within that context; indeed the university probably has a comparative advantage over other institutions in our society when it comes to gathering such knowledge and technology systematically over time and then imparting it to students through an intensive learning process. By contrast, can we say that the university also has a comparative advantage in regard to continuing education? The case for assigning responsibility for continuing education to the university is based on a conception of the university as a "learning center." Here, as developed earlier in the discussion of the Davy paper, the focus is upon the growth and development of the individual student. Faculty members become "learning counsellors" or "directors of learning." Post-entry training or education simply becomes another step in a life-long "learning process," begun during pre-entry education and carried on throughout the urban administrator's career. Does the university have a comparative advantage for extending this "learning center" concept throughout the professional lives of its graduates? If the conception of the university as an "information center" is more accurate, then is it appropriate or desirable to try to reorient the university and rebuild it so that it may take on a major responsibility for continuing education and discharge that responsibility effectively?

Such issues arose during the discussion of the Sherwood paper, but they were not finally resolved. Perhaps the nearest approach to resolution came in a cautionary note sounded near the end of the session suggesting that participants guard against an overly simple approach to the function and purpose of the university. A participant with wide experience in both government and academia observed: "We have let this discussion get into a question of whether universities do it [continuing education] or do not do it. One university can, has done, and will keep on doing continuing education. Some can do more than they are now doing, and probably will. Others, because of various constraints, are not going to be any more active than they are now. Isn't this a realistic picture? The need which has been envisaged is going to have to be met in part by the universities, in part by new institutions. We all have great hopes for NTDS. There will be other experiments also. We haven't done too well in the past and we are going to have to put a lot of energy, leadership, and blood, sweat, and tears into continuing education, and hope for a little bit of luck in order to meet the needs."

Finally, there appeared throughout this discussion of the universities and continuing education the suggestion of the possible need for new institutions to be developed outside the education system. One such new institution—the National Training Development Service—received special attention. Several symposium participants involved in the creation of NTDS commented on its potential role and the strategies devised to guide its early development. NTDS seeks to build the foundations for an effective system of continuing education for state and local government. On the one hand, this involves working closely with top officials in the state and local government to gain their understanding of and commitment to continuing education. It also means helping these officials to build an infrastructure to support on-going training processes within government agencies at state and local levels. On a broader front, the long-term goal of NTDS is to develop an extensive continuing education network linking government training officers, universities and university faculty members, professional associations, private organizations and foundations active and involved in training, and key federal, state, and local officials concerned with improving the quality of administrative leadership in government.

NTDS itself expects to play a catalytic role, and to provide assistance through a small, highly skilled staff working to improve training programs through experimentation, continuing evaluation, and feedback. If NTDS is fully successful in performing this catalytic role, it may well provide answers to two imponderable issues brought out in the discussion. First, NTDS through its work with state and local officials and agencies may help to aggregate and then to articulate effectively the demand for greater attention to and investment in continuing education for urban administrators. Second, NTDS through its continuing education network may provide the necessary link to relate universities more effectively to government clients seeking help in post-entry education. Those universities already engaged in continuing education and ready to play a more important role can find such a network helpful in broadening their access to government officials and in exchanging ideas and experiences for improving their performance. Those universities with limited past experience can overcome their lack of access and make up for their inexperience through utilizing the network.

How to Utilize the Resources of the University Effectively for Educating Urban Administrators

By Ferrel Heady

ABSTRACT: In discussing effective utilization of university resources for educating urban administrators, we face a problem of meshing what a university is capable of doing with the educational needs of urban administration. A number of trends are central to the issue: (1) the sparcity of available resources, (2) slowing growth rates, (3) tendency to limit university involvement in new ventures to those which are self-supporting, (4) avoidance of specialized programs, (5) increased university involvement in community affairs, and (6) increased attention to inter-institutional coordination. On the other side, among the developments shaping educational needs are: (1) a blurring of the roles of political and administrative leaders, (2) increased ambiguity between urban and other public administrators, (3) reduced focus on city managership, (4) greater career mobility, (5) increase in post-entry education, and (6) uncertainty of municipal manpower projections. Based upon these trends, the following guidelines are suggested: (1) prime responsibility should be centered in an academic unit oriented toward public affairs or administration with sufficient autonomy and resource support; (2) programs should be related to and interdependent with other relevant professional schools; (3) close working relationships with social science departments should be maintained; and (4) relations with practitioner groups should be strengthened. Finally, government, at all levels, must support the education of urban administrators.

Ferrel Heady has been president of the University of New Mexico since 1968 following two years as academic vice president. He earned his M.A. and Ph.D. from Washington University. He served on the faculty of the University of Michigan from 1946 to 1966 including directorship of its Institute of Public Administration. He was president of the American Society for Public Administration and is a member of the National Academy of Public Administration.

I N A "how to" discussion about effective utilization of university resources for educating urban administrators, we face a problem of meshing what a university is capable of doing with the educational needs of urban administration. It would be a mistake to start out by assuming either that a university is prepared to provide whatever resources might be requested for the education of urban administrators, or that urban administrators can be assured that their educational needs will be met satisfactorily by universities.

UNIVERSITY RESOURCES AND THEIR UTILIZATION

In order to make a realistic assessment of how well these commitments and expectations match, I will try to identify some trends both on campus and off that should be taken into account. Motivated probably by being a university president myself, I'll begin with some considerations about university resources and their utilization during the next couple of decades, and then turn to some speculations about trends in the educational needs of urban administrators during the same period.

Sparcity of available resources

The evidence is overwhelming that resources available to universities during the next few years will become less and less adequate when compared to potential expansions of university based programs. The financial plight of institutions of higher education, particularly the private ones, has already been documented. Many are in serious trouble, some are going out of existence, and even the strongest and most prestigious, such as Columbia and Princeton, have embarked on stringent economy campaigns to make ends meet. This is not a temporary emergency situation, calling for a brief period of belt tightening, but a long-range retrenchment prospect. Public support may expand for the institutions now classified as private, but the more this happens, the more all institutions will share in the common discouraging outlook for the future. As for the public institutions themselves, in many parts of the country they are now receiving less generous support on a per capita student basis than before. In view of rapidly rising enrollments and the decline in purchasing power of the dollar, increases in appropriation totals from year to year are deceiving and mask the fact of an actual deterioration in the effective level of support for public universities. These institutions are suffering from the combined impact of public disillusionment based on concern over campus activism in the recent past, and competition with other governmental programs for support from overcommitted state revenue sources. Overall, the outlook is that resource stringency will affect university programming adversely during the foreseeable future.

Slowing growth rates

Underlying this predicament is a basic fact that is new to higher education in the United States. For the first time in our history, according to projections of the Carnegie Commission on Higher Education, we are entering a decade in which the college and university student population will grow at a much slower rate, to be followed in the 1980s by a decade in which enrollment will actually be lower at the end of the decade than at the beginning. If this happens, it will reflect a lowering of the birth rate so dramatic as to reduce enrollment totals even if a higher proportion of college age youth actually attend college. The Carnegie report summarizes in these words:

Higher education in the United States has been a continuous rapid-growth segment of the nation for more than three centuries. During that time, it has experienced steady enrollment increases at a rate faster than the expansion of American society generally. Over the past century, in particular, enrollments in higher education have doubled regularly every fourteen to fifteen years. But never again.[1]

This may be a desirable social development to achieve better balance between population and resources, but it places a tremendous strain on a system of higher education that has always been accustomed to a pattern of growth, particularly since the end of World War II. Expansion of enrollments, operating budgets, and physical facilities have made it easier to enhance existing programs or embark on new ones. Basic support prospects in a slowdown or standstill situation will make it more difficult for universities to change from what they are already doing. The

1. The Carnegie Commission on Higher Education, *New Students and New Places: Policies for the Future Growth and Development of American Higher Education* (Highstown, N.J.: McGraw-Hill, 1971), p. 1.

option of innovating by adding on will no longer be available. Innovation will be feasible only in combination with elimination or reduction of existing programs that are in competition for support from general institutional resources.

New ventures

Under these circumstances, prospects are that new ventures, either in the form of additional programs or expansion of existing ones, will seldom be undertaken in the absence of special support that is earmarked for the new venture and is not readily transferable, or is not transferable at all, to some other objective. This is a fact of institutional life that may not be palatable to academic administrators who would prefer more discretion as between existing and new programs, but only the more aggressive ones who are also lucky will be able to overcome the forces of institutional inertia. For the outside group seeking a response from the university to a need that it has identified, this means that the response is much more likely to occur if the requesting group can generate support that will fund all or a substantial part of the institutional costs. With regard to the education of public administrators, this means that unless governmental units, which are prime sources of support for nearly all higher education institutions, public and private, give clear indications in their funding priorities that they value public administration education programs, the universities will be inclined to apply their energies elsewhere.

Avoidance of specialized programs

Another common response to the resource problem will be for universities to seek to avoid funneling their scarce resources into programs that have a high degree of specialization and operational autonomy, and demand a long-range nontransferable budgetary commitment. The higher the unit cost of the output, measured by academic credit hours, degrees conferred, or similar criteria, the more this reluctance will grow. Therefore, in a tight situation, expensive advanced graduate and professional curriculums will be subjected to the closest scrutiny. Most programs designed for educating urban and other public administrators fall into this category. Decisions that result may discontinue even long-established traditional professional schools, such as dentistry, or turn thumbs down on attractive current proposals, as for example those focusing on environmental problems, if the program is largely self-contained and cannot be extensively bolstered by existing programs.

Reaching outside the campus

Even with these constraints, there will be some moves in novel directions in response to urgent needs or strong pressures, or a combination of both. The most common example is the burgeoning of programs in ethnic studies and women's studies, even though these may be expensive, and are often considered threatening by disciplinary academic departments.

One such urge is to take the university beyond the campus boundaries and to involve it more in community affairs. In part this responds to student demands for relevance in their education, but it also serves to cement relations with constituencies in the community. For many kinds of professional training, including education for urban administration, this tendency to move outside the campus classroom fits in well with the aim of acquainting pre-professionals with practitioners in a way that will strengthen educational preparation for the profession. Fortunately, this trend is one that reinforces and legitimizes what has always been a feature of university public administration programs.

Interinstitutional coordination

Forces both internal and external to the university are now beginning to focus attention on better utilization of resources through institutional specialization or division of function on a coordinated basis. It does not make sense for the hard-pressed management of a university in financial trouble to persist in competition with other institutions in offering similar programs all struggling for survival. Self-interest then may bring about agreements among institutions that result in fewer but more viable programs. At the state level among public institutions, some kind of system-wide coordinating mechanism is likely to be exploring persistently the possibilities of less duplication of effort among individual institutions in the system, and to be developing the legal or financial clout to get compliance. Accrediting associations in specialized fields are in the process of thinning out marginal programs that fail to meet minimum accreditation standards. As the market situation in overcrowded professions deteriorates for the practitioner and the trainee, those already in the profession or in the pipeline may join forces to ease the competitive pressure by eliminating programs or curtailing the rate of admission. In these and other ways, momentum is building up for more coordination to achieve better overall resource utilization.

EDUCATIONAL NEEDS OF URBAN ADMINISTRATORS

Other contributors to this Symposium have a more direct assignment to identify the pre-entry and post-entry educational needs of urban administrators. Even without the full benefit of their findings and recommendations, I must set forth some hypotheses about these needs as a prelude to fitting university competencies to their realization. So I will comment on certain developments that seem to me at this juncture most pertinent in making plans for educating urban administrators.

Blending of political and administrative roles

While recognizing that the distinction between policy-making and policy execution has never been as clear-cut in real life as it once was in the literature of public administration, I would nevertheless suggest that in actual practice there is now more of a blurring of the roles of political and administrative leaders than in the past. Particularly in urban affairs under the council-manager form of municipal government, the assumption once was that the council made the public policy decisions and the city manager was responsible for carrying them out. The training of city managers placed much emphasis on the impropriety of moving into the policy field reserved to the council, and the ethical obligation of the manager to move on if he could not conscientiously implement the policies adopted by the council. Infringement by the manager upon the policy domain of the council was a legitimate, and commonly applied, reason for dismissal of an offending manager. As a reciprocal commitment, the manager presumably was to be isolated and protected by the council from the dangers of direct exposure to political forces in the community.

Even the doctrine about role propriety has changed considerably, but the shift in practice seems to have been more dramatic. Neither council members nor managers seem to have these traditional expectations about the policy neutral stance of the principal urban administrator. When administrators respond to questions about role involvement, it is evident that they do not shun policy leadership kinds of activity. They may even consider this as central to the role of the urban administrator, and use language describing him as a politically responsible, effective policy executive who can marshal total community and regional resources to solve community problems and meet community opportunities.[2] In listings of typical specific problem/issue involvements, many examples obviously are concerned primarily with policy matters. In predictions about trends, even more such involvement is anticipated. A majority of respondents project a stronger advocacy role for the urban administrator in the future.

Likewise, city councilmen appear to expect more policy input from the chief administrator, and to praise or blame him for what that input is. There is nothing new about making the performance of a city manager a political campaign issue, but the issue is more likely now to be framed in terms of his policy stance rather than his record of administrative accomplishment. His future may often turn on an indirect judgment by the electorate as to his record of policy initiation or his stand on current policy issues.

Obviously, if these trends are accurately described, their impact will be to alter, and make more complex, the task of training the future urban administrator. They also render partially obsolete the education of many practicing administrators, and indicate needs for mid-career training.

Differentiating urban from other public administrators

In a symposium on the education of urban administrators, an assumption has to be made that urban administrators can be differentiated from other categories of administrators. Without quarreling with the validity of urban administrators as a useful

2. See article in this volume by Graham W. Watt, John K. Parker, and Robert R. Cantine, "Roles of the Urban Administrator in the 1970s and the Knowledges and Skills Required to Perform These Roles," pp. 50–79.

classification, I would argue that the boundary lines for the grouping are becoming less clear, and that increasingly we face ambiguities as we try to separate urban administrators from other kinds of public administrators or, for that matter, from some types of quasi-public or private administrators.

This point is underlined by the listing of administrators included in the survey of perspectives of practitioners upon which the paper by Watt, Parker, and Cantine is based. Among those included were:

. . . city and county administrators and their assistants; department heads, planning, finance, and personnel directors; professional leaders of regional councils and other regional organizations; senior members of urban research and service organizations; executive officials of civic and community action agencies; principal staff members of professional associations; and key officials in state and federal programs directed at urban areas.[3]

I do not disagree with this selection of respondents. All are intimately concerned with urban problems and deserve to be called urban administrators. But included are administrators at various levels of government, state, regional, and national as well as urban, in a wide variety of functional fields of specialization, in organizations with primarily research or service rather than program achievement orientations, in professional and other non-public or quasi-public associations, and so forth.

This diversity reflects the fact that American society today is basically an urbanized society, and that urbanism is a prime focus for the work of an impressive aggregation of expert professionals. What they have in common is that they bring their expertise to bear on urban problems in one way or another and to a greater or lesser degree. But they differ tremendously in what they have been trained to do and in what they are actually doing. Many of them did not know when they were being educated that they would ever become urban administrators. Many have already or will later spend parts of their careers outside of urban administration however broadly defined.

The implications for planning the education of urban administrators are staggering. Put in the starkest terms, there seems to be no realistic possibility of identifying a cohesive group of

3. Ibid., p. 54.

future urban administrators for pre-entry education that could follow a common curriculum. Continuing post-entry education poses fewer problems of identification, but nearly equivalent problems of what should be taught and how.

Less focus on city managership

Another aspect of the problem of educating for urban administration is that training of young people specifically for careers as city managers is not as much the prime focus of university programs of advanced training as it once was.

I do not refer to this development because I object to it. The change in emphasis is a response to changes in urban administration. The functions of the city manager are less well defined than they were. Deviations from the classic pattern of managership, such as the new style city administrators in large cities with strong mayor systems, put management training in a different perspective. There is more recognition that a large proportion of university graduates who go into urban administration do not become city managers, and less of an attitude that only the second-rate or castoffs take other than manager positions.

This diffusion of educational objectives, however, does cause more uncertainty as to the educational needs of urban administrators and what plans should be made to meet them.

Career mobility

Another more pervasive characteristic of public employment also contributes to the problem of designing appropriate educational programs. Career mobility for individuals, especially those in professional and managerial type positions, is increasingly common. This reflects in part the mobile nature of our society generally. It is often also the result of individual desires for changes of scenery and varieties of experiences. Employing organizations plan and carry out reassignments to meet organizational work needs or to aid in career development. The advantages of a prevailing pattern of career mobility probably outweigh the disadvantages, particularly if position changes are within a limited orbit organizationally or functionally. If career shifts are dramatic enough, however, to move individuals into or out of urban administration broadly defined, this must be taken into account both in pre-entry and post-entry education.

Extended education

Notice also needs to be taken of the general movement toward education extending over a lifetime rather than concentrated in youth and early adulthood. This will probably mean for urban administrators, as well as for many other groups, more emphasis on extended or in-and-out education as contrasted to concentrated pre-entry education. As devices, such as universities without walls, are developed to meet these general requirements, they will have to be adapted to the special needs of urban administrators.

Responsiveness to changing demands

If the tasks of urban administrators have changed as extensively as practitioners think they have, and if these changes continue as they predict, a major objective of educational programs should be to anticipate and respond to these changes. This cannot be done without flexibility and adaptability. The dangers of rigidity in curriculum are real enough in any educational endeavor, but they can be unusually crucial when the objective is to provide training for urban administrators that is responsive to their current needs rather than the needs of their predecessors.

Problems orientation

Management education has for a long time tended to deal less with theoretical or doctrinal approaches to teaching and more with techniques that are problem- or case-centered. This was the result of conscious choice by teachers as to how best to get the results they wanted, and it also fitted the preferences of their students. Pioneering work with case studies, role playing, simulation, and other devices took place in management education. In this regard, much of higher education is playing a game of catch up, as similar efforts spread into other fields. Fortunately, what is needed in urban administration education is not a revision of approach but continued development of such a problems orientation.

Manpower projection uncertainties

Finally, on a different dimension, I suggest that planning for educating urban administrators must try to take better account of future manpower requirements for the whole category and for subgroups, with particular attention to variations over time during the next three decades.

Professional and managerial manpower shortages in government service, particularly at the local level, have been a built-in feature of the labor market in recent years. Depression and wartime expansions of government employment have repeatedly meant a scramble by recruitment agencies to find qualified people. More recently, when the rate of growth has leveled off somewhat, replacement requirements for retirees brought in during much earlier growth periods have sustained manpower demands. Since state and local units of government, particularly cities, have provided most of the expansion in public employment during the last decade, these units continue to face severe recruitment and retention problems. Reports from sources such as the Municipal Manpower Commission have documented the existing shortages and have projected future manpower requirements.

In summary, the prospect for the near future is that educational institutions will be hard pressed to produce an adequate output of trained urban administrators, particularly in the most rapidly expanding program areas, such as health, welfare, and education. The sharp drop-off in employment opportunities for graduating students during the last two or three years appears to be mainly in the private sector, and has not changed this outlook as far as public employment is concerned.

We do need, however, to be looking farther down the road, and I doubt that we can get a very clear view. We already know that something dramatic has happened in the rate of births during the 1960s, with a resulting actual decline in the annual number of babies being added to the population as compared to the post-World War II era. This already means lower enrollments in the primary schools grades, and this population valley will move on through secondary and higher education, and will ultimately have far-reaching effects on employment patterns and on the age distribution profile of the population as a whole.

The point is that we are facing more uncertainties in projecting manpower needs because of what has already happened in population growth rates, and this ambiguity is compounded by not knowing whether or not we are actually heading eventually toward a pattern of zero population growth. Whatever happens, it does look as though employment demands will be more erratic than in the past, with the impact of population shifts being superimposed on the effects of fluctuations in the economy, and with dramatic changes likely among the various functional areas in their requirements for skilled manpower. Unless the agencies that are educating urban administrators can anticipate and adjust quickly, they may add to the complications that seem inevitable anyway in meeting manpower needs during an extended period of population variations.

GUIDELINES FOR MATCHING RESOURCE CAPABILITIES AND EDUCATIONAL NEEDS

Based upon these trends as to both university resources and urban administration education, I will try to suggest some guidelines as to how university resources can be used most effectively for this purpose.

I might as well admit at the outset that I will not come up with any revolutionary action program that would scrap what many universities have already been doing, and substitute some entirely new concept for educating urban administrators. The situation, as I see it, does not call for a brand new start, but there are choices to be made among limited options, some things should be emphasized, and others should be de-emphasized—all within a realistic assessment of the resources that can be allotted to the task.

Centrality of a public affairs-oriented academic entity

In organizing within the university for the purpose of educating urban administrators, as is the case with most organizational decisions, there is no one right way, and any choice involves a balancing of advantages against disadvantages. Given the variety among American institutions of higher education, characteristics of individual institutions may be crucially important. These and other reasons cast doubt on the wisdom of recommending a uniform standardized plan for fitting urban administration education into the overall structure of the university.

Nevertheless, for any sizable university intending to offer programs of direct benefit to urban administrators, it does seem to me essential, with only rare exceptions, that prime responsibility should be centered in an academic unit which is oriented toward public affairs or public administration education, and which has sufficient autonomy and resource support to be able to plan and offer a coherent program.

The preferred form in most cases, as I see it, would be a graduate professional school of public affairs or public administration, with a core faculty offering a core curriculum which the school controls. At some universities, divisional status may provide these essentials without placing the program in an existing school or college and without creating a new one. Another option is a more comprehensive school of administration or administrative sciences, incorporating education for management careers in government with other kinds of management training. Given the longer history and greater size of schools of business, which are usually the base for such an academic entity, this is a hazardous choice for purposes of educating public, and specifically urban, administrators. Unless a sufficient degree of operating autonomy and identity can be provided with the larger structure, results may be unsatisfactory or too diffuse to be evaluated.

I do not regard it as either feasible or necessary that an urban administration program should be set up separately from other programs for educating public administrators. For most institutions, the proliferation of academic units that would result from such an approach does not seem feasible, nor is it called for to meet educational objectives or to satisfy student preferences. Of course, some urban universities may choose properly by their academic structure and program offerings to emphasize education for urban administrators to the exclusion of, or with less attention to, other levels of public administration.

Relations with other professional schools

Equally as important as basic autonomy on essentials is interdependence on nonessentials with other relevant professional schools at the same university. Unless this happens, university resources are apt to be squandered, and the education of at least some potential urban administrators may be neglected.

In saying that the urban administration program should have identity but not be self-contained, I have several things in mind. One is that even common courses for the students should be offered directly by the public affairs unit only if the content really requires special treatment, or the course is not already available elsewhere. Many course offerings are equally relevant for the training of a variety of future managers, such as courses in statistics, accounting, quantitative analysis, computer usage, and organizational behavior. Considerations of economy, as well as benefits from a student mix, point toward concentrating responsibility on a university-wide basis for each such course, and it is not likely to be in a small and specialized public affairs unit.

For a future urban administrator, it is also important that he have access to the diversity of courses available in such professional schools as business, law, engineering, public health, social work, architecture, and planning. Unless he has individual flexibility in course selection, he will be thwarted in trying to map out a program as closely adapted as possible to his perceived career plans.

Finally, ways must be open for students enrolled in these other professional schools to take advantage of the curriculum in public and urban administration. Many of them already anticipate that they will be practicing their professions in an urban setting, and that their careers may lead to heavy managerial responsibilities. Past experience indicates that this actually happens in many instances when it is not anticipated. Hence, every encouragement should be given to cooperative arrangements among professional schools that will reach as many of these potential or actual urban administrators as possible, either through pre-entry or post-entry programs.

Relations with social science departments

Professional programs for education of administrators have evolved from parent social science departments, typically economics for business administration and political science for public administration. Whatever the organizational relationship between the parent department and its offspring, a professional program in administration must maintain close working relationships with these two social science departments. The degree of dependence is not much less on other social sciences, particularly sociology and psychology. Trends in educational needs already discussed point toward a growing relevance of social science-based knowledge for the urban administrator.

A happy frictionless relationship between professional and social science academic units is difficult, perhaps impossible, to achieve. Professional programs have a problem-solving orientation. They are heavily concerned with preparing students for careers by acquainting them with real problems and equipping them to become practicing professionals. They want to bring social science knowledge to bear in professional training, but are not primarily committed to the advancement of knowledge in the social science disciplines. Students in the professional program are likely to have different interests, priorities, and approaches than advanced students in a social science discipline.

For such reasons, there are serious problems in trying to maintain a viable professional program for educating urban administrators which avoids the resource leakage resulting from making these programs self-sufficient in their social science capabilities, and at the same time assures that their needs will be met by social science departments with only a peripheral interest in what they are doing. The key element for success is a mutual desire to cooperate by faculty members on both sides of the line. If this doesn't exist because of past experiences, current differences of opinion, or concern over future developments, it must be nurtured. Practices such as joint appointments, joint course offerings, time-sharing arrangements, cooperative research projects, and so forth often help. The attitude of central administrative officers of the university may be critical. If they insist on a reinforcing relationship, and show it in decisions about position allotments, staff appointments, administrative assignments, and budget allocations, this may bring results that would not happen otherwise.

Relations with practitioner groups

Professional schools customarily maintain close ties with alumni, and hence with at least this group of practitioners. Associations of professionals take a direct and active interest in what is going on in the professional schools.   In the traditional well-defined professions, such as law or medicine, this continuing relationship is much closer than it is between working alumni who graduated in disciplinary specialties and their university departments or colleges.   This closer affinity is also characteristic of professional programs in management and their graduates, except that the alumni are apt to be more widely diversified in where and how their training is being put into practice.

These contacts between educators and practitioners can be strengthened at various levels and in various ways.   Nationally, more intercommunication is needed between such groups as the International City Management Association and the National League of Cities on the one hand, and the National Association of Schools of Public Affairs and Administration on the other.   Educational groupings on a regional basis, such as the Western Interstate Commission on Higher Education, might give more attention, in collaboration with practitioner groups, to the education of urban administrators, as they are already doing in such fields as medicine and public health.

The basic task, however, is for particular universities to work with their own practitioner constituencies of alumni and nearby urban administrators, by such measures as using practitioners as adjunct faculty members, as participants in advisory committees regarding curriculums, as supervisors of administrative interns and in similar ways useful both to the student and the practitioner. The prescription is not for the academics to surrender the control of the program to the practicing professionals, but to make sure that their views are known and taken into account.   This is likely to improve pre-entry education, and it is sure to enhance mid-career training.

Mobilizing resources for educating urban administrators

Finally, in achieving maximum availability and utilization of university resources for the education of urban administrators, it is essential to emphasize again the impact of general considerations with regard to resource mobilization.   In a time of resource undernourishment, universities are unlikely to extend themselves in the support of programs for government administrators unless governments show in a tangible way that they value these programs.   University decision-makers are well aware of the liberality of government funding for manpower training in the health sciences, for example.   They are looking for at least token indications of such interest in university-based programs for professional public administrators.   This is why legislative authorization for support, followed by actual funding even in relatively small amounts, is so important.   The significance is not only that such direct resource input may serve as a primer for releasing other discretionary resources.   There is also a psychological effect when government as employer of administrative talent recognizes and encourages university efforts to train urban and other public administrators.

The universities, for their part, can impress educational coordinating agencies and legislative bodies by demonstrating that they are concerned about avoiding duplication of effort in educating administrators, both in how they organize and operate internally, and in how they coordinate among themselves through interuniversity cooperative arrangements.

Commentary on the Heady Paper

By John D. Millett

ABSTRACT: University resources to undertake the education of urban administrators are limited, and too much in the way of innovation cannot be expected without new sources of financial support. The identification of urban administration for which universities might educate a professional practitioner remains troublesome. Urban services are specialized and are performed initially through the efforts of professionally competent individuals as engineers, architects, doctors, nurses, teachers, social workers, police, firemen, and others. Education for public administration or for urban administration may focus its attention upon management specialists, upon professional students during their professional education, or upon professional practitioners already in the public service as they move from that stage in their careers wherein they become generalists rather than specialists. Education for urban administration must draw upon the social sciences and upon professional education. It may also need innovative endeavors, endeavors not too easily introduced into the practice of university education.

John D. Millett, Ph.D., has been professor of public administration at Columbia University, president of Miami University (Oxford, Ohio), and chancellor of the Ohio Board of Regents. In the summer of 1972 he became vice president of the Academy for Educational Development in charge of its Management Division. His books and articles are well known to students of public administration and of higher education.

I T IS always much easier to criticize than to be constructive. The commentator has a much simpler role than the proponent. In the observations which follow I hope I may be able to voice as much appreciation as concern for the proposals submitted by President Heady.

It is entirely appropriate today for a university president to begin any paper involving higher education activity with an admonition: don't expect too much from the American university. We live in a period when our society, in spite of its anxieties and its misunderstanding, continues to look upon higher education as a promise of future benefit rather than as a threat of current subversion. Yet the resources available to higher education to promote this future benefit have begun to be more restricted than at any time in the past twenty-five years.

Although President Heady devotes a lengthy introduction to the subject of university resources and their utilization, this whole matter is too complicated to receive the consideration which it deserves. The demands upon the university for various services seem to be unabated, and the expectations of the faculty profession for substantial remuneration appear to be undiminished. Yet the resources society is willing to offer toward the costs of these services and these expectations are not apt to expand in the next ten years as they did in the decade of the 1960s. These circumstances justify President Heady's admonition that desirable as may be new and augmented university activities, such services must also be financed in some way if they are to be rendered.

In the discussion of his assigned topic, President Heady dwells upon two major issues: (1) the educational needs of urban administrators, and (2) guidelines for matching university capabilities with these educational needs. In the course of his consideration of these two issues, the author makes many helpful suggestions drawn probably more from his extensive experience as director of an institute of public administration in one of our great state universities than from his role as a university administrator. As a commentator I must still express the wish that the problems might have been more sharply delineated.

I find myself in complete agreement with the various items considered under the heading of educational needs. It is profoundly true, as some have been maintaining for many years, that there is increasingly a blending of the political and administrative roles in the public service. Any simplistic belief, if it ever did exist, that politics and administration are two separated and separable roles, must surely have been amply refuted by the events of our recent past. But even as we discard this conventional wisdom of an earlier day, we must still confront the need to determine how administrative expertise is to be harnessed with the representational role of elected legislators and executives.

I am troubled by the failure of President Heady to come to grips with the primary problem, which is whether or not there is a profession of urban administration. To be sure, the argument about this issue has been with us for at least forty years. Because it is an old problem does not mean, however, that it is a resolved problem. In a simpler day we might perhaps properly have talked about educating young people at the master's degree level to become city managers. President Heady says it is time to forget about this objective, and I agree. But unless we find a professional career ladder which we can identify as one of urban administration, we shall continue to flounder in our efforts at devising an appropriate professional education for entry into the profession.

It is all well and good to call attention to the prospects for career mobility in the public service, to the changing needs of the American city, to manpower uncertainties, and to a problems orientation for an educational curriculum. The tasks of urban administration are not too different from what they were several decades ago; the tasks are more urgent, more complicated, and more burdensome. There are still such concerns as urban design, land utilization, traffic flow and parking, water supply, sanitation and refuse disposal, adequate housing, health, family income maintenance, recreation, education, law and order, fire protection. To these are now added the more recent concerns with pollution of air, water, and land. These problems require a great variety of professional talents: architectural, engineering, medical, nursing, social service, recreation leadership, teaching, police, fire, and economic. The urban community can maintain itself only if it can staff its services, house them, supply them, direct them, and finance them. The urban community can survive only if it develops a political leadership prepared to cope with every one of these problem areas.

Who then is the urban administrator? I can define this individual only as the supervisory and directing personnel for every one of these essential services which the urban community must render. At the top reaches of these services, but increasingly throughout all echelons or subdivisions of a service, the urban administrator is also an urban politician. The administrator must be alert to the concerns of urban citizens in urban neighborhoods, he must seek within the limits of statutory authority to respond to human needs in a sympathetic, humane manner. He must collaborate with group leaders and elected representatives to maintain an urban environment which is livable, satisfying, and hopeful. It is no mean assignment.

The American public service throughout its history has struggled to find a method of accommodation between the specialist and the generalist. When the American university—and more particularly the political scientist or other social scientist within the American university—speaks of the urban administrator, they are really speaking of the urban generalist rather than of the urban specialist. This generalist is supposed to have two principal attributes. He sees his problem area in the larger context of the total urban community; he realizes that police maintenance of law and order is possible only when there is a community circumstance and commitment which makes law and order a desirable objective. This generalist, moreover, understands that municipal services have a unity as well as a specialized identity; he realizes that urban design, transportation, housing, water supply, health, income maintenance, refuse disposal, recreation, education, pollution abatement, police and fire protection are all intimately related one to the other. This generalist understands further that services require direction in order to achieve purposes, and financing in order to accomplish intentions.

I take it that President Heady is really discussing how to educate specialists who can become generalists, or how to educate generalists who can deal effectively with specialists. And if we know how to educate this generalist, how does he obtain employment as a generalist? President Heady does not answer the question either of education or of employment because he doesn't know the answer. I don't know the answer, either. And I have been waiting forty years to meet the man or woman who does know the answer.

The public administration fraternity over the years has tried several answers. It is still trying them. One approach has been to educate individuals for the staff jobs in governmental administration: the specialists in personnel, budgeting, organizational analysis, procedures, purchasing, accounting who in the due course of events might become generalists because they were not identified as such with architects, doctors, nurses, engineers, teachers, police administrators, fire administrators, social workers, and so on. I know of no study which has ever been undertaken to determine the utility or the accomplishment of this approach to education for public administration.

A second approach has been to infiltrate the professional education of architects, engineers, doctors, nurses, teachers, social workers, economists, and others. To some extent these specialists have resisted such infiltration because of the heavy demands of their particular educational requirements. To some extent these specialists have welcomed participation in their educational endeavor in the interest of a broader preparation for professional practice. My observation is that professional students themselves often resist these broadening efforts simply because they seek mastery of immediately employable skills.

A third approach has been to offer education for public administration as a post-entry graduate program of professional education. In this arrangement the specialist who has been in service for a number of years, has risen several promotion steps, and who foresees the prospect of advancement to general management duties seeks to broaden his own capacities for handling a new administrative role. This kind of educational interest has frequently appeared among engineers, scientists, and other specialists within industrial and business enterprises, and in various ways schools of business administration within our universities have met this educational demand. Schools of public administration may do the same thing.

Although I have no statistics with which to quantify my observation, I believe that there are schools of public administration which do, in fact, undertake simultaneously to effect all three approaches to their professional education. I see no basic fault in such an eclectic endeavor, although there may be some evidence to suggest that varied objectives, or at least a varied student clientele, in professional education tends to result in an instructional program which satisfies no particular need in full.

President Heady insists that it is increasingly difficult today to differentiate education for urban administration from education for public administration. I agree with this position and take the statement as one reflecting the rediscovery of the complications of urban life in America in our day. In the federal government two concerns have been dominant since the 1930s: one has been a concern with national security—foreign affairs and military posture—and the other has been a concern with the impact of governmental activities upon the functioning of the American economy. It is surely no accident that the last several directors of the budget in the federal government have been economists. Today, partly because of our disillusionment with our role in international affairs and partly because of our fears for the future stability of American society itself, we as a people have become increasingly introspective. And however much we assert that the overwhelming difficulties of our day are population, poverty, and pollution, it is in the urban environment where all three come into sharp focus. It is to be expected that governmental interests as a whole—federal and state—will be increasingly directed toward urban affairs. It is no exaggeration to declare that the business of government in the United States in the 1970s will be urbanism.

If governmental preoccupation—economic, social, and political—is to be the urban environment, higher education has an obligation to determine how to contribute effectively and appropriately to this concentration of attention. One answer is at least clear-cut; at least it is clear-cut to me. The university response must be that of education. The university cannot properly in our society aspire to a role of decision-making; its institutional assignment is to provide an educational background or preparation for individuals, families, groups, professions, business enterprise, and government as they undertake to advance urban welfare.

President Heady insists that political scientists and instructors of public administration cannot assay the tasks of urban education alone or by themselves. They must first of all enlist the collaboration of all the social sciences. It is for the behavioral sciences, which are at once both empirical sciences and a branch of moral philosophy, to provide the broad backdrop of intelligence whereby a rational and ethical action in urban affairs must be undertaken. Similarly, schools of public, or urban, administration must be prepared to collaborate closely with their colleagues in other professional schools: law, engineering, medicine, nursing, social work, education, and so forth. Urban administration needs their specialized expertise in instruction and their students as well. And undoubtedly President Heady is correct in urging increased attention within education for urban administration to clientele groups. Participation is the new watchword in public administration. Just as the politics of deference disappeared several decades ago, so a public administration of popular deference has disappeared in our day.

Like criticism, prescription is relatively easy to offer as an intellectual exercise. Administration, governmental and academic, is a process of action. The academic community does not readily alter its long-established procedures. Faculties find an inherent security in routines to which they are accustomed. University education in urban administration will require considerable effort in order to achieve effective organization and appropriate service. In this respect certainly university education and urban administration share a common interest and an urgent need.

Commentary on the Heady Paper

By Donald C. Stone

ABSTRACT: The failure of universities to educate urban administrators is not for lack of resources. It is due basically to the resistance of collegial academic bodies to accept new professional fields and to curtail teaching that no longer has societal priority. This lack of innovation could have been overcome if foundations and government had exercised initiative as they did in agriculture, medicine, health, science, business administration, and language study. Any valid strategy needs to be based on analysis and forecasts of manpower and research requirements. Since there is no national leadership and no serious, informed concern about education and research to solve the nation's urban problems, there is no strategy, and very little of significance is being done. Among the elements of an adequate strategy is a major infusion of federal funds into forty or fifty universities in the larger metropolitan areas for public/urban/affairs/administration education and research; a tenfold increase in funding of the Intergovernmental Personnel Act; initiation of doctoral programs to produce the necessary instructors and researchers; broadening of National Science Foundation grant provisions to cover operationally oriented research; assignment of local, state, and federal officials to universities to remedy their educational deficiencies, and incorporation of an adequate training and research component in every major urban field or program.

Donald C. Stone is dean emeritus and professor of political science at the University of Pittsburgh, where he guided the development of the School of Public and International Affairs with a Department of Urban Affairs offering five different urban master's and a Ph.D. program. He has held a variety of administrative posts and consultancies at all levels of government and is author of numerous articles, monographs, and books on urban and other public problems.

WHAT Ferrel Heady says about the utilization of university resources has vision and insight. Who would take issue with any of his theses, other than persons who believe that administrative knowledge is intuitive and that the way to gain competence is by trial and error. Unfortunately, there seems to be a lot of such persons.

I shall deal much more concretely with the problem of tooling up universities with resources and capabilities to develop high quality urban administrators, and other urban professionals. The ultimate aim of such an effort is to provide the insights, skills, and operational competences essential to make the federal-state-local system manageable in the service of an urban nation.

TESTED OPERATIONALLY

These comments are derived from struggle over a span of forty years in trying to improve urban administration and to educate urban and other public administrators. As an official of or consultant to city, county, state, and federal agencies, I developed great conviction about the feasibility of university preparation of persons armed with administrative knowledge and competences.

I recall vividly the day in London while representing the United States in the Fifth Committee of the United Nations Preparatory Commission when I said to myself, after observing the ignorance of diplomats about urban problems in particular, and economic and social affairs in general, "some day I shall organize a school in which we shall educate foreign service officers, urban planners, and city managers under one roof." And that is exactly what happened.

If fifty universities had sought and used resources twenty years ago to establish professional schools of public/urban/affairs/administration, the nation's urban programs would be far more effective today and the local-state-federal system far better managed. My views on the need for urban affairs education and research are easily ascertainable.*

* "Manning Tomorrow's Cities," *Public Administration Review*, June 1963, pp. 99–104; "To Serve an Urban America," *Civil Service Journal*, October-December 1967, pp. 8–12; "The Present and Future in Urban Affairs Education," Boston University, 1967; "Urgent Need for a National

EDUCATIONAL PRIORITIES

Ferrel Heady rightly points out the scarcity of university resources as an obstacle to initiating educational programs for urban administrators. Nevertheless, during the past ten years the resources available to universities have increased enormously. Philanthropic gifts to universities have reached an all-time high. If universities had been interested in developing programs for urban administrators and other fields of public service education, they could very well have done so. It is quite true that resources are not coming so easily and costs have mounted, but scarcity of resources is not the problem.

The problem is the sluggishness with which most universities respond to changing societal conditions and needs. The greater the degree of academic self-governance and faculty control over budgets, the stronger the resistance to innovation and to curtailing low-priority programs.

In respect to urban life and service, colleges and universities need to respond resourcefully to four educational needs:

1. Undergraduate education that gives youth a realistic understanding of urban life and its environment, how to live in it, what is needed to make it more inhabitable, and how college graduates can do something about it. Many institutions are assigning higher priority to doing this.

2. Advanced disciplinary education in urban aspects of economics, political science, social psychology, the physical sciences, and humanities to develop scholars, analytical methods, and knowledge. In view of the oversupply in some of the disciplines, universities should move with caution in starting new or expanding programs.

3. Specialized professional and technical education to provide the engineers, nurses, accountants, lawyers, public health officers,

Commitment to Public Service Education and Research," National Association of Schools of Public Affairs and Administration (NASPAA) Circular #18, May 1971; "The Response of Higher Education to the Administrative Needs of the Public Service," NASPAA, April 1971; "An Agenda for Advocates," *Bureaucrat*, Spring 1972, pp. 89–93; "Career Development for Administrative and Professional Personnel to Serve an Urban America," Presidential Task Force on Career Development, October 1966.

policemen, clerks, and hundreds of other categories to staff the
nation's urban services. More resources—including those of
junior and community colleges—are being assigned to such purposes.

4. Urban professional education to produce the thousands of
administrative-oriented professionals to plan, organize, and manage the vast range of urban policy, program, and operational
services and functions. This is a major underdeveloped area of
universities.

INTERRELATED ADMINISTRATIVE FIELDS

In my report for the Presidential Task Force on Career Development, I recommended that professional education embracing
twelve urban administrative fields or specialities be accorded
immediate federal support. (See attached references below.)
Slightly modified in light of the changing urban scene, these are:
urban executive management, urban and regional planning, community social planning and administration, urban development,
renewal, and housing administration, public works and related
environmental protection administration, urban economic and
industrial development planning and administration, social welfare planning and administration, administration of criminal justice, education planning and administration, administration of
recreation and other leisure time functions, metropolitan organization and administration, planning and management of the federal-
state-local system.

Public health and hospital administration were omitted because the federal government is already providing very substantial
financial assistance to universities.

Substantively, these are all in whole or part subfields or adjunct fields of urban administration, which from the standpoint
of education are part of the rubric, public affairs/administration.
A number of these subfields are greatly advantaged when incorporated in a comprehensive school of public/urban/interna-
tional/affairs/administration. The early practice of organizing
urban planning curriculums in one part of a university and a
program to prepare urban administrators in a totally different
part makes no sense whatever.

Some subfields may advantageously be based within a public

affairs school with cooperative linkages with other professional schools. Public works administration together with related environmental protection functions is an example, with linkages to engineering and public health. Another example is administration of criminal justice with linkages to law, social work, sociology, and so on.

On the other hand, university resources and capabilities may be best utilized by basing some of the urban adjunct fields in a school of education, social work, public health, and so forth, with a collaborative or joint input by the public/urban/affairs school.

INSTITUTIONAL IMPLICATIONS

In this context, planning and financing a program in urban administration cannot be separated from a broad range of decisions regarding public affairs education and allocation of university resources.

It should be apparent, but Ferrel Heady does not speak specifically to the point, that only a limited number of universities should attempt to establish the professional educational apparatus to produce urban and other administrators and to make claims of excellence in so doing.

There are a number of reasons for this which do not seem to be widely understood. First, a curriculum in urban administration does not constitute a discrete set of courses that can be packaged by a political science department or any other discipline.

Second, urban administration narrowly conceived is but one element in a far broader urban professional and public affairs spectrum. It is one orientation in a diverse mosaic.

Third, urban administration requires a multidisciplinary and multiprofessional faculty.

Fourth, a substantial research element is essential both to produce the knowledge and materials required for instruction and for operational guidance.

Fifth, continuing education including non-degree programs are as much needed as pre-service degree programs.

Sixth, only in a comprehensive professional school is it possible to provide graduate education and research involving a desirable diversity of subfields, a pluralistic faculty, effective substantive interfaces, external relationships, and institutional capability essential to cope with the size and complexity of the task of achieving a livable and viable urban society.

Such a professional school requires considerable resources, equivalent to those of a school of business, law, agriculture, or medicine. No school should have a faculty of less than 25 to 50 full-time faculty (100 would be a good target) or enrollment of less than 100 to 200 full-time students.

In principle, it is no more realistic to organize a school of urban/public affairs/administration as an appendage of a political science department than to establish a school of medicine as a dependency of a department of biology or anatomy.

Within the United States there are only a handful of schools of public affairs/administration which approach the scope of resources required and which offer a favorable setting for the strengthening or the addition of high quality programs in urban administration. And most of these are impoverished.

In the long run, a university in each of the thirty to forty principal metropolitan areas of the country might well have a comprehensive school engaged in a cluster of public/urban/affairs/administration programs. Universities with a full complement of professional schools are desirable in order to permit collaborative programs in functional fields. New York and Chicago areas might be able to support two or three such centers. The specializations and approaches of these schools may well differ considerably.

What about other less strategically located or smaller universities which have aspirations or which already have announced programs in urban studies/administration? Several have made important contributions in a field which has been virtually ignored by universities, government, and philanthropy. However, most programs are flimsy and attract little academic or external respect. Let them continue, but do not label them as professional if they aren't, and let us discourage all universities from continuing or initiating fragmented urban administration programs. Complementing professional urban programs, much long-term value would be derived by having more social scientists and other disciplinarians focus on urban phenomena, policy issues, and methodology. Some may move into administrative positions.

Causes of Institutional Lag

Why have individual prestigious universities ignored urban administration and related public services? Why is it that a chain of prestigious comprehensive schools covering priority public service fields has not been established?

The reason is in part university decision processes, or lack of them. This could have been overcome if the federal government and foundations had exercised initiative as they did in medicine, health, agriculture, and science. Basically the cause is ignorance and apathy within and outside of the universities in respect to the urban condition and the urgency of education and research to cope with it. Professors are preoccupied with their own thing. New undertakings are a threatening claim on resources.

A university which seriously wishes to make savings in graduate education to enable allocations to a new program can find many possibilities by adjustment of its master's and doctoral fields and enrollments to the needs of the market place. Fewer naval architects, mining engineers, ancient history majors, agronomists, archeologists, political scientists, or whatever with an excess of scholars would provide the resources to get on with urban administration.

Universities undertake new programs only:

1. When university administrators, faculties, councils, or senates conclude that a new school or program should be established or accede to the establishment of a new undertaking when it is clear that traditional budgets and curriculums will not be adversely affected; this seldom happens as a result of initiative by an elected faculty organ.

2. When pressed to do so by persons who have enough influence to offset academic resistance, for example, when initiative is taken by university administrators, planning organs, a convinced group of influential professors or trustees, or by state legislators, professional societies, leading citizens;

3. When grants or endowments are made by philanthropists or foundations;

4. When government decides that some field of education and research is crucial to the public interest and provides fellowships and funds for its support.

One or more of these conditions has produced great growth and achievements in science, agriculture, elementary and secondary teacher education, public health, medicine, space technology, atomic energy, and foreign languages. With the exception of public health, and some aspects of social welfare, none of the necessary conditions has existed in the past in urban and related public service fields. Without external pressures and financial assistance, universities will not—and indeed cannot—initiate prestigious educational and research centers.

MANPOWER AND RESEARCH PLANNING

For these reasons, more than the circumstances cited by Ferrel Heady, there will probably be little reallocation of present funds to the education of urban and other public administrators. The federal government is the key to the future. It is the proper instrument, because the nation is an urban society and the federal government is the only unit capable of developing in partnership a system of federalism which can serve all urban citizens equitably and cope with the great range of public policies and administrative requisites to make the system workable.

The starting point is the conduct of manpower studies to determine the categories and qualifications of personnel needed during the next decade or more. The Municipal Manpower Commission produced an excellent report which showed that the requirements are vast and that a lot of action was needed if requirements were to be met. Unfortunately, the Commission spent its $500,000 on producing a book without following through to foster the kinds of action necessary to implement its recommendations. No one else picked up the ball.

A companion step to manpower planning is that of research planning. The urban policy, program, operating, and institutional problems which call for intensive study should be identified and steps taken to foster research as has been done in science, agriculture, and health.

The Executive Branch has developed no strategy, and has even suppressed initiatives authorized by the Congress which would have contributed significantly to education and research in urban administration. Voices are heard in the halls of Washington that we have an excess of educated persons ready to fill present and future needs. Are we destined permanently to a system of urban administration by intuition and trial and error?

The root of the problem is that most local, state, and federal officials responsible for urban policies and programs have never been educated in urban administration. Within Allegheny County where I am writing this, there are 126 municipal governments, one county, and dozens of state and federal agencies serving a dense metropolitan area. I doubt that more than fifteen percent of all persons with administrative responsibility ever read a single book on administration of urban affairs.

The simple fact is these officials do not know enough about the knowledge and competences achievable through professional education to provide a basis for judgment of who has essential qualifications when filling positions. As a result, most positions are filled by persons who fall far short of having the qualifications which would be possible if the need for higher standards was recognized and if the programs of universities were substantial and respected.

In the long run the quality of and respect for a profession is dependent upon the recognition and respect accorded its educational underpinning. The nation does not yet begin to have a system of professional education in urban/public/affairs/administration which can enlist this respect.

Lack of Support for University Initiatives

The 1973 federal budget provides cheerless reading. Favorable features are: (1) an increase in funds budgeted for the Intergovernmental Personnel Act, at a fraction of the level needed; (2) continuation of some grant funds for education and research in urban mass transportation and environmental protection; and (3) higher appropriations recommended for the Law Enforcement Assistance Administration. These provide a few crumbs for universities.

On the other hand, Title IX, Education for the Public Service, would be terminated on the assumption that the education of urban administrators and other public service professionals is a problem of aid to higher education and not part of the strategy of the federal government to improve the administration of the federal-state-local system. No request was made in the budget for

Housing and Urban Development (HUD) fellowships which provide an exceedingly important mechanism for encouraging universities to produce urban administrators. In terms of commitment to university education and research of the kind discussed in this Symposium, the federal budget, despite its gigantic size, is a cipher.

No, there is one exception, namely, public health. The 1973 budget says "federal outlays for training health manpower are estimated at $727 million in 1973, an increase of $358 million over 1969. These outlays will help health professions schools expand their enrollment, provide scholarship and loan assistance, and—for the first time—assure financial support to these schools based on enrollment."

Why, for heaven's sake, is it not equally urgent to provide federal funding for other equally important and even more basic public service fields to that of health? Why should the Executive Branch support public health fellowships and not urban administration fellowships?

Why should the President destroy a first-rate education for public service act which was designed to establish and strengthen a network of urban/public/administration centers which would carry forward initiatives and collaborative programs vital to staffing the public services of federal, state, and local governments?

Why should public health schools be given such enormously generous support when schools designed to produce public works engineers and administrators essential to plan and implement $50 to 60 billion of physical infrastructure and environmental services annually are provided with no funds whatever, except some small grants by the Urban Mass Transit Administration?

Improving the Strategy

A strategy to enable universities to make a comparable contribution in urban administration and other elements of the federal-state-local system that they have made in health and medicine, agriculture, science, and public education, has several facets.

The federal elements should include:

1. transfer of the Education for the Public Service Act to the Civil Service Commission and its funding at a level of at least $500 million annually;

2. ten times larger funding of the training and fellowship provisions of the Intergovernmental Personnel Act with greater utilization of university resources;

3. expansion of the HUD fellowships program;

4. initiation of doctoral fellowships and instructional grants to produce the instructors and researchers essential to fulfilling the university contribution;

5. expanded assignment of federal employees for short-term and academic development at schools of public/urban affairs;

6. broadening of the National Science Foundation policies to support grants to universities under which public/urban/affairs schools in cooperation with other professions and disciplines may undertake research to deal broadly with urban, social, environmental, and other multifaceted problems in which planning, operations, and management as well as technology are primary elements.

Complementing these federal initiatives each state and large municipality, county, and public authority should (1) activate a training policy which provides released time and financial assistance for employees to enroll in public/urban/administration courses and degree programs; (2) develop more resourceful recruitment and utilization of the graduates of such schools and programs to enhance administrative capabilities; and (3) assist universities in providing internships, field work, and research assignments for students.

Many of the social, economic, medical, poverty, public works, and other urban and environmental oriented programs of the last ten years have failed to realize their potential and many have floundered because of the unavailability of competent public administrators and because of the lack of research and development funds to engage in the essential planning and development of delivery systems. To overcome these miscarriages, federal and state governments and the larger municipalities should incorporate an essential component of training and research in each major function or program to assure effective implementation and administration.

Three other steps would round out the strategy. One is greater utilization by governments at all levels of the expert resources of universities to conduct research and provide consultative services in improving governmental policies, plans, programs, administration, organization, personnel, and the application of advanced technology.

Second is the appointment of a university programs officer within the federal Office of Management and Budget, the Civil Service Commission, and all major federal departments, and a similar step in the office of the chief executive of states, large cities, and counties. The purpose is to open up channels of communication and mutual assistance and to facilitate these strategic and cooperative endeavors.

The third measure is to incorporate in all fellowships a substantial supplement fund to help cover the costs of educating students assigned to universities under such programs. It costs two to four times as much to educate a person in high quality graduate programs as tuition covers, even in a private university. Most federal fellowships now carry a small supplement. Most foundation programs carry none. The supplement should at least equate the rate of tuition.

CONCLUDING NOTE

Supplementing government action, foundations have a rare opportunity to get the ball rolling by giving inducements to selected universities to apply substantial resources to the education of urban administrators. Foundations have made enormous contributions in this same way by providing seed money in many other fields. Is it not time that they do something significant for the public service?

If the foundations will take the initiative to stimulate a network of comprehensive schools in which urban administration is a prime ingredient, governments will soon pick up the ball as they have done in other professional fields.

In the long run a university should not be expected to allocate to an urban/public/affairs/administration school much more of its general funds than the amount generated by tuition. There is no other new source of general university income except from foundations, personal philanthropy, and public appropriations. State governments should help programs in state institutions and provide sponsored assignments, and even fellowships. The federal government, however, must be the prime mover.

Commentary on the Heady Paper

By York Willbern

ABSTRACT: The constraints upon university resources imposed by changing patterns of growth and public support are unmistakable. Yet, these constraints may operate differentially with regard to different types of institutions. Current pressures may force universities to give much more conscious attention to program priorities than they have in the past. The pressures of tightened resources may actually be stronger in overcoming academic inertia than were the opportunities presented by continuous growth. The difficulty in fitting educational programs precisely to demand suggests that two major guidelines for university policy may be more important in the future than they have in the past. One is a strong emphasis on educational programs of sufficient breadth that they may be used by persons going into a variety of fields; the other is a much more heavy reliance upon in-service education as a method of helping people adapt to changing situations. To meet this latter demand, universities may need to pursue methods other than formal instruction to apply their resources to the education of urban administrators.

York Willbern is professor of political science, Indiana University. He is former director, Institute of Public Administration, Indiana University; chairman, Committee on Urban Studies, Indiana University; director, Bureau of Government Research, Indiana University; director, Bureau of Public Administration, University of Alabama; chairman, Southern Regional Training Program in Public Administration; editor, Public Administration Review; and president, American Society for Public Administration.

A COMMENTARY can add little to the carefully reasoned and obviously sensible paper contributed by President Heady; even temptations to amplify his discussion are minimal. But there may be some value in trying to supply a different emphasis or perspective on some of the points.

The constraints upon university resources imposed by changing patterns of growth and public support are unmistakable. It may be significant to note that these constraints may operate differentially with regard to different types of institutions. Clearly, as Mr. Heady says, private institutions are frequently those most drastically affected; they will be required not merely to limit the addition of new activities, but in many cases they will have to eliminate or cut back existing programs. In public administration education as in other areas of higher education, some of the pioneering and best known efforts have been in a few of the great private universities. They have difficulty in maintaining these activities, as well as in extending them. Among public universities, the central state universities have generally hit growth ceilings somewhat earlier than have the regional public institutions. Opportunities for innovation and expansion may be most significant during the next few years in the newer regional state universities.

Mr. Heady may be correct in suggesting that program innovations and changes will be considerably more difficult with current resource restraints than was the case during the long period of rapid growth by higher educational institutions. He seems to feel that vested academic interests are so strong that, in the absence of growth, existing programs and activities will be continued and there will be little room for new ones. It is also possible, however, that current pressures and constraints may force universities to give much more conscious attention to program priorities than they have in the past. In the past, it was not so necessary to make priority choices, because new opportunities and fields could be exploited and added without having to replace older ones. Most major universities are now considering program priorities much more seriously than they have ever done before. These deliberations may produce significant changes; the pressures of tightened resources may actually be stronger in overcoming academic inertia than were the opportunities presented by continuous growth. If, as he suggests elsewhere, personnel needs and demands in the private sector tend to become surfeited by the output of educational institutions to a somewhat greater degree than do those in the public sector, there may be shifts in the direction of public service training programs, even in a period of financial and support constraints.

It does seem, as Heady's discussion of manpower planning indicates, that the nation as a whole, and not just the higher educational system, is at a stage of stock-taking and consideration of new directions. Since the nation emerged from the great depression and World War II, the existence of a powerful base of capital and technology, accumulated national and international demands, and a surging population growth combined to produce a long period in which mistakes and weaknesses and even growing pathologies in the system were hidden and obscured by the overwhelming fact of high levels of economic activity and production. Now our world economic pre-eminence seems fast disappearing, our demographic patterns are rapidly changing, and even our values and goals seem to be shifting substantially.

These reassessments and shifts in direction are nowhere more evident than in regard to higher educational programs. The concern of students for relevance, evident in other areas as well as in the increased emphasis on ethnic studies and women's programs, is probably even less significant than the clearly apparent shifts in the markets for university graduates. Both students and faculty members are keenly conscious of the newly discovered difficulties in placing particular types of graduates. When the need for educated manpower was so great in nearly every area that placement was no problem, mistakes in program planning, either by students or by institutions, were not important—nearly any product of an educational institution could be readily marketed. Now, disparities between production and demand are much more costly.

Although it is important to try to anticipate the areas of surplus and and of shortage, it is very hard for a university to keep up with shifts in national needs. There is a lag of several years between program planning and the output of students. The difficulty of fitting educational programs precisely to demand suggests that two major guidelines for university policy may be more important in the future than they have been in the past. One is a strong emphasis on educational programs of sufficient breadth that they may be used by persons going into a variety of fields; the other is a much more heavy reliance upon in-service education as a method of helping people adapt to changing situations.

Heady's approach to the first of these guidelines proposes concentration upon schools or divisions of public affairs, suggesting that persons trained in such programs could reasonably be expected to fit into a wide variety of public service employments. Some might argue that a combined professional program in public and private management would provide an even wider range of options. But President Heady thinks, and I agree, that the attitudes and understandings which are basic in the private sector differ sufficiently from those which are basic in the public sector to justify organizational and program separation.

He does not give extended consideration to the relationship of a general program in public affairs or public administration to the various specific educational programs which are designed to prepare people for particular public service occupations. In many universities, for example, there are increasingly well-established programs in city and regional planning, in police administration, in public welfare—or social work, as it is more commonly designated, with the assumption that here the profession is one that clearly spans public and private segments—in public health, and always, of course, in the largest and best-established of the public service occupations, education. It may be true that the knowledge and skills involved in these particular occupations are so distinct and so well-established that they may not be easily integrated with other areas. But the logic of trying to frame basic programs capable of application in a variety of specific fields certainly leads in the direction of giving serious consideration to approaching such efforts in integrated fashion to the highest feasible degree.

Heady suggests the desirability of using common courses for students in various professional areas when their needs for a particular subject matter or skill area overlap. He gives two reasons for these combinations—economy of scale and the desirability of mixing students from differing professional programs as an educational device. With regard to the second of these reasons, there are two sides to the coin. A course, or some other educational experience, is appropriate for a mixed student population, or may be useful to a particular student in a wider range of later activities, if it is as broad and comprehensive and basic as possible. But, on the other hand, what it gains in breadth of applicability it may lose in directness of relevance. If there are enough students who are certain enough that they wish to use competence in statistics in connection with urban public affairs, for example, a special course for them can be far more effective than an arrangement in which they are lumped together with many other potential users. And this may be true with regard to the basic disciplines as well as tool skills.

It is this reasoning, of course, that probably provides the primary motivation for the establishment of any particular professional school or program. Specialized education is considered more effective than general education, in preparing a person for an occupation. The basic disciplines, economics, sociology, political science, and so on, constitute the most fundamental educational preparation, and there are many who suggest that these are all that are really important at the pre-entry level for so ill-defined an occupation as public service, or even urban administration. These persons would argue that specific professional training can best be secured on the job or through later in-service programs.

But the logic of a professional program does not rest merely upon the need for a sharper degree of intellectual specialization than is secured in the underlying disciplines. It rests also upon the utility of a program of education which, recognizing that competence rests upon understanding, presumes also that competence is more than understanding. Or, to put it more accurately, professional programs may be best justified by the presumption that the competence which comes from understanding is more likely to be acquired if the understanding is sought for the purpose of achieving a particular goal than if it is sought for its own sake alone.

Universities, in defining programs for urban administrators as well as in other areas, will be caught in a continuing dilemma which may become more acute as resource constraints are intensified. Educational programs may be more effective as they are more sharply defined and specialized, but difficulties of precise definition of output goals as well as the need for a higher degree of scale economy will lead in the direction of broader rather than sharper programs. Separate programs for city planners and city managers, for example, may be justifiable on effectiveness criteria but not on efficiency criteria.

President Heady does not discuss extensively the potential growth of mid-career education. For a good many reasons, some of which have been suggested above, this aspect of education may become much more important in the future than it has been in the past. Both the basic knowledge upon which professional understanding is based, and the specific technologies through which it is applied, are changing more rapidly than ever before. Furthermore, personal mobility and changes in community and society thrust individuals into different roles at a rapid rate. Although Mr. Heady used the traditional terminology in speaking of pre-entry education and mid-career training, what is increasingly required is not just new training but also continuing education of the most basic and comprehensive character.

The direct and formal role of a university in this process of continuing education may be significant but not predominant. Educational stimuli may come to urban administrators through reading, through professional associations and activities, through civic activities, through continuous exposure to and interaction with a diversity of other individuals and groups. Formal courses, either short or long, at a university may continue to be relatively exceptional. The indirect contribution of the university to these processes may however be much more important than its direct and formal input. Universities are at the heart of our intellectual communities, whether they be national or state or local. The research and writing and public discussion and teaching of scholars continually conditions the world of ideas and of intellectual interchange. Without fully defining it, the society has come to sense the tremendous importance of the universities in this regard. As Stephen Bailey (I think) put it once, the modern university is the cathedral of our secular society. Its resources can be brought to bear upon the preparation of urban administrators not only through professional programs directed at students who presumably will enter the field, and not only through formal course offerings for persons already on the job, but even more importantly through the vigorous and active participation of its members in study and teaching and writing and discussion about the constantly changing forces and problems of urban life. This can be effectively achieved only if there is a high volume and quality of continuing interchange between practitioner and scholar.

Summary of the Discussion of the Heady Paper

By Frederic N. Cleaveland

THIS final session of the Symposium started on a somber note. Early comments and responses focused on the plight of universities trying to stretch present resources to cover both rising costs and those things the institutions believe they ought to be doing. In that context whenever a university wants to start something new or expand significantly something it is doing modestly, the institution must first decide what has to be curtailed or phased out to provide resources to finance the desired growth. It is much harder to undertake new things in education for urban administration when the institution must cut back somewhere else first. Nor is there much reason for optimism that many institutions are prepared to make cuts elsewhere to make it possible to strengthen professional education for urban administration. Moreover, many institutions face growing pressures from state legislatures, boards of higher education, and their own administrative officers to justify present resource allocation patterns by demonstrating adequate return per dollar invested through such measures as student contact hours, teaching loads, and so forth. Faced with measures like these, professional education for urban administrators is likely to fall into the class of high cost programs.

Others among the participants rejected this gloomy view. While they acknowledged the atmosphere of retrenchment and fiscal concern on most campuses, nevertheless they insisted that there were signs of considerable promise. One participant wise in the ways of the university and of government, pointed out: "We are in a period of stock-taking and appraisal and a reordering of priorities in the educational world. This is a period that provides some opportunity for change." Another observed that some eight or nine new university programs devoted to public and urban affairs had recently been established. He speculated that in at least some of these cases, where the institution serves a major urban-metropolitan population, the involvement of the city governmental leadership had probably helped to persuade the university to launch a public affairs program rather than some other new academic undertaking. A third participant, also a university representative, insisted: "We don't have to make a massive demand [upon those responsible for financing higher education]. It just takes a little more of a push for a governor and the state legislature to do more. And it does not take much more money. We [university public affairs faculty and practitioners] need to start working as a team to do the job."

Several participants expressed concern over how the federal government could allocate substantial sums for the support of professional education in other fields—public health, for example—yet provide no more than token support for public affairs education. Most felt that this federal action reflected a conviction that better professional education in public health "will do more for the public than public administration can." But it is the business of public administration educators and practitioners to cope with this problem. As one participant put it, ". . . the time is coming when the public will feel that we [in public and urban affairs] can do more for them." Another participant argued against wasting time over the absence of general government support for urban affairs education. He urged greater ingenuity and imagination in the search for resources. "People go for problem-centered activities. You could 'piggy back' on public health in Title I [of the Education Act] for instance." Another educator participant suggested that each school had to think through what is "legitimate" for it to undertake in the way of focused training. "Is it legitimate for schools of public affairs to be training for civil defense, the administration of justice, and so on? Maybe the next conference should be on schools of public affairs and designing support strategies for the kinds of activities they think are legitimate for them to do."

A younger practitioner in the group grew increasingly impatient with the educator participants and finally pointed the finger directly at them: "Maybe the title of this Symposium should be 'educating urban educators.' The people in this room include many who are tops in their profession. If you don't see where you fit into this total picture [of meeting learning and educational needs], if you don't see that times are changing, then the new programs just being established will grasp the action. There are some simple things that can be done by the people here to alter the structure—things that do not take any resources, for example, changing course content. So, get your own house in order first." His challenge hit home as these several responses suggest:

"We have not spent enough time thinking about the quality of what we are doing and what we could do."

"I had hoped we would come away with what constitutes a valid curriculum. We didn't."

"I'm not sure we understand each other. I am not sure everyone knows what experience-based learning is. I think it is a problem in communication."

"If someone came in today and gave us $1 million, we would not have a sense of where to put it."

But a long-time academic participant redirected the group into a more constructive path by recalling the value of sharp analysis and a questioning approach: "No revelation has come from on high as to where the path is. . . . I think a fair number of us have been moved somewhat. We have engaged in a degree of learning through what we may have gotten from this [discussion]. We have a desire to learn more, to explore the need further, and to raise further questions and experiment, and try some things out intellectually. If our thinking has been shifted somewhat, and the patterns of ideas encourages us to explore further things—that is what we are trying to work on. That is what education is."

With this impetus the participants turned to consider ways to strengthen the capacity of universities and their schools of public affairs to respond more creatively to the forces of change. One participant offered the American Council on Education institutes for university presidents or business officers as a model. He went on: "I am impressed by the various levels of sophistication present in this Symposium in the grasp of problems to be addressed in this business and in experience in dealing with them. I think we have within us the resources to stage such institutes."

Other participants talked about how to equip faculty members of public affairs schools to work effectively in academic programs organized around experience-based learning. Some suggested that the Federal Executive Institute take on responsibility for developing "a program whose function would be to make better teachers and educational planners out of administrators and faculty in schools of public affairs." Another participant observed that one of the basic purposes of the National Training Development Service (NTDS) is to help build in universities the capability to perform more effectively as learning-centered institutions. Clearly NTDS can play an important role in training to help develop effective faculty learning counselors.

The group identified two other essential functions to be performed if schools of public affairs are to be reoriented to meet the needs defined in this Symposium. The first is the function of curriculum development. Here the critical requirement is continuing research focused upon curriculum development, research, for example, probing alternative approaches in terms of content, problem selection, teaching format and methodology for accomplishing defined curricular objectives. Such research is a continuing responsibility of every institution engaged in educating urban administrators, as well as a responsibility of professional organizations like the National Association of Schools of Public Affairs and Administration (NASPAA) and the International City Management Association. Agencies like NTDS can also play an important role in research-based curriculum development for urban administration.

The second essential function noted was the need for special attention to the development and exchange of effective teaching and learning materials designed to fit the interests and reflect the needs of student learners in public and urban affairs. Again each school has a responsibility to devote major attention and resources to this function. The associations like NASPAA and NTDS also have an important place both in the development of materials and in devising ways to insure exchange of materials among institutions.

Two closing comments, one by a practitioner and one by an educator, sought to put the symposium discussion in context: "We [practitioners] have seen our own jobs changing and we have found it necessary to adapt to the changing character of our roles. We have seen changes in the education of persons seeking to pursue the careers we are following. We are not well-equipped to evaluate all these changes, but we are nevertheless keenly aware of how important it is for the educational programs to reflect what we know to be the reality of the changing world of the urban administrator. We are optimistic that more resources will become available for this whole area of education. If we have been able to spark new thinking on the part of educators about what you in the universities are doing, and if you in turn have been able to stimulate new thinking on our part, then this Symposium has been a success."

The final comment came as part of the informal summary at the close of the last session:

"We have wrestled with real problems, serious problems and in many cases perplexing and perhaps insoluble problems. We have spent a lot of time confronting differences in perspective, especially in the perspectives of the urban administration practitioner and the urban administration academic. Many symposium participants have held both roles in their careers. We have no doubt identified as many areas of disagreement as we have found areas of agreement, but we have found far more areas of common concern and this is an important finding. Hopefully we go away a little closer to understanding.

"We have found many things wrong with the institutions in which we are working—universities, professional associations, urban governments. We talked about the need for new institutions, and perhaps we now have more insight into how our institutions can be strengthened and improved.

"We can take hope, I believe, from the fact that we are meeting in a time of ferment for that situation gives us significant opportunity. Had we met on this subject ten years ago we would have been far more complacent. We lacked adequate resources then, too, but I suspect that we were more self-confident in what we were doing to educate urban administrators. Indeed I suspect that we knew less well then than now what we were about.

"This is especially a time of ferment and change in our universities. Indeed there has already been more change on the campus in the last five years than in the previous fifteen years. It is a time when reform is possible. In part this is true because it is a time of fiscal stringency rather than of fiscal affluence. When budgets are tight you can often get results from asking hard questions. It is a time to ask hard questions and to re-examine priorities. Significant changes are possible in universities, even changes of the kind necessary to address some of the problems identified in this Symposium.

"The same kind of ferment is apparent in our cities. This is why the roles of urban administrators come out looking the way they do in the paper by Graham Watt, John Parker, and Robert Cantine. The practitioners they surveyed were responding to new forces and new demands in their experience. So it is a time of ferment and of change in the city and in urban government.

"Finally, we should not apologize because we at this Symposium have not found all the answers. If we thought we knew the answers, they would in part, I believe, turn out to be wrong answers. But the important thing is for us to continue the search for answers, and to continue to search together—educator and practitioner—and to ask each other hard questions as we have at this Symposium. Out of this process will come progress towards better definition of the real world of the urban administrator and more effective approaches to preparing people for this demanding career."

Achieving Effective Education for Urban Administrators: Action Requirements Derived from the Symposium

By John K. Parker

ABSTRACT: Symposium participants identified significant needs for initial and continuing education to enable urban administrators to perform effectively in the increasingly complex social and governmental environment. Vigorous action is required by universities, governments, and professionals in urban administration. Universities throughout the nation must develop strong programs in public administration, with emphasis on urban administration, in order to fulfill their responsibilities to the public and governments in their own geographic areas. Greater cooperative efforts by universities can increase effectiveness and improve program quality and funding. Federal, state, and local governments must demand university performance, take an active role in program development, and ensure availability of requisite funding. Professionals in urban administration must exert results-oriented leadership through national and regional associations and through individual effort with universities in their locality. Foundations can play a unique role in accelerating change. Especially needed are individuals in universities, governments, foundations, and professional associations who will commit themselves to decisive action and serve as catalysts to bring about long-term change.

For biographical statement see: "Roles of the Urban Administrator in the 1970s."

ON THE third day of the Symposium at which the authors of the papers in this volume discussed the merits and demerits of each paper, there was evident a general belief that the experience had been highly stimulating and had succeeded in mapping the principal features of the rugged terrain to be traversed in achieving quality education for urban administrators.

Elsewhere in this volume is contained a summary of each of the symposium discussions. Those summaries, and the individual papers and commentaries, reveal a body of consensus clothed in as many spines of controversy as any porcupine could hope to wear. But it is the body of the porcupine, and not the spines, upon which action must be based.

Briefly, there can be found general agreement that there is a vast, unmet need for able, motivated, educated, and continuously developing public executives who were identified for this discussion as "urban administrators." These urban administrators must function in an increasingly complex social and governmental environment, and will occupy a diversity of positions and fill a variety of roles during their careers. It was agreed that we need many more such people than are now available or seem to be becoming available in the foreseeable future, and it was further agreed that vigorous action was needed to recruit and train young people to meet this enormous need. It even was agreed that responsibility for vigorous action was shared by universities, governments (as the prime users), and public officials—especially including urban administrators now in the field.

Of course there was enthusiastic consensus among the educators that if only the public officials and governments would carry out their responsibilities, the universities would then be able to do what they have been trying to do all along. With equal unanimity, the urban administrators felt that their own educational prescriptions would be quite effective if the universities and the governments would only take action as clearly indicated. Of course, the government representatives felt their staffing needs would be met if the universities and the professional urban administrators would take appropriate action. Despite this predictable consensus, there was a strong undercurrent of agreement that all three—universities, governments, and urban administrators—would have to exert initiatives on their own part and on their own behalf if any substantial progress toward mutual goals in educating for urban administration was to be made. Despite the attractions of the let George do it approach, and despite all the interdependency arguments that have been and will be advanced, this paper will address as evenhandedly as possible the actions that participants proposed to be taken by each involved interest group.

Action for Universities

One of the most significant conclusions arising in the discussion was that all universities should develop strong programs in public administration and urban affairs, with an emphasis on education for urban administration. This conclusion seemed to be based on three principal factors: first, governmental clients— federal, state, and local governments dealing with urban matters—and students are located throughout the United States, and universities draw students mainly from a local population, who in turn tend to pursue their careers in the geographic areas in which they were educated; second, large numbers of doctors, engineers, school teachers, social workers, and other functional specialists are educated by nearly all universities, and a strong public administration program was seen as essential to enable the university to provide specialists with a broad understanding of urban society; third, the geographic dispersion of sites of government employment makes it important that universities in each locality be able to conduct research and provide continuing education for elected and appointed local government officials and technical employees.

This focus on universities in general should be kept in mind, for the suggested actions were directed not just toward those major universities with known programs of public administration and urban affairs, but to each university throughout the nation. Consequently, emphasis was placed on the urgent need for universities to work together in identifying sources of funding, in planning and developing programs based on one another's experience, in educating and equipping faculty members to establish and conduct programs for urban administrators, in recruiting students, and in planning and evaluating curriculums.

The magnitude of the opportunity for effective joint action by universities was illustrated by the fact that none of the educators participating in the Symposium were aware of any reasonably comprehensive study or publication identifying the principal sources of governmental and foundation funds available for the financial support of programs in public administration and public affairs. Even with the competitive outlook perhaps necessarily adopted by many universities at the present time, the absence of commonly available information about sources of funds is symptomatic of the urgent need for improved communications among universities, so that those who have established programs can more promptly improve them and those that wish to establish programs may benefit from the knowledge and experience of their colleagues.

Joint efforts, of course, are most likely to occur where a university has some existing program in public affairs or public administration. One of the participants in the discussion pointed out that a recent survey by the National Association of Schools of Public Affairs and Administration was able to identify only 125 campuses at which there was an on-going program at either the undergraduate or graduate levels. This number included multiple campuses of universities. For these universities, and for those that have yet to begin a program of education in urban administration, the symposium participants have urged the following actions:

Organization

Each university should organize a core teaching unit in public affairs and public administration, able to compete politically with the organizational units established in other disciplines and professions. For most universities, the preferred organizational unit would be a school of public administration and public affairs or a school of urban administration. In a smaller number of universities, a strong, separate department similarly titled would be the more appropriate unit. Whether a school or a department, the unit must have full-time faculty solely devoted to its program in order to be a meaningful teaching unit. Part-time faculty from other schools and departments of the university can be valuable supplementary participants in a program but, used alone, prove sorely inadequate.

Goals

Each university and school should examine its own unique strengths and comparative advantages in building its program in urban administration. It should be standard practice to define goals, set priorities, and monitor progress toward goal achievement.

Coordination

The school would have the responsibility within the university of providing a bridge to the other teaching units within the university engaged in preparation of people for careers in the public service. This would include doctors, nurses, city planners, welfare specialists, civil engineers, and so forth. At the same time, the school should bring to the students enrolled in its own program the skills and special knowledge of the members of related teaching units, and provide the means for the individual student to achieve program flexibility while pursuing a core program.

Faculty development

The school would of necessity recruit and develop the faculty required for its own program and for the broadening of programs of students throughout the university. The faculty must be able to look to its own school for career opportunities, and not be subject to the divergent values and interests of departments of political science, or business administration faculty members. The school also should exert major emphasis on career development of its faculty, including arranging sabbaticals for faculty members, so that they may gain experience in urban administration at least every few years throughout their careers. Such sabbaticals have been arranged by agencies of the federal government, and it was believed by the participants in the Symposium that states and cities would gladly cooperate with the universities to provide similar faculty experience in the professions for which faculty members are endeavoring to educate their students.

Program scope

It was observed by one of the participants that there may be only one university in the United States that has a program leading to degrees at the bachelor, master, and doctoral levels. Participants placed strong emphasis on programs that reach into the undergraduate level rather than being concerned solely with the master or Ph.D. levels.

Program content

Schools and departments educating for urban administration must provide professional—not disciplinary—programs. More attention must be devoted to developing skills in interpersonal relations, formal and informal communications, management, and program and policy implementation. Good policy is not nearly enough, for even the best policy is not self-implementing. This will require concerted, joint, organized, and immediate attention to the development and use of fresh teaching materials and to the use of teaching methods far more effective than lectures and term papers. Every program should include faculty and student research useful to governments in the locality, especially emphasizing research in applied areas of operational needs.

Continuing education

Several of the symposium participants expressed strong disbelief that universities were capable of providing effective continuing education programs for urban administrators. There was, nevertheless, equally strong belief that universities must indeed look beyond the degree-granting episode and focus on the career-long requirements of the public executive, and especially the change-buffeted urban administrator. Examples were advanced of successful university-based programs in public administration, as well as university successes in continuing education for business executives, physicians, attorneys, and other professionals.

Student recruiting

The characteristics of the students recruited by the university may be, in the opinion of a number of symposium participants, the most important factor in determining the educational and career success of the student. Consequently, universities must aggressively recruit potential students at both the undergraduate and graduate levels, with special emphasis on minority groups that in the past have often been excluded from university programs. The tendency of some universities to rely on accidental discovery of a public administration or urban affairs program by a diligently searching student, or for students to be delivered personally by a friendly political science professor would be inconceivable approaches to recruiting were they not so widely practiced. Closely linked to aggressive and intelligent recruiting of students is the matter of student financial support. It was pointed out that this support can take the form not only of scholarships and fellowships, but can include, for educational as well as financial reasons, a strong field work and internship program.

Internships

Students in public administration, and particularly those preparing for a career in urban administration, must be provided field work experience in public organizations involved in urban action if their educational experience is to be meaningful. The field work experience can take many forms, including summer work, work experience during the academic program, or the more traditional internship following the academic program with continuing communications between the university faculty and the employer. The field work experience can be an important means of keeping programs current with the rapidly changing character of urban society and urban administration.

Funding

While more will be said about funding responsibilities of governments, there is clear responsibility on the part of the universities to actively seek and make use of funds that are now available for educating urban administrators and functional specialists in public administration. Further, the university cannot escape responsibility for allocating funds under its control to schools or departments of public administration and urban affairs. As one university president participating in the Symposium remarked, nearly every university can reallocate as much as ten percent of its total funds in any given year, and it is the university that sets priorities for allocating funds among competing demands. He further remarked that the demand for improved programs in urban administration or even public administration was seldom strongly brought to bear on the university administration. Several participants also thought that universities may be slow to recognize that most students of public administration and public affairs can and do pay full tuition.

GOVERNMENTS CAN'T SHIRK MAJOR RESPONSIBILITIES

It should come as no surprise that the symposium participants handed to governments the greatest responsibility for action to achieve effective education for urban administrators. Governments are the employers of urban administrators. Yet it was noted with at least a touch of irony that federal, state and even city governments have been pressured into funding a multitude of professional and technical university programs throughout the nation, as well as underwriting universities as institutions, while failing to demand that those same universities prepare the executives and key program specialists urgently required by the governments themselves. Thus action proposals for governments focused equally on special funding for educating urban administrators and upon the necessity for governments to express emphatically their demands that universities establish and strengthen programs for urban administrators. Specific action proposed includes:

Express demand

A significant number of universities obtain a major part of their funding through the state, and in some cases city budget process. Thus states and some cities have a direct responsibility and opportunity to ensure that universities take vigorous action to meet the needs for educating urban administrators and functional public administration professionals. In addition, governors and other public officials appointing members to boards of regents and boards of university trustees should ensure that their appointments include persons able to ensure that universities adequately meet their responsibility for preparing future public executives. Governments should also consider appointing special review commissions to ascertain to what degree universities are meeting their public responsibilities in educating executives and specialists for the public service and to recommend remedial action where universities have failed to meet their responsibilities.

Funding

Symposium participants recognize that for the most part governments have gotten from universities pretty much what governments were willing to pay for and demand. It would be appropriate at this point for the reader to review Donald Stone's paper in this Monograph from which I quote the following passage relevant to federal funding:

The federal element should include:

1. transfer of the Education for the Public Service Act to the Civil Service Commission and its funding at a level of at least $500 million annually;

2. ten times larger funding of the training and fellowship provisions of the Intergovernmental Personnel Act with greater utilization of university resources;

3. expansion of the Housing and Urban Development fellowships program;

4. initiation of doctoral fellowships and instructional grants to produce the instructors and researchers essential to fulfilling the university contribution;

5. expanded assignment of federal employees for short-term and academic training at schools of public/urban affairs;

6. broadening of the National Science Foundation policies to support grants to universities under which public/urban affairs schools in cooperation with other professions and disciplines may undertake research to deal broadly with urban, social, environmental, and other multifaceted problems in which planning, operations, and management as well as technology are primary elements.

It is obvious that each state and most cities similarly can take initiatives to make direct appropriations for scholarships and fellowships in urban administration and urban affairs for residents of their jurisdiction, or may in some cases, make direct appropriations for such purposes to universities within their jurisdictions.

Require professional education

Several participants observed that one of the reasons governments have not more actively required professional education of their officials and employees is that many elected and appointed officials themselves have little formal education in public administration and hence little understanding of the value of such education in improving the effectiveness, efficiency, and responsiveness of the governments and programs for which they have responsibility. Yet governments must require appropriate professional education for key employees at the managerial and technical levels if they expect to make any significant progress in solving the problems thrust upon them.

Arrange employee education

Governments also should take more vigorous action to establish programs whereby current employees may, on a part-time or full-time basis, participate in university education programs that meet professional qualifications. Some cities and states do presently have tuition assistance and leave of absence provisions. What is needed is a more widespread and more vigorous effort by governments to arrange for employee participation in programs of formal education. Also needed is a strong effort by governments to initiate and fund executive development and continuing education programs to be carried out by universities and by other qualified educational organizations.

Provide internships

Although many cities and some federal agencies and states have long-established internship programs for recent college graduates and degree candidates, educators participating in the Symposium stressed that it is still extremely difficult to place all qualified students in meaningful internship assignments with governmental units, especially when summer internships and academic year field work assignments are considered. It is strongly suggested that every governmental unit involved in urban programs should have an active internship program in cooperation with one or more universities. Most governments, and larger agencies of state and federal governments, should have a designated individual responsible for arranging internships and field work assignments.

Create sabbaticals

During the discussion of the role of the university in continuing education, the thought was raised and promptly confirmed that one of the principal roadblocks in developing and conducting worthwhile educational programs for urban administrators was that few faculty members have any idea of what the professional urban administrator does. The discussion pinpointed the widespread neglect of the continuing education of university faculty members, and strongly underscored the need for governments to create positions that could be filled for one-year terms by mid-career faculty members, so that the faculty members might gain practical experience and firsthand understanding of the nature of urban administration.

Governments must establish such positions and sabbatical programs and then persuade universities to release faculty members to fill those positions on sabbatical leave, since the universities are unlikely to take the initiative themselves. Precedent exists for these programs in the federal government, and some financial assistance may be available through the Intergovernmental Personnel Act.

URBAN ADMINISTRATORS MUST ACT FORCEFULLY

Much of the opportunity for bringing about significant changes in the availability and value of education in urban administration depends upon vigorous action by public executives already in the field of urban administration. Symposium participants identified critically needed individual and group endeavors.

Agenda for professionals

John Fishback's article in the February, 1972 issue of *Public Management* was cited as a reminder that the International City Management Association's *Program of Professional Development for Urban Management* reported that the older professions such as law, medicine, engineering, and so forth have developed a close, cooperative relationship between the profession and professional schools that includes the following areas:

1. organizing to enlist new sources of financial support for maintenance and enlargement of professional schools' research and educational facilities;

2. promoting extensive refresher training, special institutes, and course offerings by the professional schools so that the practitioners can keep abreast of rapid changes affecting the professional field;

3. taking the initiative in sponsoring working conferences between faculties and practitioners to discuss joint concerns;

4. encouraging the research efforts of the schools and assisting in various aspects of research design;

5. assisting in the recruitment, selection, education, and retention of highly qualified faculty;

6. interpreting the professional field and career opportunities
to high school and college students, and helping to recruit talented
students for the professional schools;

7. counseling and assisting in curriculum development so that
the schools reflect the true needs of the profession and of society;

8. assisting the schools in raising their standards for admission
and improving the level of education for degree candidates; and

9. calling upon the school faculties for work as advisors and
consultants on operational, organizational, policy, and research
questions of the operating agencies.

Association action

The highest priority must be given by urban administrators
to the urgent and continuing need for concerted action by their
local, regional, and national professional associations. Professional associations such as the American Society for Public Administration and the International City Management Association,
for example, must take vigorous action in cooperation with universities and associations of schools of public administration and
urban affairs to assure the rapid development of improved programs. The professional associations also have the ability and
the responsibility to take the initiative in working with national
associations of elected officials such as the National Governors'
Conference and the National League of Cities, and with related
professional organizations such as the American Society of Planning Officials, the International Association of Chiefs of Police,
and the American Public Works Association to inform them and
enlist their support for joint-action programs. While the professional associations have engaged in some activity in this area
in the past, it is considered essential that they significantly expand
the scope and intensity of their action programs. Initial action
would, logically, include communicating to their membership the
substance of this Monograph and other relevant information.

Professional associations must also take the lead in ensuring
the establishment of appropriate educational standards for entry
in the field of urban administration, and must also consider
standards for career development educational requirements. It

was noted by one of the participants in the discussion that at least one state medical society requires a prescribed minimum of continuing education for all physicians in the state in order for them to be annually eligible to retain their qualifications for practice in the state. Guidelines in this critical area of continuing qualification to practice need to be developed, widely understood, and acted upon.

Organizing for local action

Even with vigorous action by national professional and governmental associations, there is a key role to be played by urban administrators at the local levels. Urban administrators in each metropolitan area should organize themselves to work with individual universities in their areas. Such work groups, whether independently organized or acting as part of the chapter activities of a national or state association, should meet regularly with administrators and faculty members of local universities to assist them in developing effective programs for educating urban administrators. Areas of opportunity for such work groups include: developing and participating in expanded programs for recruiting students, especially students from minority groups; developing and providing internships; through state professional and governmental associations, supporting appropriate budget requests of universities receiving state funding; involving faculty members in urban government activities, including the provision of research opportunities; and, participating as lecturer, discussion leader, or resource person in the academic program.

A NOTE TO FOUNDATIONS AND PHILANTHROPISTS

At one point the symposium discussion turned to the exceptional opportunity for private foundations and individual philanthropists to get the ball rolling. Types of grants that could provide an unusually high level of results include:

1. funding staff and program in national professional associations and national associations of schools of public administration and urban affairs to establish close communications and working relationships among governments, urban administrators, and universities;

2. funding the conduct of regional workshops of educators,

urban administrators, and government officials to develop action programs and set priorities for action by each group;

3. establishing scholarship funds at universities for the education of urban administrators;

4. endowing new schools of public administration and urban affairs, or professorships in that field; and

5. sponsoring a project to develop a comprehensive program guide for the establishment of effective schools of public administration and urban affairs with attention to undergraduate, graduate, and continuing education.

NEEDED: VOLUNTEER CATALYSTS

The contents of this Monograph should make it evident that no one organization and certainly no one individual can bring about the urgently needed changes which must take place for there to be adequate education for urban administrators. That situation has not changed over the past decade, and it is not likely to change now just by happenstance. What is needed is for individuals in universities in the field of urban administration, foundation officials, association executives, elected and appointed government officials, individual professionals, and interested citizens to commit themselves to action. The initiative must be taken by many individuals in many organizations and at locations throughout the nation if the opportunities outlined by the participants in the Symposium are to be achieved.

The changes that are required will not be accomplished quickly. It will take a concerted effort of all the interest groups involved to make a significant long-term change. At the same time, individuals, acting as catalysts in their own areas and within their own organizations, will make the decisive difference as to whether any change at all is achieved.